IMAGES
of America

THE LAND BEFORE FORT KNOX

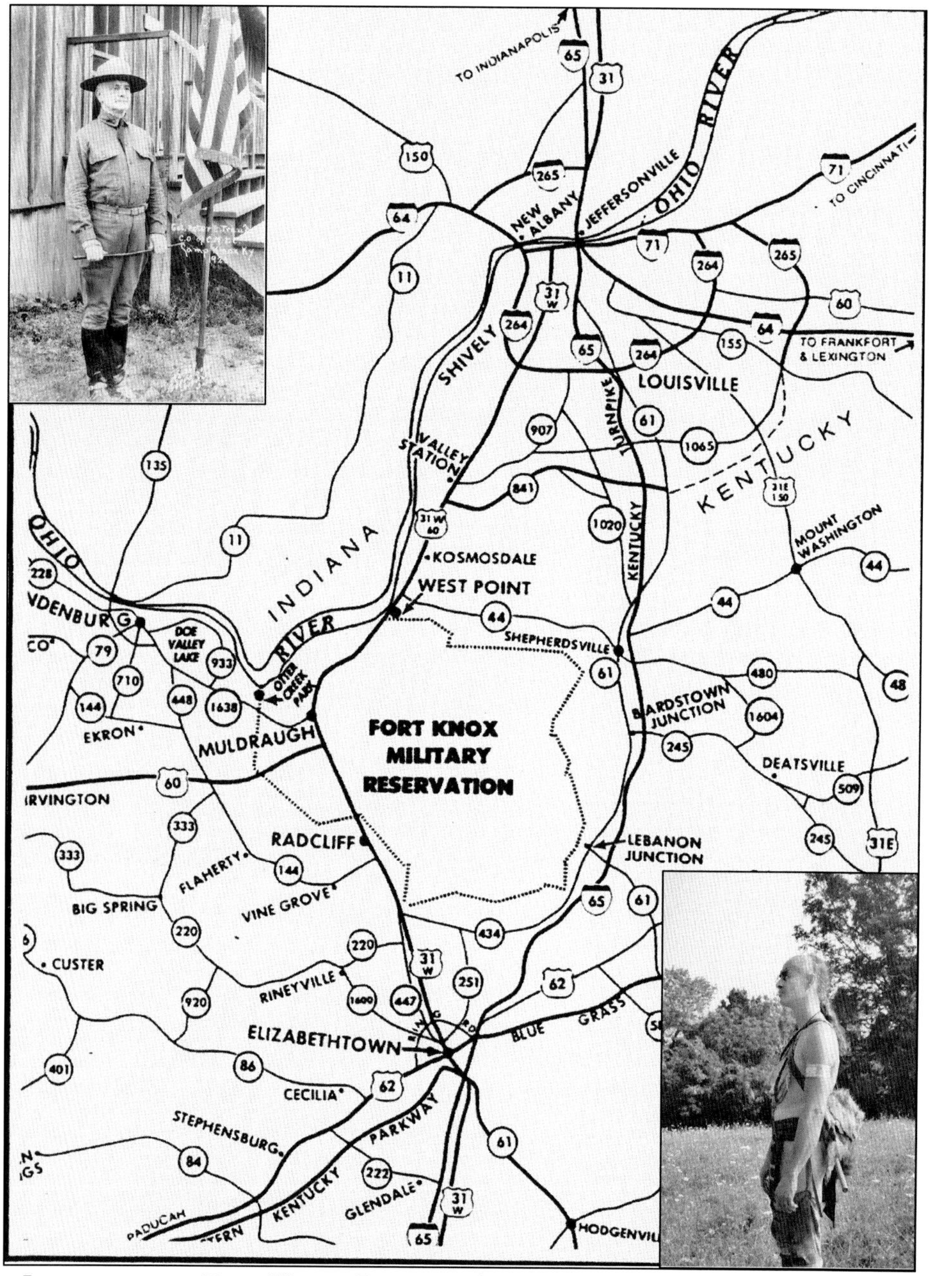

THE LAND THAT IS FORT KNOX. For more than 1,000 years Native Americans hunted, camped, and battled upon the land that is now Fort Knox. In the 18th century European settlers entered the area and eventually drove out the Native Americans. Isolated cabins came first and then clusters of cabins that became towns offering services to the rural, agricultural area. By the time the government acquired the land for the establishment of a military installation, the isolated cabins of early settlers were a thing of the past. Prosperous farms and communities existed on the land. Eventually the land became the home of mounted warfare for the United States Army. Where many hundreds of buffalo once established trails throughout the hills and valleys, wheeled and tracked vehicles now engage in military training.

IMAGES
of America

THE LAND BEFORE FORT KNOX

Gary Kempf

ARCADIA
PUBLISHING

ISBN 978-0-7385-1686-8

Published by Arcadia Publishing
Charleston, South Carolina

Printed in the United States of America

Library of Congress Catalog Card Number: 2004107295

For all general information contact Arcadia Publishing at:
Telephone 843-853-2070
Fax 843-853-0044
E-mail sales@arcadiapublishing.com
For customer service and orders:
Toll-Free 1-888-313-2665

Visit us on the Internet at www.arcadiapublishing.com

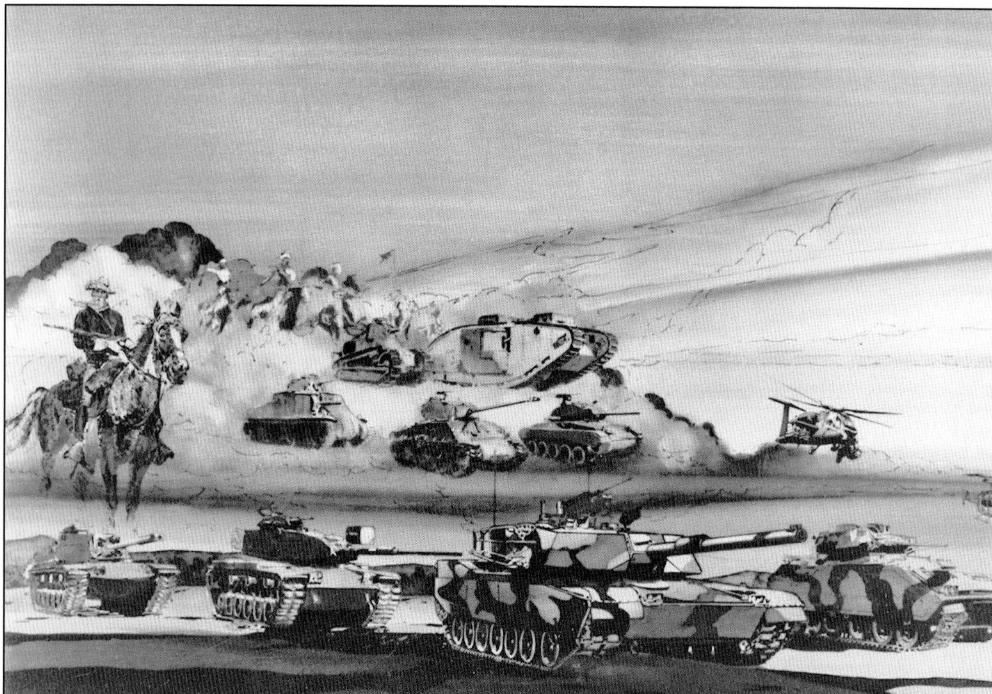

FORT KNOX, THE HOME OF CAVALRY AND ARMOR. Fort Knox, Kentucky, located 35 miles southwest of Louisville, is known as the "Home of Mounted Warfare." Although famous as the site of the United States Bullion Depository, the "Gold Vault," and now the United States Army Recruiting Command, the primary mission of Fort Knox is to develop leaders and train soldiers for the armored forces worldwide. What is known to few, due to the passage of time, is what occupied the land before the inception of Fort Knox. The depictions and narratives herein give the viewer a glimpse of the people, places, and events on the land before it became Fort Knox.

Contents

ACKNOWLEDGMENTS

In 1991 I began a project to visit, photograph, and copy all of the known cemeteries on the Fort Knox military installation. This effort resulted in the location and recording of 131 cemetery sites on about 110,000 acres of Fort Knox land. However, not all of these cemeteries remain in Fort Knox; some were relocated and some were combined. The official Fort Knox cemetery map now shows 119 cemetery sites.

During this project I found that much existed on the land before the coming of Fort Knox. There were towns, churches, schools, farms, businesses, and much more. I found that little was written and few were left who remembered what the people and their land were like before Fort Knox. Thus began a journey for me that will not end. I sought to acquire and archive as much information as I could find regarding the history of the land and people before Fort Knox. This involved searching state and local records, newspapers, church documents, deeds, obituaries, wills, and numerous other sources. The most enjoyable and enlightening of my endeavors to find and preserve a bit of history was the locating and interviewing of people who had actually lived upon the land or who had intimate knowledge of it. This resulted in volumes of transcribed interviews, as well as photographs generously provided by those interviewed.

I list here those whom I visited and who graciously agreed to be interviewed, in some cases numerous times, in order to capture their memories of the past so that a piece of history would not be lost. These people gave me considerable joy and contributed greatly to the preservation of a portion of Kentucky history. This book drew heavily upon their willingness to share memories and photographs. Their kindness and consideration will not be forgotten. The contributors are as follows: Virginia Able, Vera Applegate, Lois Baird, John Beisel, Al Burton Bennett, Allen Brown, Edith Byerly, Richard Briggs, John Carlberg, Dewey Chapman, Iva Mae Clark, Mildred Corbett, Joe and Laverne Corbett, Wes Cowley, Nina Crutcher, Barbara Davis, Dr. John Davis, C.L. Dawson, Jane Dooley, Porter Douglas, Woody Dawson, Thelma Grotlenthaler, Velma Daugherty Harned, Artis Hargan, Louis Holston, John Howlett, Barbara James, Paul James, Maime Ruth Jackson, Lilie Lewis, Maraguerite Lewis, Lloyd Mattingly, Inez McCubbins, Olive McMillen, Paul Morrison, Mildred Morris, Lucille Mudd, George and Julius Muth, Cornelia McIntire Nicholson, Burlyn Pike, Laverne Ray, Agnes Rice, Hazel Roberts, Robert and Lawreene Ruff, Ken Sherrard, Alice Sipes, Nellie Slaughter, Don Stovall, Paul Urbahns, Marvin Veirs, Wesley Walker, Bert Watts, Ann Viers Weaver, Jeanne Whitehouse, Claude Withers, Cliff Woodridge, and Ruby Zepperlein.

Some of those listed here are deceased, many are in the seventh or eighth decade of full and productive lives, a few are in their ninth decade, and one (Agnes Rice) celebrated her 103rd birthday in 2004. I am grateful to all.

INTRODUCTION

Fort Knox is the United States Army's home of Armor and Cavalry and has served as a military installation since 1918. The post spans 170.4 square miles in Hardin, Meade, and Bullitt Counties. The post's boundaries encompass a wealth of cultural heritage and natural beauty unparalleled on most military installations. Motor pools, military housing, firing ranges, bivouac sites, maintenance bays, and the University of Mounted Warfare now stand where small communities and farms once flourished.

The history of the land that is now Fort Knox goes back over 200 years. The land once witnessed settlers battling the elements, Native Americans, Civil War skirmishes, and numerous other events that reflect Kentucky's evolution and history.

Historic figures such as Abraham Lincoln and Daniel Boone walked upon the land. Bathsheba Lincoln, the grandmother of Abraham Lincoln, is buried on Fort Knox, as is Enoch Boone, the nephew of Daniel Boone and son of Squire Boone. The 119 known cemeteries on Fort Knox contain veterans of every war from the Revolution to Vietnam. Some cemeteries date back to the late 18th century. The names of over 3,800 people are recorded in the Fort Knox cemetery names database.

The Louisville and Nashville Turnpike ran through the land that is now Fort Knox. Construction of the pike began in the 1830s; the pike carried thousands of Civil War soldiers and material, and it remained a major north-south highway through Kentucky until the 1950s. A one-mile section of this bygone highway, with its bridges and stonework, has been preserved and exists today as the "Bridges to the Past" hiking trail on Fort Knox.

Towns and communities that appeared on maps 100 years ago, such as Stithton, Tip Top, Easy Gap, Dorrett's Run, Plain Dealing, Wigginton (also known as Pleasant View), Bloomington, Pitts Point, Garnettsville, Grahampton, New Stithton, and Bartles exist no more—they were consumed by the purchase of land for the establishment, and later expansion, of a military installation. Also seized were stores, churches, schools, farms, railroads, mills, bridges, and roads.

Long before settlers began moving into the region that became Kentucky, the area around present-day Fort Knox served as a hunting ground for many Native American tribes and the scene of numerous skirmishes between war parties. No single tribe made the area a permanent home. Instead, many different tribes utilized the land for over 10,000 years. Today 11 tribes with past links to the land that was occupied by Fort Knox have established relations with the federal government. Large herds of buffalo also once roamed the area, and their movements left traces that served as roads for Native Americans and early European settlers alike. Buffalo and other game were attracted by the extensive salt licks that existed near Shepherdsville.

Pioneers, including Thomas Bullitt, Michael Stoner, and Daniel and Squire Boone, began to arrive in the area in the late 18th century. In 1776 Samuel Pearman led a group of settlers to the mouth of the Salt River, laying claim to vast tracts of land along the Ohio, Salt, and Rolling Fork Rivers. At the confluence of the Salt and Rolling Fork Rivers, they built a small log cabin. Native American attacks, however, forced Pearman and followers to return to their homes in Virginia. Later settlers transformed the area around their cabin into the town of Pitts Point, which was consumed by expansion of Fort Knox in 1941–1942.

The failure of Pearman's expedition did not prevent continuing efforts to build permanent settlements in the area. In 1780 John Carr and Squire Boone arrived to explore the region. Carr's family later settled at the base of Sugar Loaf Mountain, near where the Rolling Fork and Salt Rivers join. Native Americans, however, resisted all such settlement efforts. In 1802 Carr died while defending his homestead. He and his wife are buried near the site of their cabin at the base of Sugar Loaf Mountain.

The end of the Revolutionary War accelerated settlement of the land that is now Fort Knox. The Mill Creek and Cedar Creek Valleys witnessed the emergence of small communities in the 1780s. Col. John Conley established a mill and farm in the Mill Creek Valley about 1800. John Moore operated a distillery in the valley. Abraham Lincoln's grandmother moved into the area in 1802. Following her death in 1833, she was buried in the Old Mill Creek Cemetery (now the Lincoln Memorial Cemetery), which was the site of a Baptist church built in 1783. A thriving community developed in the Cedar Creek Valley and included a Methodist church established in 1801. A cemetery was located around the church and is visited every Memorial Day by descendants of those buried within.

The growing number of settlers determined to live in the area, coupled with an aggressive defense of their homesteads, drove the Native Americans from the land. It became safe for a wider dispersal of individual farms, and these farms came to need access to markets and services. In the 19th century the development of towns occurred in response to continued population growth and demands for specialized goods and services unavailable on local farms.

The development of towns and communities stimulated the building of roads, bridges, and ferries to link the growing population in the area. Ferries at West Point operated across the Ohio and Salt Rivers. Pitts Point became the site of a ferry that crossed the Rolling Fork River. Wooldridge Ferry Bridge crossed the Rolling Fork River where a ferry once operated. Fort Knox now encompasses all of the original ferry sites. All that once was, is no more. It is present only in fading memories, documents, and photographs.

In 1903 extensive military maneuvers within and around West Point demonstrated the suitability and desirability of the land for a military installation. In 1918 approximately 40,000 acres of land in Hardin County, as well as a small part of Meade County, were purchased for a permanent military installation. In 1941–1942, 45,000 additional acres in Hardin, Meade, and Bullitt Counties were purchased for the expansion of Fort Knox, and in 1953, more land was purchased in Bullitt County for additional expansion.

One

THE LAND BEFORE FORT KNOX 1776–1942

Early Settlers and Their Descendents

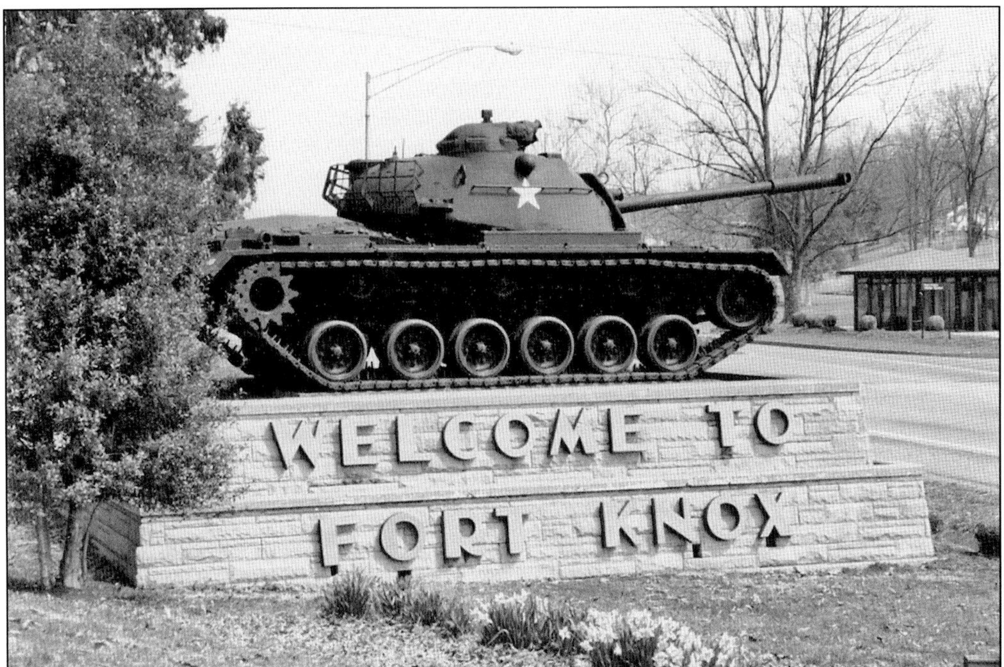

ENTERING FORT KNOX. The main entrance to Fort Knox is located off Highway 31 West in Radcliff. Fort Knox is the home of Cavalry and Armor. The Patton Museum of Cavalry and Armor, located in Keyes Park just beyond this welcome monument, is the Armor Branch Museum for the United States Army.

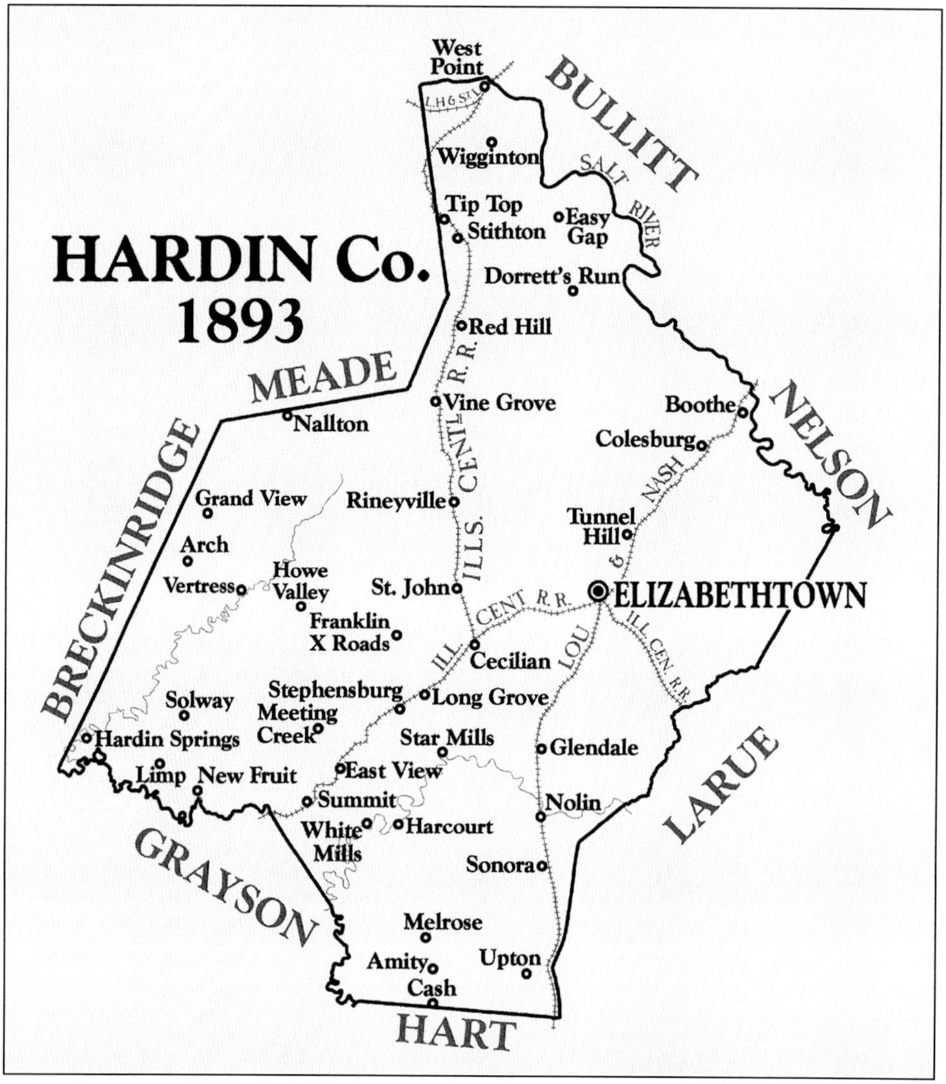

HARDIN COUNTY, 1893. In 1903 large-scale military maneuvers around and within West Point, in northern Hardin County, established the area as an army training installation. When land was purchased in 1918 for establishment of the installation, approximately 40,000 acres of land in Hardin County, as well as a small portion of Meade County around the town of Muldraugh, were included. The "towns" of Wigginton (also known as Pleasant View), Tip Top, Stithton, Easy Gap, and Dorrett's Run were seized. Schools, churches, farms, and businesses came to be known only in memory, documents, and photographs. However, these towns were not incorporated; throughout the 19th century and beyond, areas were placed on maps and regarded as towns by inhabitants if it had a post office, store, church, and/or school in close proximity. Stithton was the largest of these towns, with three churches, two schools, hotels, a train depot, a post office, a blacksmith shop, stores, and other characteristics of a town. A cemetery close by also helped define an area as a town. Dorrett's Run had only a store, a post office (for a short time), and a school. In the 1950s Red Hill, outside the boundaries of the military installation, became the town of Radcliff. It must be noted that in earlier times the spelling of place names was not always consistent. Some early historians, and often newspapers, did not regard a name worthy of use unless it could be spelled several different ways.

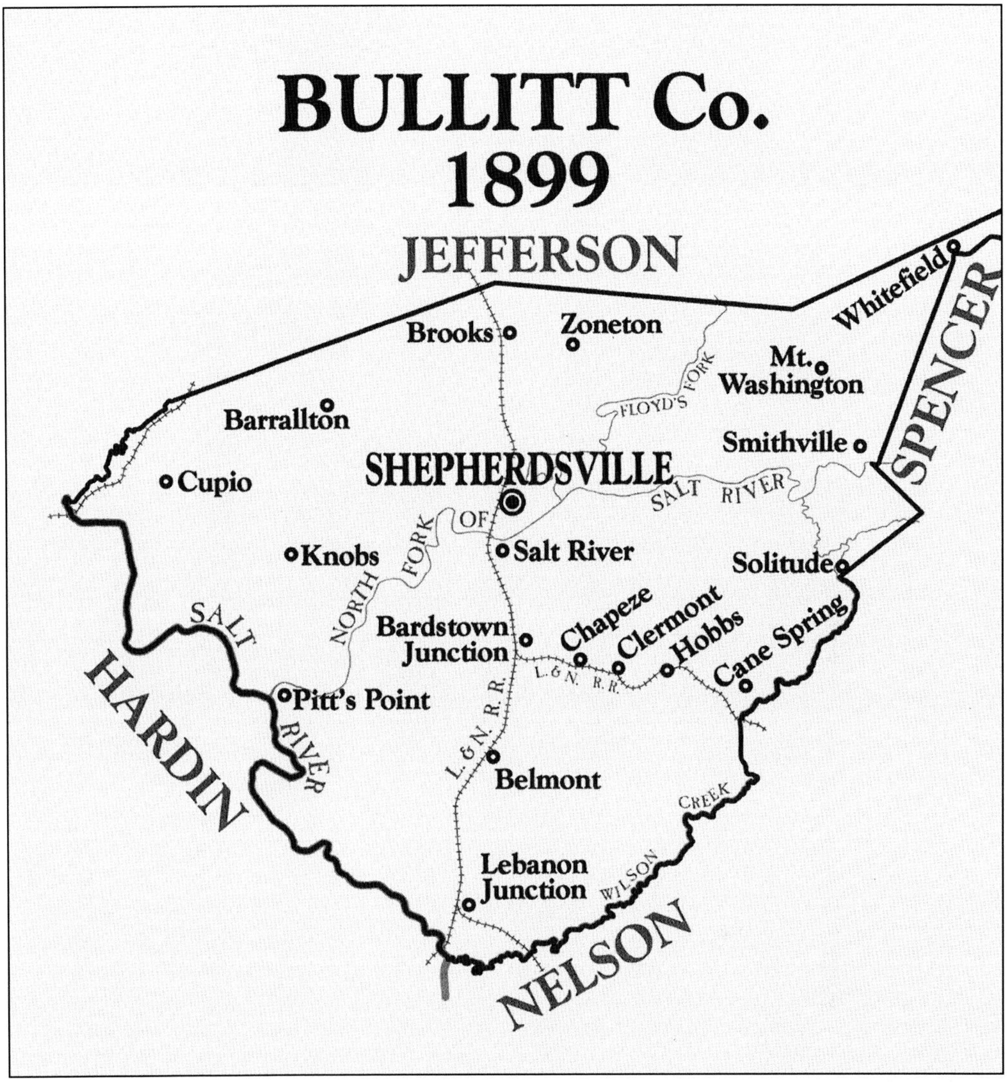

BULLITT COUNTY, 1899. Initially, Bullitt County was not greatly affected by the military maneuvers of 1903 and the establishment of Camp Knox in 1918. In 1941–1942, the expansion of Fort Knox resulted in the acquisition of approximately 40,000 acres of land in Bullitt County and some additional land in Meade County. The town of Pitts Point, in Bullitt County, was consumed; its two churches, school, hotel, and all else associated with the town were no more. The area south of Pitts Point and west of Belmont was known as the Flats; this area had some of the finest farm land in the area and perhaps in the state. What were once farms, churches, schools, and businesses is now an area where guns fire and shells explode as part of Fort Knox military training. Farms that had been held by families for five generations were purchased by the government, and the owners were sent to seek new homes and livelihood elsewhere. The area that was the site of Native American battles with settlers, Civil War skirmishes, and steamboats plying the Salt and Rolling Fork Rivers has no visible evidence of its past but for the numerous cemeteries that contain the remains of the earliest settlers.

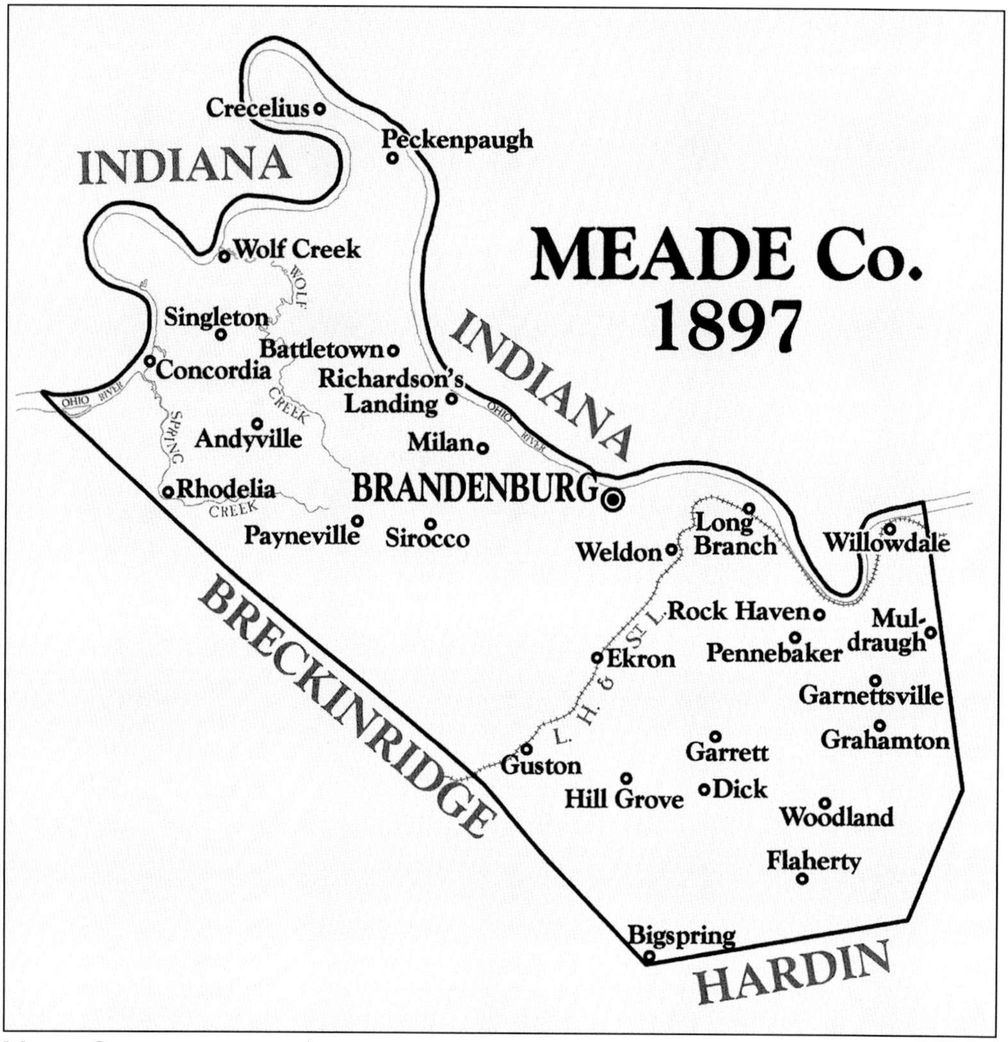

MEADE COUNTY, 1897. In the 1918 purchase of land for the establishment of Camp Knox a small portion of Meade County south of Muldraugh and extending west of Highway 31 West was taken. The town of Muldraugh was spared. The 1941–1942 expansion of Fort Knox took another larger portion of Meade County; Muldraugh was again spared but was then completely surrounded by the military installation and thus denied future expansion. Fort Knox extended to Otter Creek in Meade County and beyond. The once flourishing mill towns of Grahampton and Garnettsville on Otter Creek were taken and are now only memories. One building that was once a residence in Grahampton remains as silent evidence that these towns once existed along this section of Otter Creek. Highway 1638 over Otter Creek passes through the center of land that was once Garnettsville. No visible evidence of the town remains except for the Garnettsville cemetery that rests atop the hill just north of the highway and east of Otter Creek. Highway 60, at the point where a bridge carries the road over Otter Creek, passes through what was once the town of Grahampton.

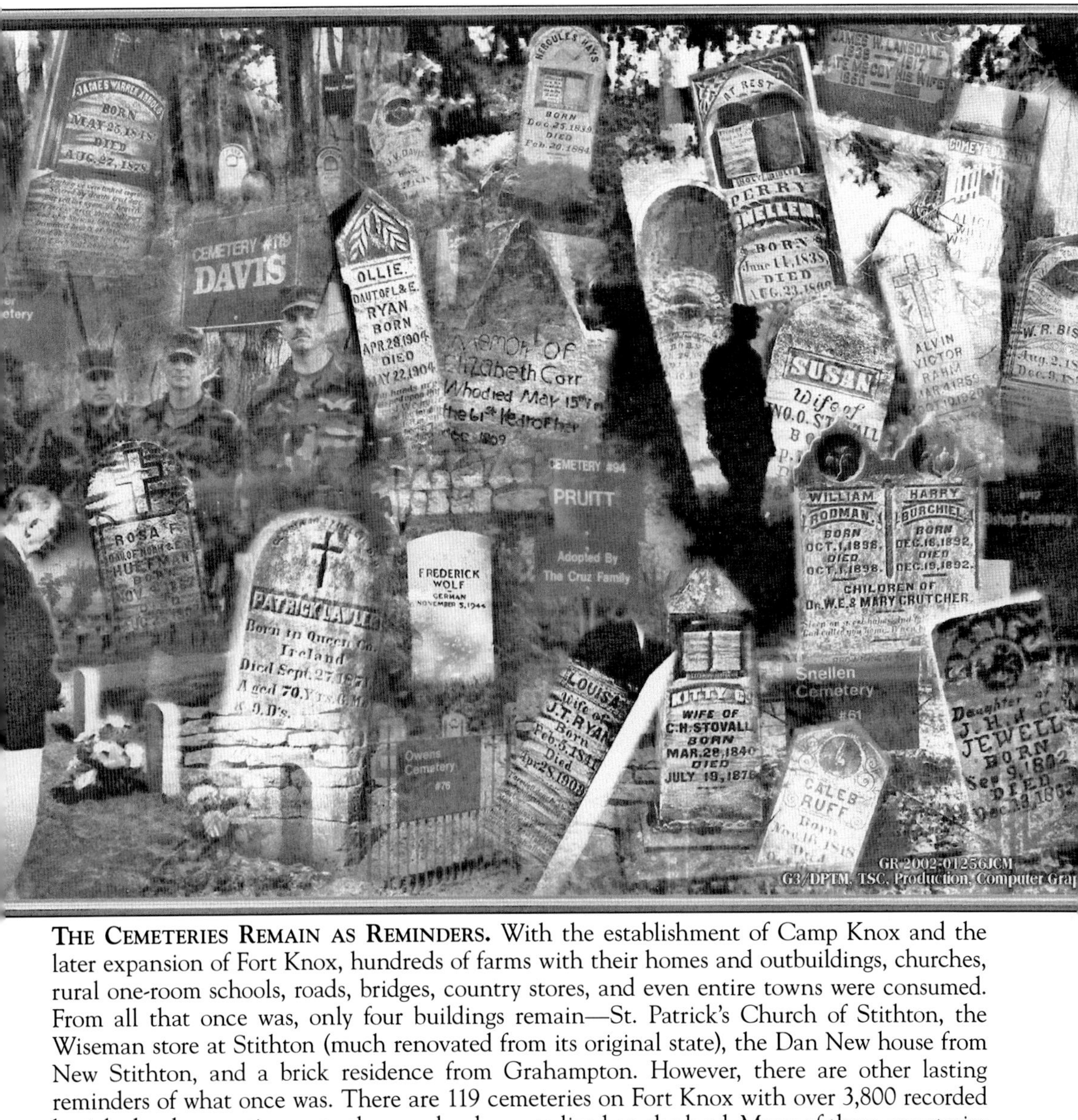

The Cemeteries Remain as Reminders. With the establishment of Camp Knox and the later expansion of Fort Knox, hundreds of farms with their homes and outbuildings, churches, rural one-room schools, roads, bridges, country stores, and even entire towns were consumed. From all that once was, only four buildings remain—St. Patrick's Church of Stithton, the Wiseman store at Stithton (much renovated from its original state), the Dan New house from New Stithton, and a brick residence from Grahampton. However, there are other lasting reminders of what once was. There are 119 cemeteries on Fort Knox with over 3,800 recorded burials that bear testimony to the people who once lived on the land. Many of these cemeteries contain the graves of the earliest settlers in the area, as well as some of the most prominent citizens of Kentucky and the country.

FORT KNOX, KENTUCKY
1776 - Present

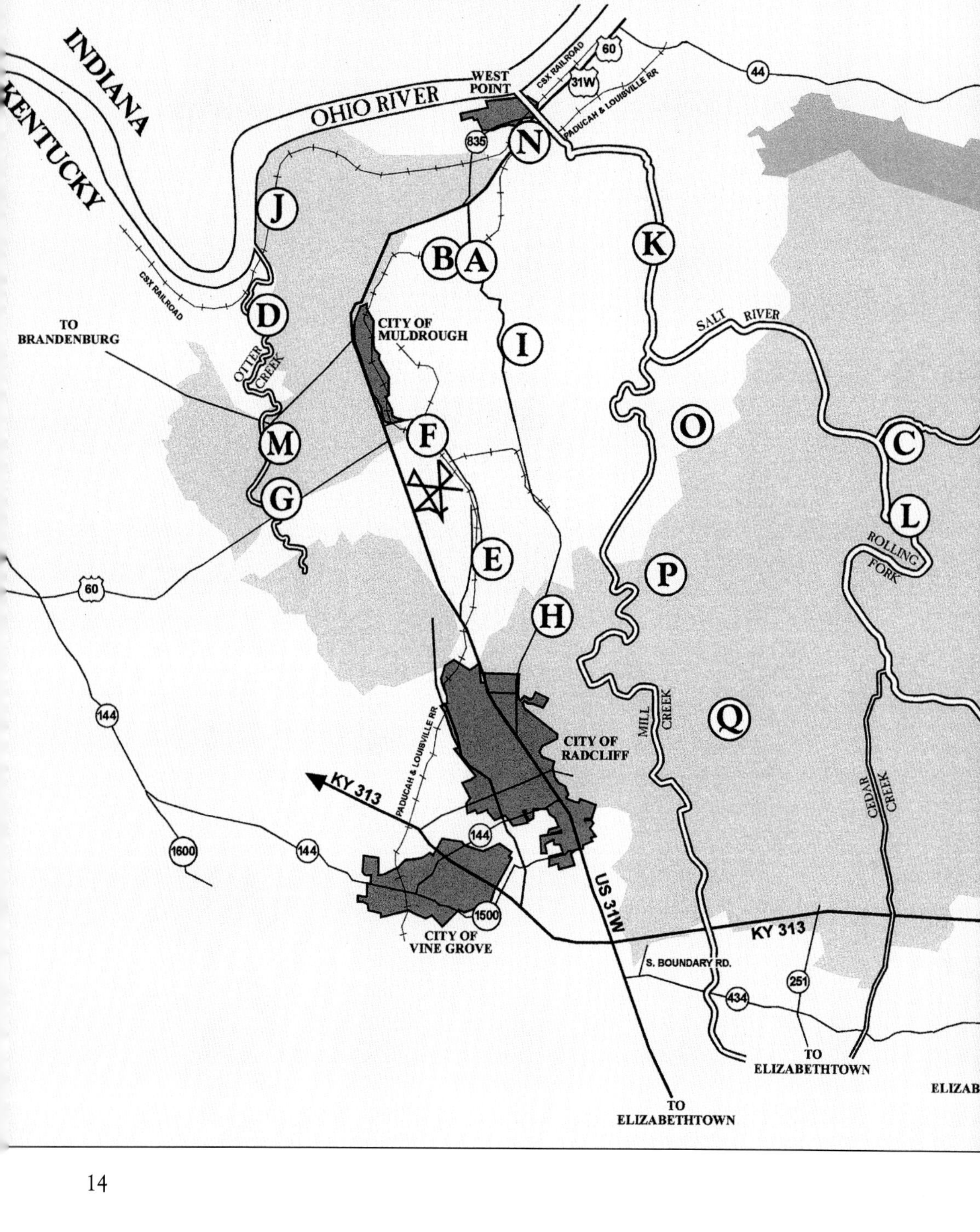

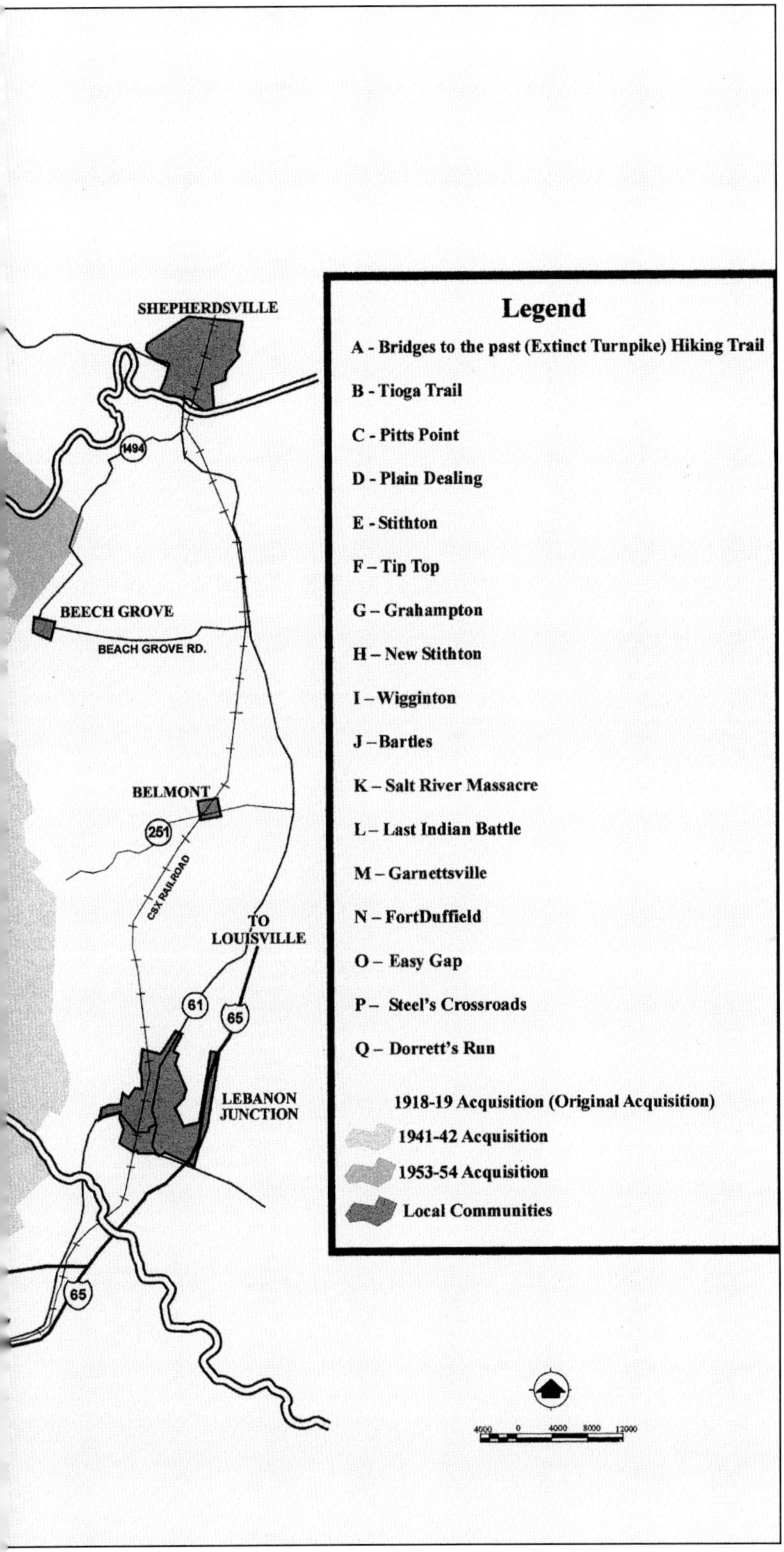

EARLY PLACES AND EVENTS ON THE LAND. The time of initial Euro-American entry into the Fort Knox area is uncertain, but by the last quarter of the 18th century numerous hunters, surveyors, explorers, and fortune-seekers had traversed this part of Kentucky. Such well-known pioneers as Thomas Bullitt, Michael Stoner, and Daniel and Squire Boone had been active in the area. The earliest known attempt to settle this area took place in 1776, when Shane, Sweeney, and Company, led by Samuel Pearman, traveled by flatboat down the Ohio River and then up the Salt River to the junction of the Salt and Rolling Fork Rivers. Here, they built a log cabin before numerous Native American attacks forced their retreat back to Virginia. Samuel Pearman later returned and with James Young established the town of West Point.

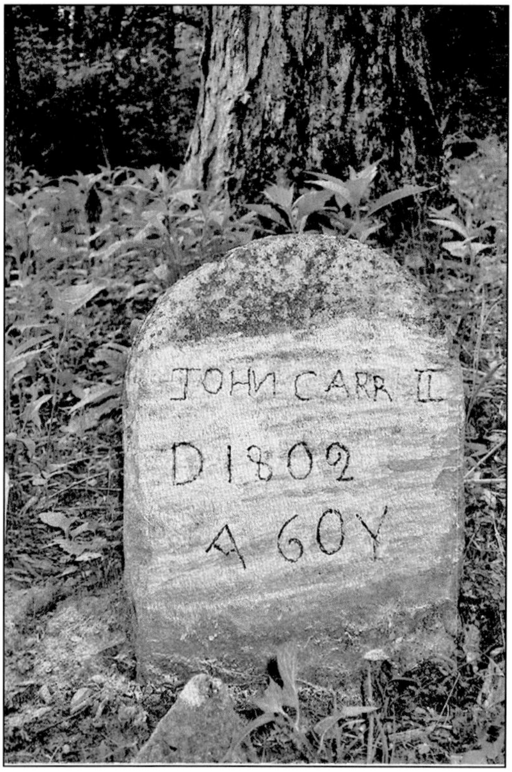

Pioneer Settler. John Carr was known to have been in Kentucky as early as 1780, exploring the area that later became the town of Pitts Point at the confluence of the Rolling Fork and Salt Rivers. He departed and returned some years later to build a log cabin west of the Rolling Fork River at the northeast base of Sugar Loaf Mountain. It is known that John and his wife, Elizabeth, had two sons and a daughter at this time.

The Death of John Carr. In 1788 eight miles below the mouth of the Rolling Fork River, Henry Crist, Soloman Spears, one woman, and ten other men in a boat loaded with kettles in transport to the salt works at Bullitt's Lick (just west of Shepherdsville) were surprised by a large party of Native Americans. A fight ensued and most of the men were killed or wounded, and the woman was captured and taken prisoner to Canada. This became known as the "Salt River Massacre" or the "Battle of the Kettles." In 1792 the last major battle between Native Americans and settlers occurred south of Pitts Point where Browns Run empties into the Rolling Fork River; this was the "Battle of Browns Run," where the Native Americans suffered a major defeat. However, minor skirmishes with Native Americans were not over; in 1802 John Carr was attacked and killed by Native Americans while tending his crops. He was buried not far from his cabin, and his wife was later buried beside him.

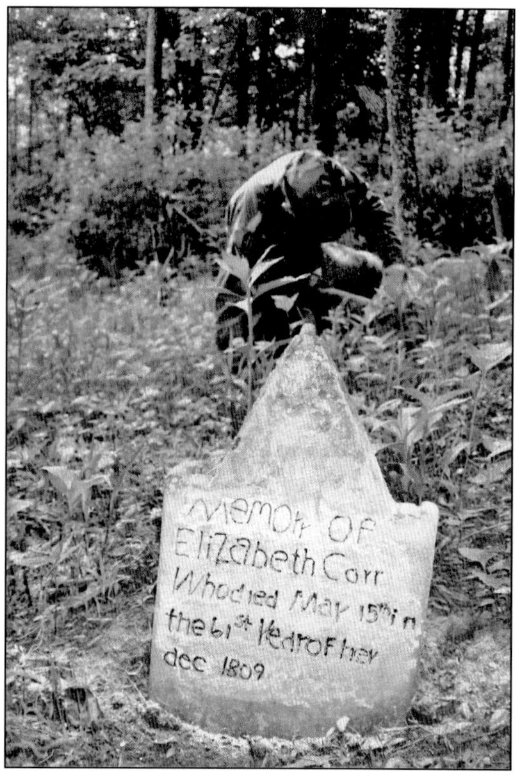

PIONEER SETTLER ENOCH BOONE. Daniel Boone and his brother Squire, along with John Carr, explored the area that is now Fort Knox. Squire Boone was a preacher and is said to have preached in Mill Creek Baptist Church, which was on land purchased for the expansion of Fort Knox in 1941–1942. Enoch Boone was the son of Squire. Enoch and his wife, Lucy, settled with their children in a log cabin atop Muldraugh Hill. Nearby, a cemetery was established where some of the earliest settlers in Kentucky were buried. Enoch and his wife were buried in this cemetery, which is now part of Fort Knox. Enoch was buried in 1862 and Lucy in 1858. Their daughter Lucy Jane and her husband, Collins Fitch, along with other members of the Boone family, are also buried here.

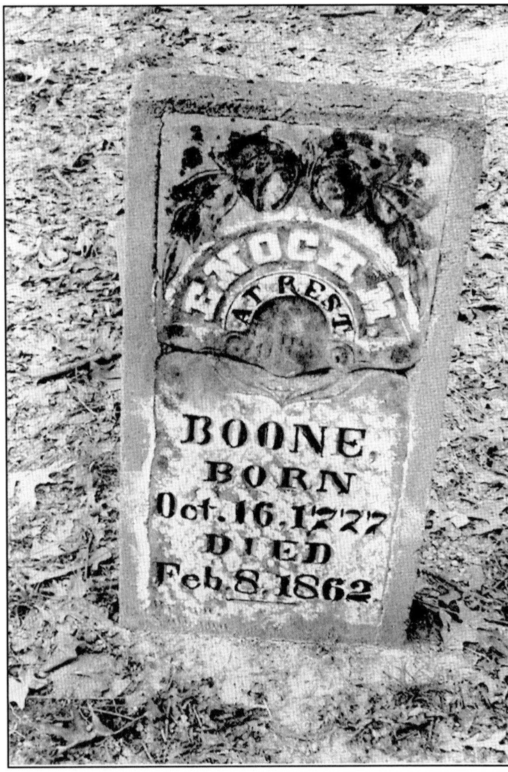

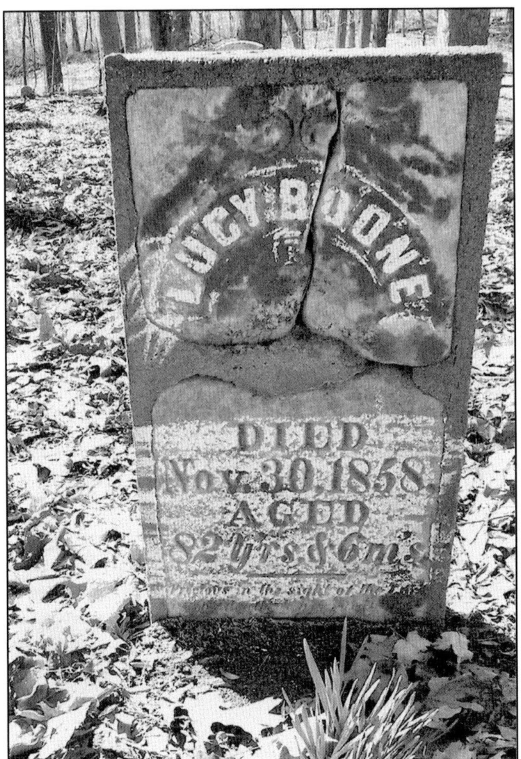

THE "TOWN" OF PLAIN DEALING. Southwest of the Boone Cemetery, on the banks of Otter Creek, a town known as Plain Dealing arose shortly after the arrival of the Boone family. The town had a post office, store, and tavern at one time. Collins Fitch, son-in-law of Enoch Boone, built a fine home near Plain Dealing. If one knows where to look, the remnants of Collins Fitch's home, barns, and blacksmith shop can be found along with remnants of the road that led from the Fitch home to Plain Dealing. Enoch Boone and Collins Fitch operated a merchandise store at the confluence of Otter Creek and the Ohio River. Collins Fitch was a prominent citizen and judge in Meade County.

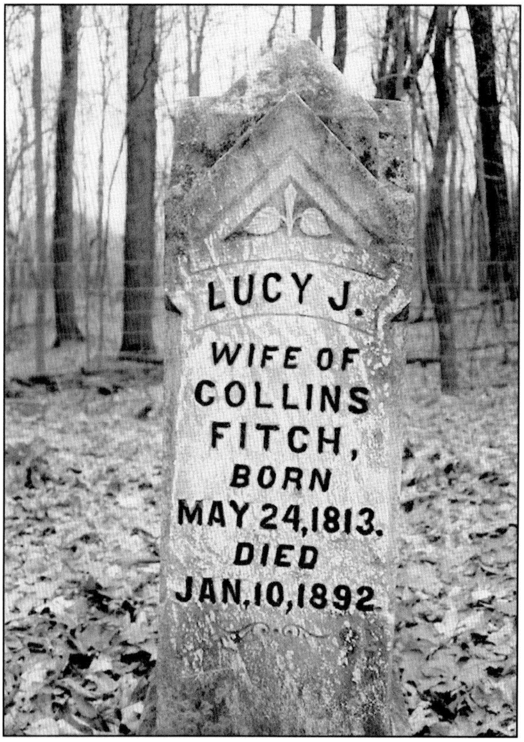

THE BOONES ON THE LAND THAT BECAME FORT KNOX. Lucy Jane Boone, the daughter of Enoch and Lucy Boone, married Collins Fitch and lived a comfortable life on a farm just east of the now extinct town of Plain Dealing. Remnants of their handsome farmhouse are visible today. The post office at Plain Dealing was used by Collins, Lucy Jane, and other farm families in the area. Farms in the area along Otter Creek were prosperous and raised corn and often pumpkins that were sent to a cannery in Austin, Indiana, which still operates today. In the time of Enoch Boone and Collins Fitch, the land along Otter Creek was not forested as it now is; it was flat, productive, fertile farmland.

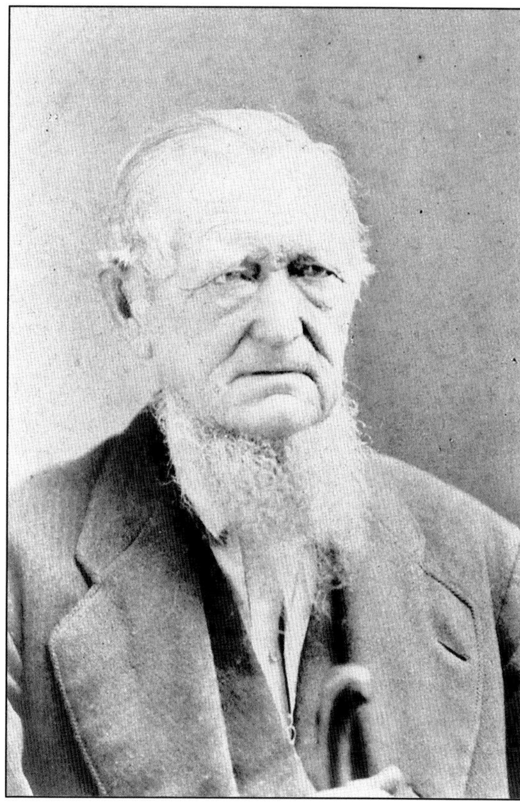

COLLINS FITCH, MEADE COUNTY JUDGE. Collins Fitch operated a store at the mouth of Otter Creek with his father-in-law, Enoch Boone. Collins became prosperous and prominent, and then he became a Meade County judge. He lived to be nearly 100 years old. Descendants of Collins and Lucy live throughout the area to this day. The *Elizabethtown News* of March 6, 1891, contained the obituary of Collins Fitch: "Judge Collins Fitch died last Wednesday at his home near Garnettsville in Meade Co. Born May 13, 1792 in Washington Co., N.Y. Was in the War of 1812. Came to Lexington in 1817. In 1832, he settled in Meade Co., where he married a daughter of Enoch Boone, a nephew of Daniel Boone, and the first white child born in Kentucky."

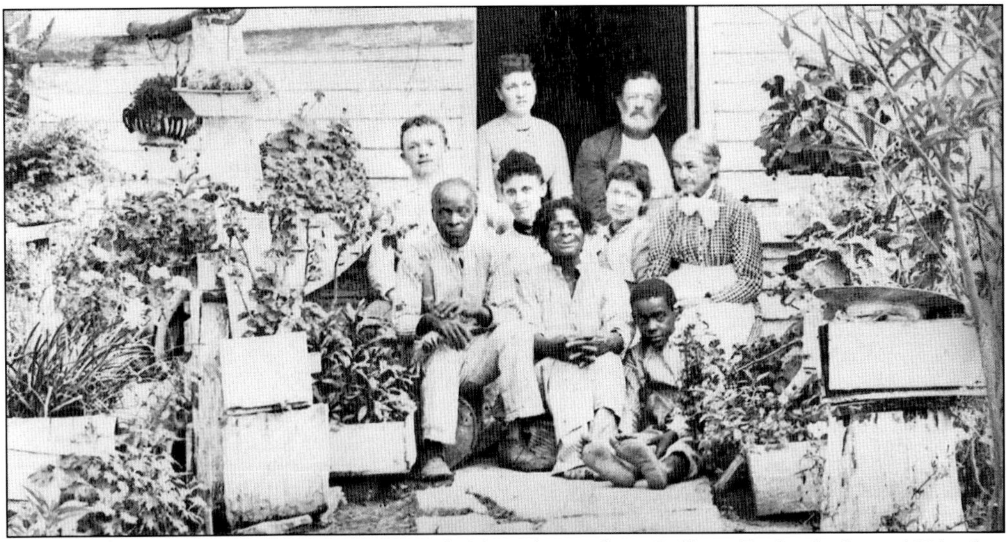

COLLINS FITCH HOME, C. 1890S. Probably taken after Collins Fitch died in 1891, this photograph shows, from left to right, (front row) "Uncle" Dick Fitch, Henrietta Bischoff, unidentified woman (possibly Dick Fitch's wife), Emma Kunnecke Schooler, unidentified child, and Louise Behrens Kunnecke; (back row) William R. Kunnecke, Bertha Fitch, and William Tandy Fitch, Collins's son. Dick Fitch and his wife, once slaves of Collins Fitch, remained with him as farm workers after the Civil War. In his handwritten will, which survives today, Collins left 30 acres of land and a house to a man named Dick Fitch.

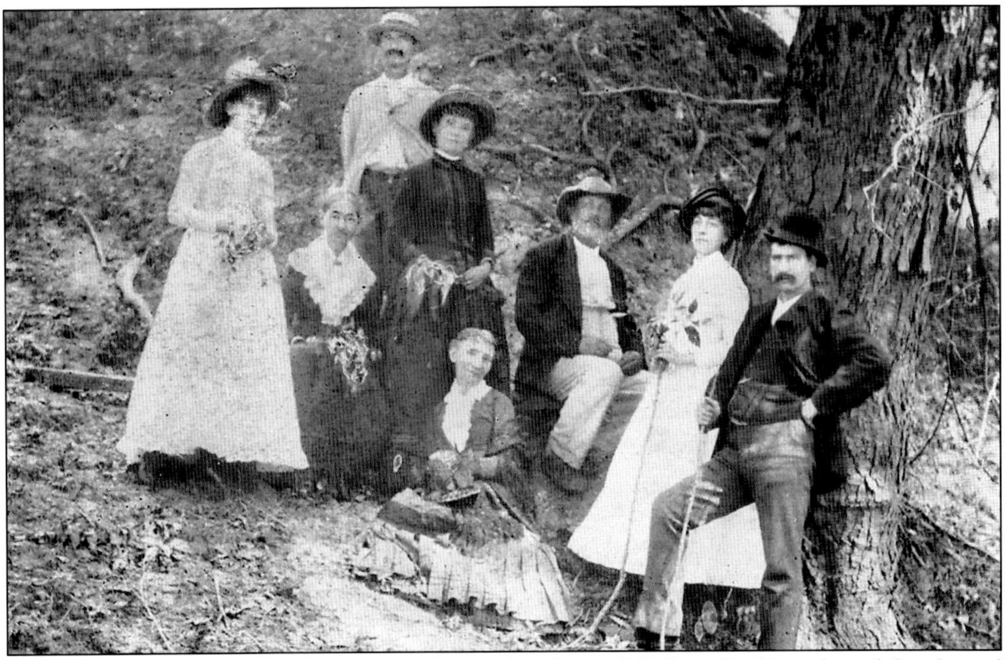

NEAR THE COLLINS FITCH HOME, C. 1891. The dress of Collins Fitch's wife and family and the will Collins Fitch left attest to the family's prosperity. Lucy Jane Fitch (daughter of Enoch Boone) died soon after this picture was taken. Pictured from left to right are Emma Kunnecke Schooler, Lucy Jane Fitch, Herman F. Kunnecke, Margaret Hogan Kunnecke, Louise Behrens Kunnecke, William Tandy Fitch, Bertha Kunnecke Fitch, and John H. Schooler.

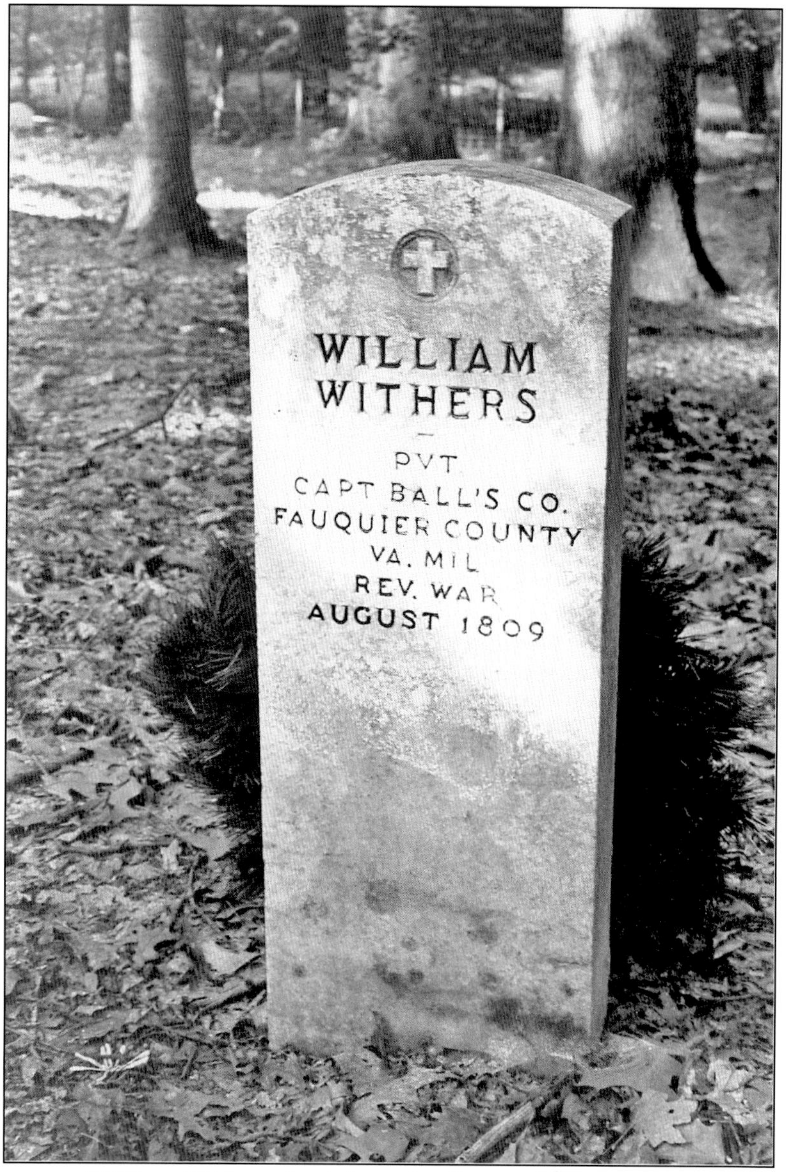

EARLY SETTLER. William Withers, buried in the Boone Cemetery, was a veteran of the American Revolution; many veterans received land in Kentucky as a pension for their war service. Withers planned to leave Culpepper County, Virginia, and migrate to Kentucky around 1805; however, his wife's death prevented him from leaving until 1808. Leaving Virginia with 11 members of his family and 19 slaves, William claimed most of the land that later became known as Bartles, Kentucky, and the range of hills east of Iron Mountain. He built his home on top of a hill overlooking the Ohio River in two directions, near Round Hollow. Withers did not live long enough to enjoy the benefits he hoped to achieve in Kentucky, as he died slightly over a year after his arrival. His older children kept the family together. The 1810 census listed the oldest son, William B. Withers, then 24, as the head of the household. William Withers was the first to be buried in the Boone Cemetery, and the last known was John Allen Medley on October 21, 1945. The last owner of the land on which the cemetery rests was Claude Lewis Withers.

REVOLUTIONARY WAR LAND GRANT. Michael Hargan is buried in Patterson Chapel Cemetery. Michael was a Revolutionary War veteran and, as such, was given 400 acres of land along the Rolling Fork River in what became Hardin County. He married Elizabeth Wallingford in 1791 and then moved from Virginia to his land in Kentucky. Many of Kentucky's early settlers were veterans who received land as pensions for military service, and most grants bore the signatures of Patrick Henry or Thomas Jefferson, Virginia governors. Michael rested in an unmarked grave until Memorial Day, 1993, when his descendants, some from as far as California, placed this monument in the Patterson Chapel Cemetery, which is associated with a Methodist church that once sat nearby.

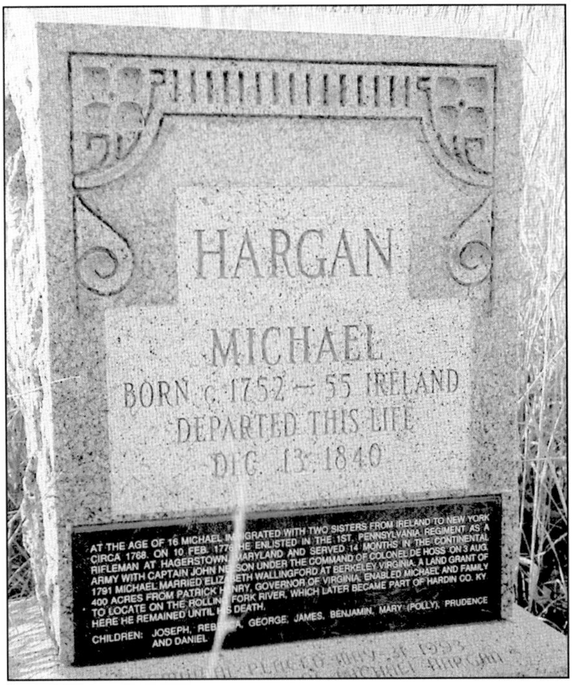

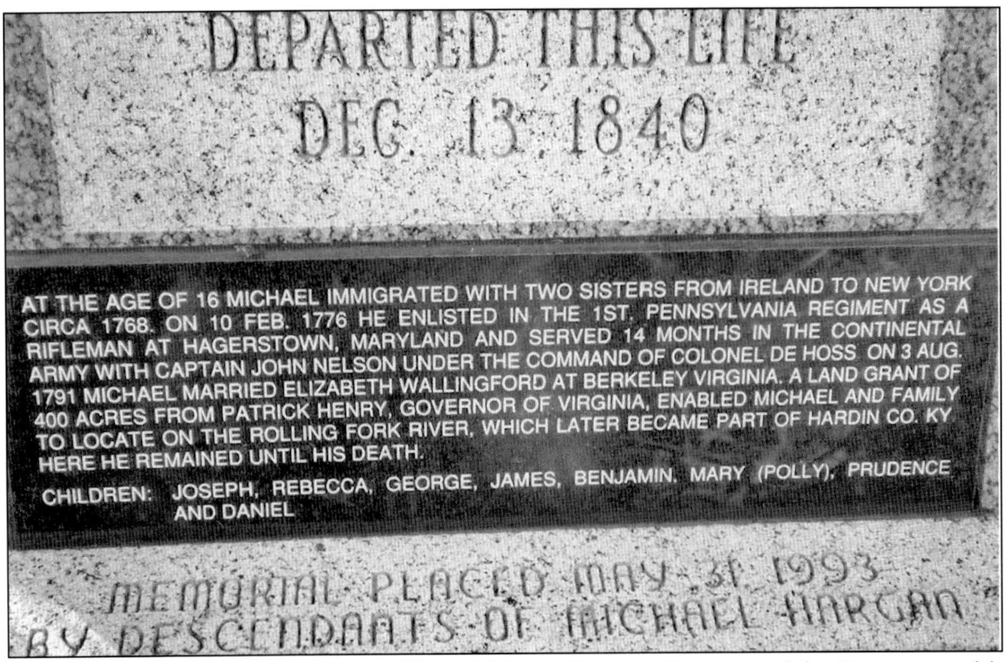

MICHAEL HARGAN'S LAND GRANT. "Patrick Henry Esquire, Governor of the Commonwealth of Virginia, to all to whom these presents shall come Greeting. Know ye that by virtue and in consideration of part of a land office Treasury Warrant Number 19114 issued the 2nd day of September 1783 this is granted by said Commonwealth unto Michael Hargan assignee of Andrew Hynes a certain tract or parcel of land containing four hundred acres by survey bearing date 20th day of November 1784. . . ." The grant delineates the land using the Salt River, Cedar Creek, two white oak trees, and two dogwood trees; it bears Patrick Henry's signature.

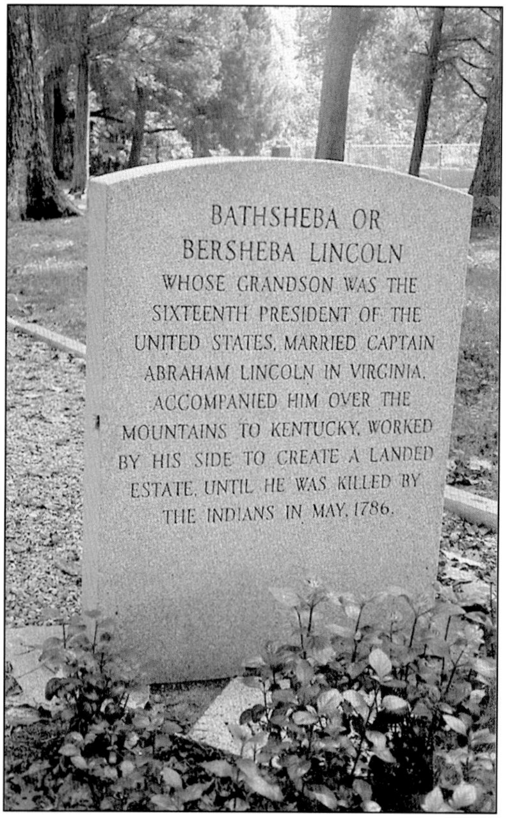

The Lincoln Connection to Fort Knox. The Mill Creek area of the land that is now Fort Knox was one of the earliest areas to be settled. The *Elizabethtown News* of September 6, 1878, reported, "The flouring mill located on Mill Creek known as the James Stovall Mill, caught fire one day last week and burned to the ground." It is known that a mill existed much earlier than the Stovall Mill. A Baptist church was erected in the Mill Creek Valley in 1783. Capt. Abraham Lincoln, grandfather of our martyred 16th President, helped build the church. The Mill Creek Valley lies entirely within the boundary of Fort Knox. In 1803 and for a time thereafter, Thomas Lincoln, father of President Abraham Lincoln, owned and lived upon a farm in the valley. Bathsheba Lincoln, grandmother of our 16th President, also lived for a time in the valley and was buried in the Mill Creek Cemetery, now known as the Lincoln Cemetery.

The Mill Creek Valley. The site of the Mill Creek cabin of Thomas Lincoln was located near the Baptist church. The stone foundation of this church can still be seen today within the cemetery that surrounded the church on three sides. Thomas's mother Bathsheba is buried in this cemetery along with several other Lincoln kin. The earliest known burial in the cemetery, now known as the Lincoln Cemetery, was that of Susan Calvin on March 11, 1830. Much of Mill Creek Valley remains as it was when the pioneer families first settled upon the land. The Mill Creek Valley was taken for the expansion of Fort Knox in 1941–1942. The gravestone of William Brumfield, shown here, has suffered from the action of time and the elements.

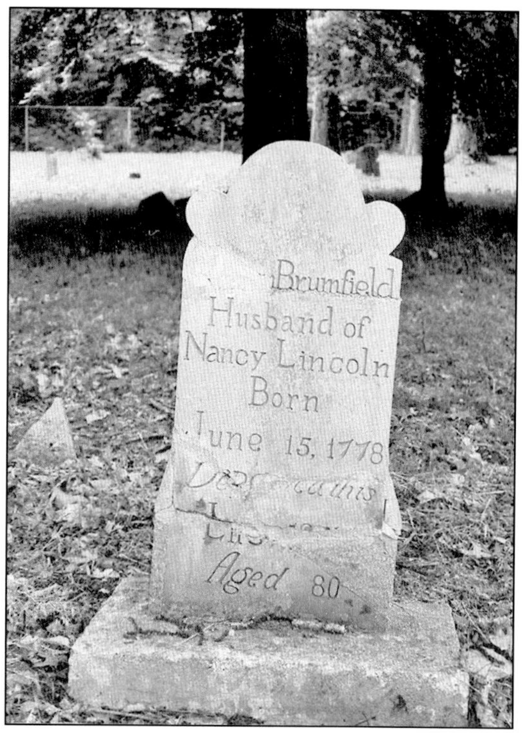

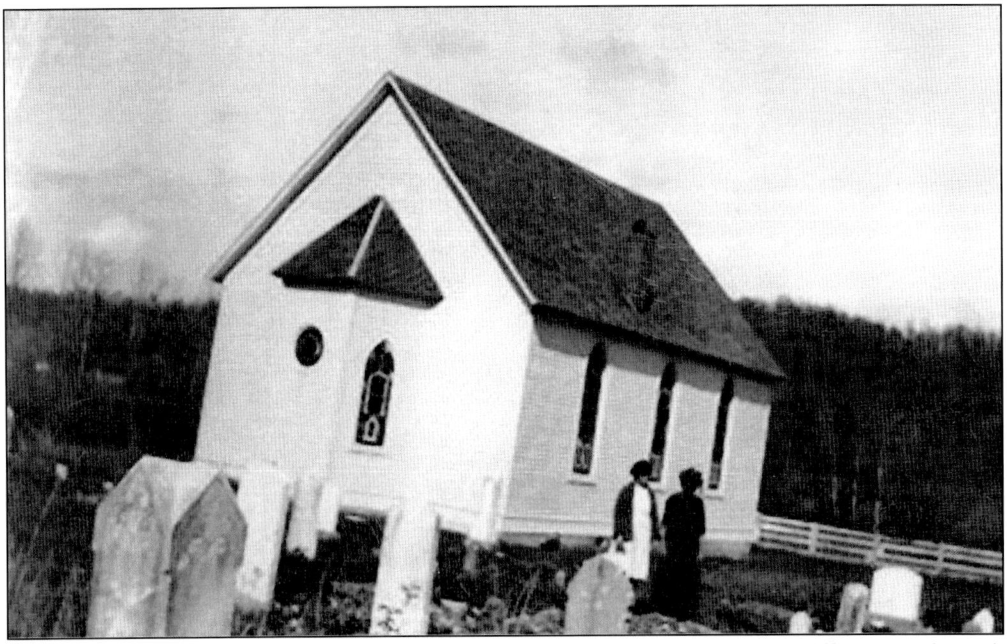

THE CEDAR CREEK VALLEY OF FORT KNOX. Virginia preachers Louis Chastine and Jacob Enlow organized a church that was built in 1801 by a Methodist congregation in the Cedar Creek Valley. Nathan Viers, at 94 years old, was one of the first received into it. The first church in this valley was a log structure, later replaced by a wood-frame building. Like Mill Creek, Cedar Creek and its valley lie within the boundaries of Fort Knox. It is east of Mill Creek and flows into the Rolling Fork River; Mill Creek flows into the Salt River.

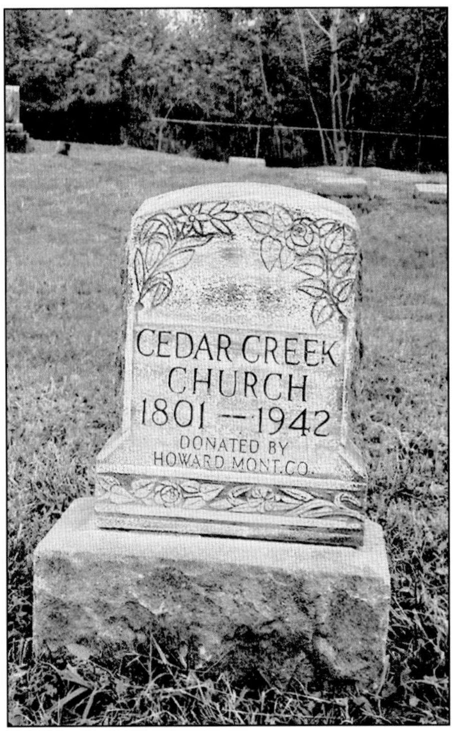

THE CEDAR CREEK CEMETERY. The cemetery around the Methodist church contains graves of some of the area's earliest settlers. Cedar Creek was taken in 1941–1942 for the expansion of Fort Knox but is opened each Memorial Day for visitation by descendants of those buried within. The earliest known burial in the cemetery was that of William W. Viers on January 10, 1857, and the last burial was Robert L. McCullum on November 9, 1949. There are 143 known and recorded burials in the cemetery; however, more are suspected of being buried within, but their names may be forever lost.

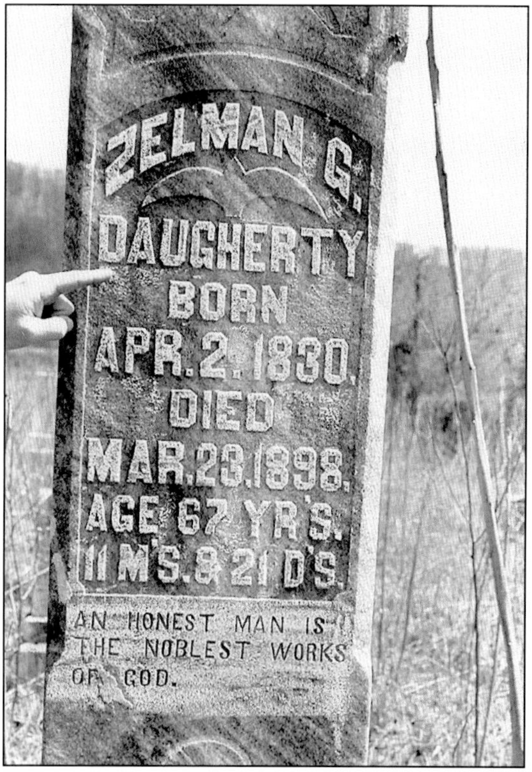

ZELMAN G. DAUGHERTY—FARMER, SLAVE HOLDER, ECCENTRIC. Some of the early settlers of Cedar Creek brought slaves with them or acquired them later. Zelman G. Daugherty was a slave owner. He was wealthy with extensive land holdings in Texas and California, yet he lived the life of a poor hermit in his dilapidated farmhouse with his slave William Daugherty. When slaves were set free following the Civil War, William remained with Zelman. Rev. Cornelius S. Daugherty, brother of Zelman, was pastor of the Cedar Creek Methodist Church in the early 20th century. Cornelius is buried in an unmarked grave in the Cedar Creek Cemetery.

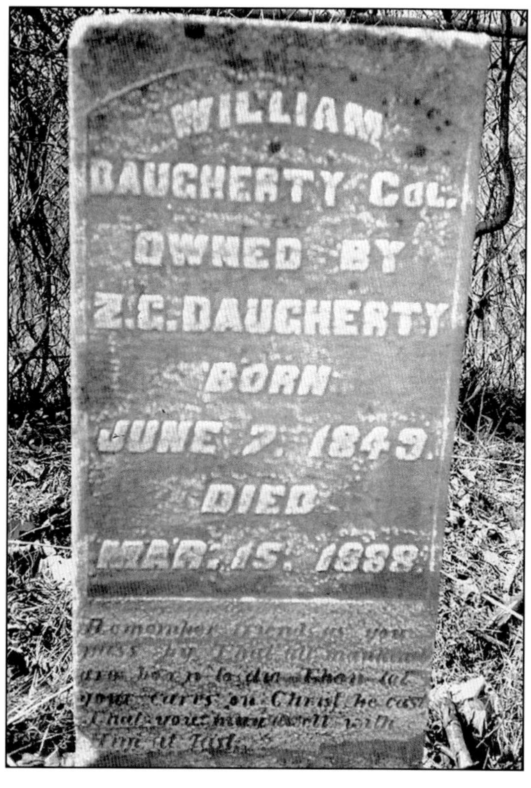

WILLIAM DAUGHERTY—ONCE A SLAVE. In a far back corner of the cemetery is the grave of William Daugherty, one-time slave of Zelman. Though William died in 1888, Zelman evidently thought he still "owned" him as evidenced by careful reading of the inscription on William's gravestone. A poetic inscription on the bottom portion of the stone reads: "Remember friends as you/ Pass by that all mankind/ Was born to die. Then let/ Your cares on Christ be cast/ That you may dwell with/ Him at last."

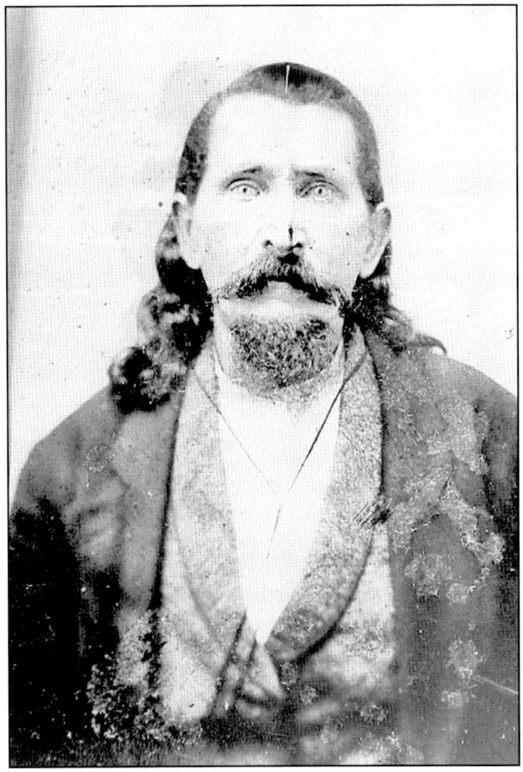

ZELMAN DAUGHERTY, 1890. Zelman Daugherty was a fearsome looking man, eccentric in appearance and actions. Though wealthy, he allowed his niece to live in poverty and eventually to be placed in the "poor house" in Elizabethtown. It has been said that his niece would have refused to live with her uncle if an offer had been made, as his house was unkempt and had received little or no repairs while Zelman lived there. In August 1892 the *Elizabethtown News* reported, "Mary Margaret Meyers, age 26, filed a breech of promise suit for $10,000 against Zelman Daugherty for trifling with her affections." At this time Zelman was not a young man. His 1898 obituary in the Elizabethtown newspaper was not kind to Zelman. It noted, "He never allowed his hair to be cut so it would dangle just above his waist."

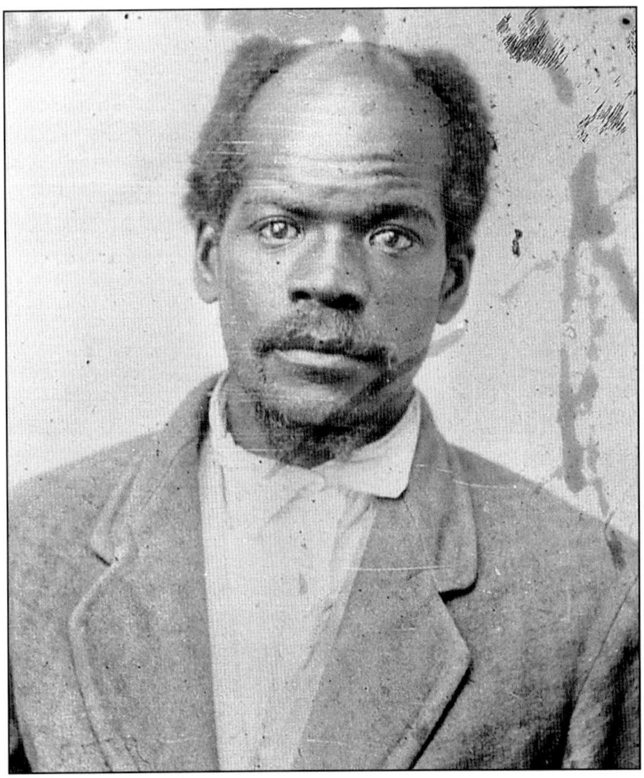

WILLIAM DAUGHERTY, 1885. William Daugherty was once a slave of Zelman and remained with Zelman following the emancipation of slaves after the Civil War. The 1880 census lists William as (shown here as it appeared on the census record) "Wm. Daugherty, black man, farm worker, suffering of T. Fever, and living with Z.G. Daugherty." It was common in the dark days of slavery in America for slaves to be given the name of their "owner." It was also common for slaves, once freed, to remain with their one-time "owners" as hired help or tenant farmers.

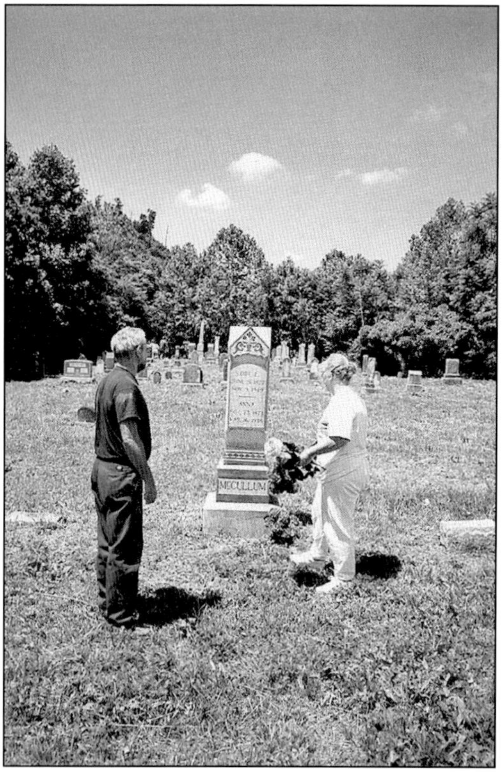

CEMETERY VISITORS AT CEDAR CREEK. Each Memorial Day since the seizure of land in 1941–1942 for the expansion of Fort Knox, 119 cemetery sites have been opened for visitation by descendants of those buried within. Visitors come from near and far to pay respect to those deceased. Fifth and sixth generation descendants now visit the cemeteries on Fort Knox. Some have first-hand recollections of life in the Cedar Creek Valley, as well as the church and school that united the community for over 100 years.

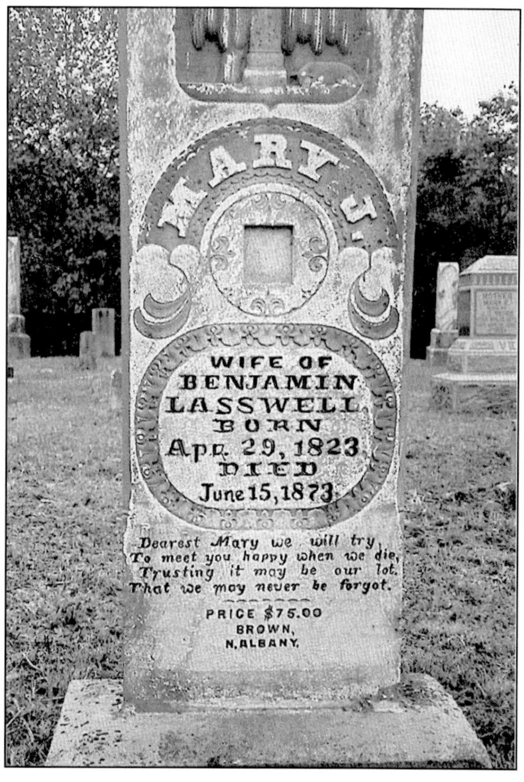

STRANGE INSCRIPTIONS. There are 153 known graves in Cedar Creek Cemetery and almost that many gravestones. The gravestones come in a great variety of sizes and shapes and bear a variety of poetic inscriptions and symbols. One of the more difficult inscriptions to fathom is that of Mary J. Lasswell. No one has been able to explain why the price of the gravestone was prominently inscribed on its base.

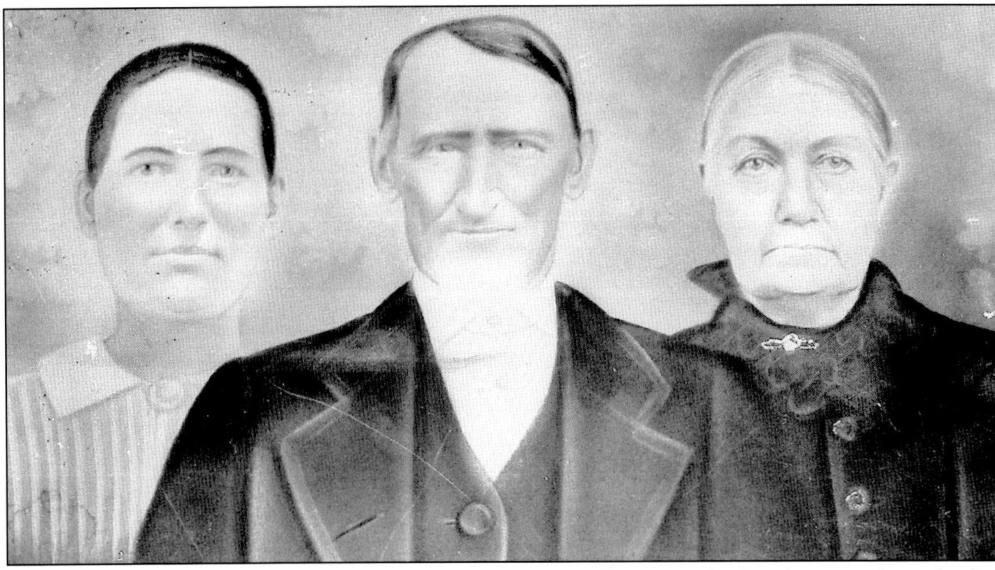

Benjamin Laswell (Lasswell) and Wives, c. 1895. Benjamin had a photograph made that superimposed an image of his first wife onto one of himself and his second wife. His first wife, left, was Mary Jane McWilliams. Her father was James McWilliams, son of James McWilliams, a Revolutionary War soldier who came to Kentucky via the Cumberland Gap around 1794. After her death in 1873 Benjamin married Nancy M. Clark in 1876. It is unknown why the price of Mary Jane's gravestone was carved onto its base ($75.00). All three are buried in Cedar Creek Methodist Church cemetery.

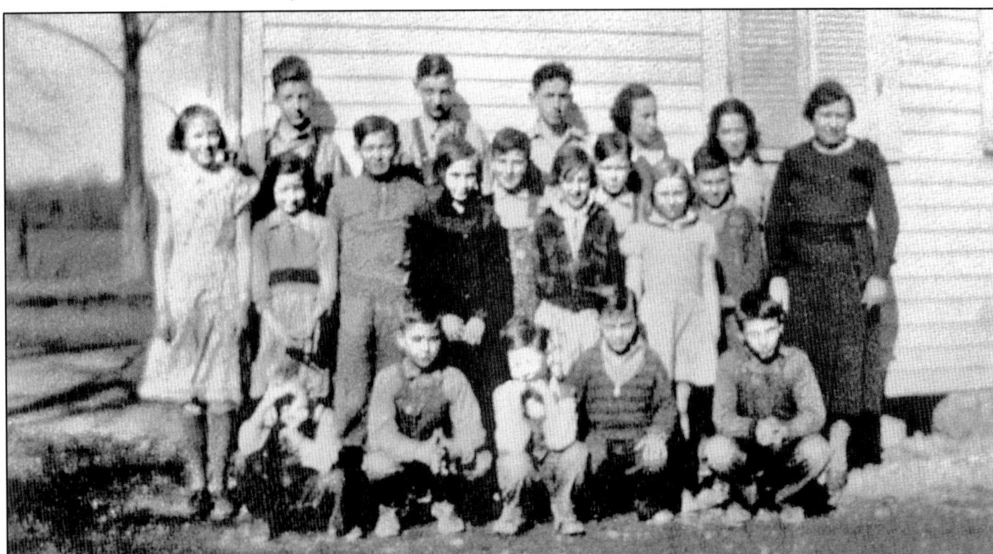

Cedar Creek School, c. 1938. Schools like Cedar Creek School, located two miles southeast of Patterson Chapel cemetery near Rolling Fork River in Hardin County, provided early education for future professionals. Students, from left to right, are (front row) Kenny Masden, Wilbur Sherrard, Harold Wise, Charles Henry Phillips, and Robert Lee French; (middle row) Inez Masden, Iris Wise, Clarence Boling, C.E. Crewz, Jerldine Judd, Charles Moore, Lillia Judd, and Nelis Stanley Phillips; (back row) John Hallet, Leo Smock, Chester French, Tina Jewell, and Lucile Earls. (Note: These names are spelled as provided.)

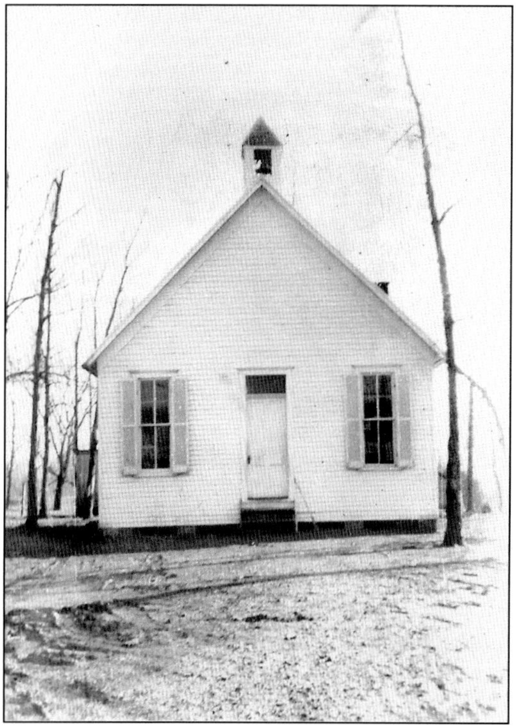

CEDAR CREEK SCHOOL. The Cedar Creek School was much like the other grade schools in Hardin, Meade, and Bullitt Counties that were seized as part of the establishment of Fort Knox and its later expansion. Most were one-room schools, but a few had two rooms. Cedar Creek and Mill Creek, as well as the towns of Stithton, Garnettsville, Grahampton, Stithton, New Stithton, Bartles, Pitts Point, Wigginton (Pleasant View), and Dorrett's Run had schools of this type. Other schools such as Harboldt, Liberty, Triplett, and Zion were located in areas between the towns.

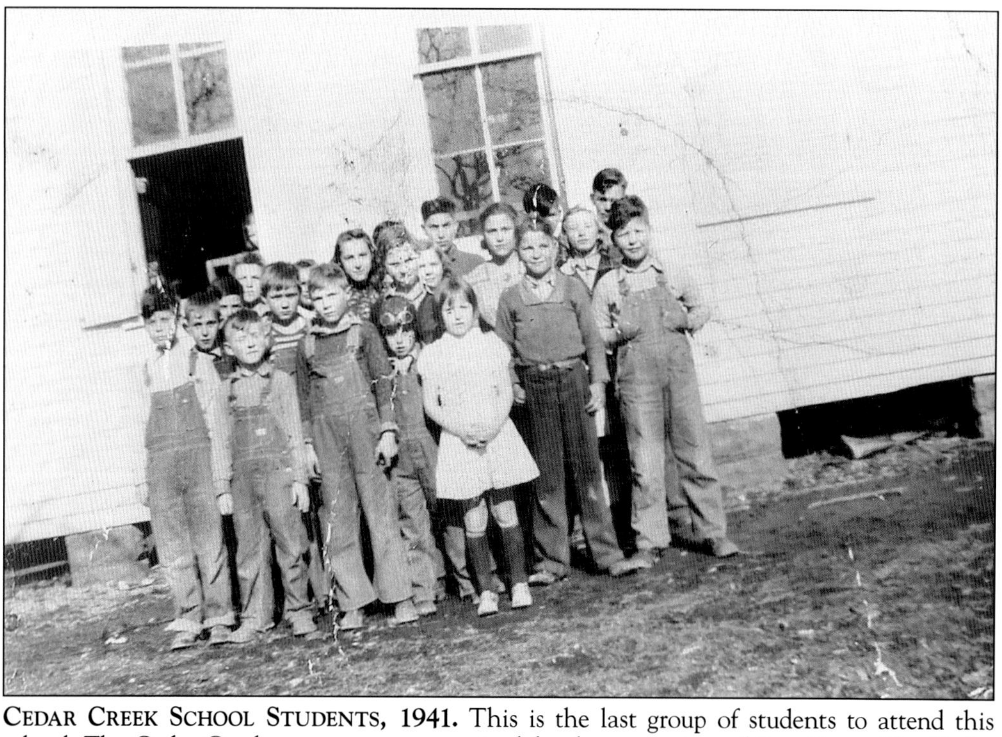

CEDAR CREEK SCHOOL STUDENTS, 1941. This is the last group of students to attend this school. The Cedar Creek area was soon acquired for the expansion of Fort Knox. The Cedar Creek School was opened as early as 1878 under teacher I.G. Stone. Where the school once stood and students played, the ground is now disturbed by rolling tanks and the fire of guns.

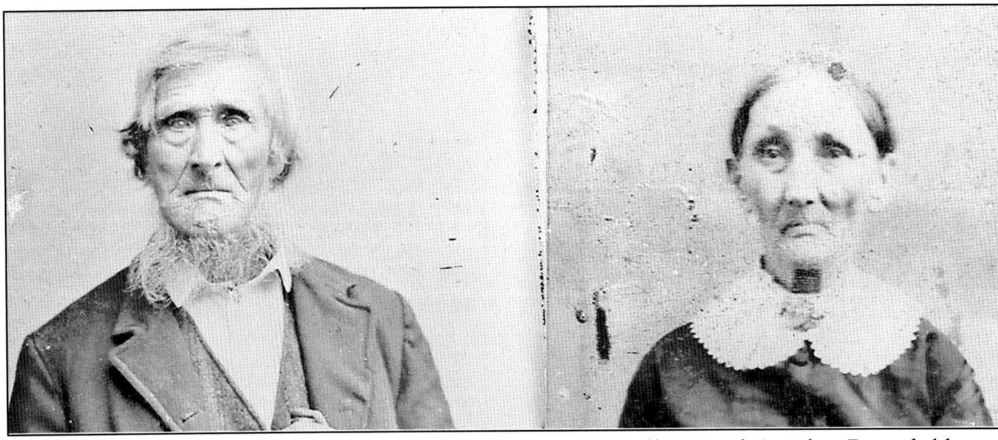

The Land West of the Rolling Fork River, 1895. William and Cynthia Brumfield were typical early farmers. They worked hard, prospered, and raised a family. When their children married, William and Cynthia gave the new couple a piece of land to raise their own families. William and Cynthia lived for a time in the now extinct town of Pitts Point. Their farm was west of the Rolling Fork River in Hardin County. The *Elizabethtown News* of August 1889 reported a dinner given by the Horticultural Society of Hardin County that honored "old folks over 70." William Brumfield was listed as a guest at 77 years old.

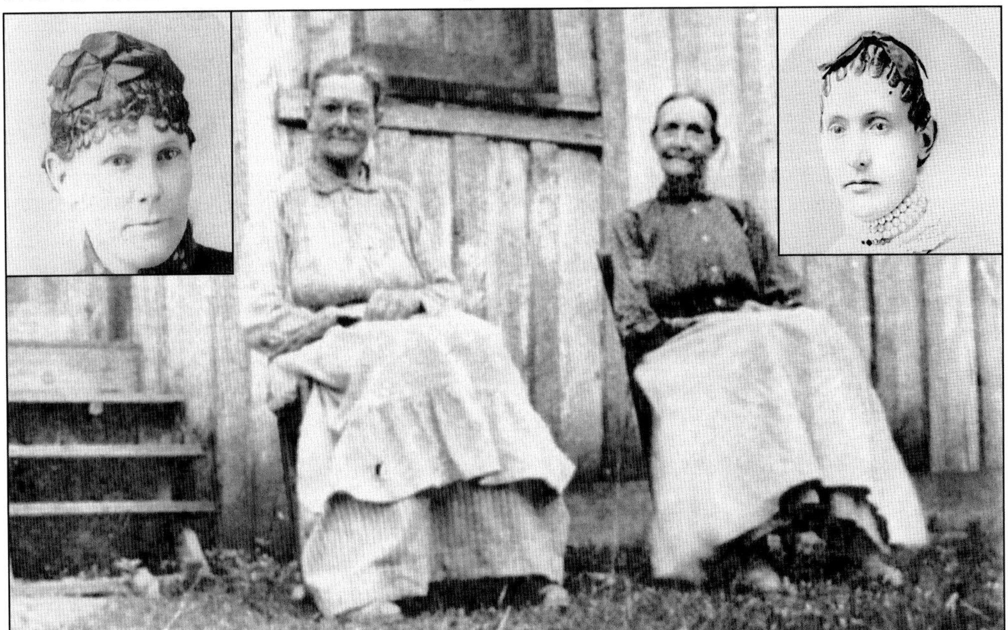

Second Generation Brumfields. Two of the Brumfied children were Joanna (1850–1925) and Mary Ellen (1844–1925). They lived together in the house they are sitting in front of in this photograph; it was near the Crandall cemetery where they were both buried. Mary Brumfield has her name erroneously spelled Broomfield on her gravestone. A misspelling is not uncommon on the gravestones in the 119 cemeteries on Fort Knox. Family members such as the Brumfields, like many others, would be born, live productive lives, and come to be buried all in the same area. They would seldom have traveled more than a few miles from their home, which was generally within close proximity to their parents' home. Each sister was born before the Civil War and lived to see men fly through the air in machines

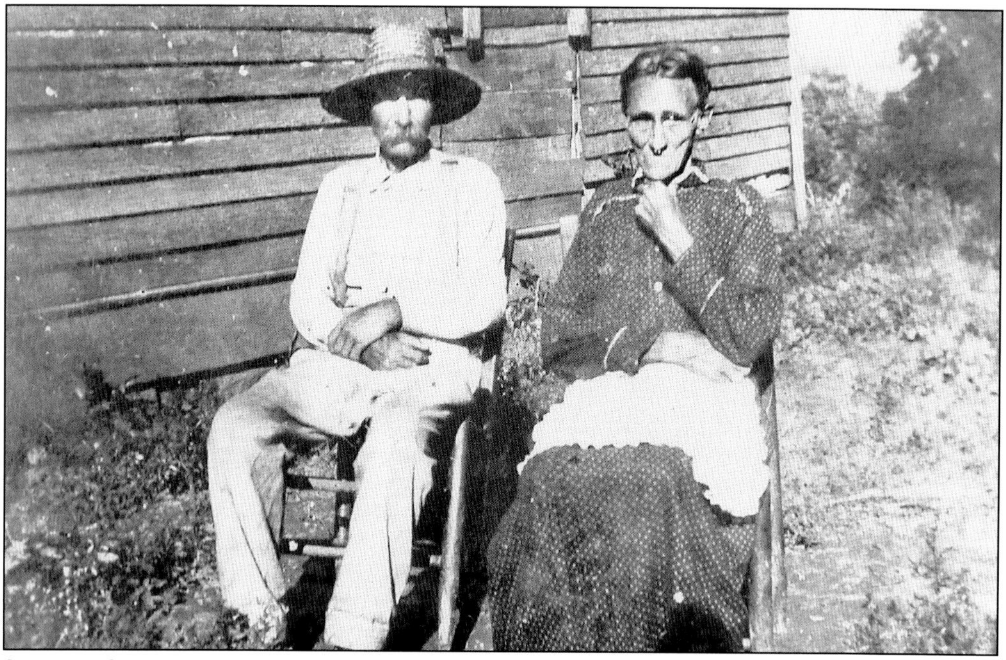

Second Generation of the Brumfield Family. George W. (1856–1931) and Angeline Brumfield Clark (1853–1936) sit at their home in 1930. Like their parents, George and Angeline were born, lived, married, had children, grew old, and were buried within a short distance of home, their parents' burial places, and their children's homes. William and Cynthia Brumfield, Angeline's parents, gave them this land when they married.

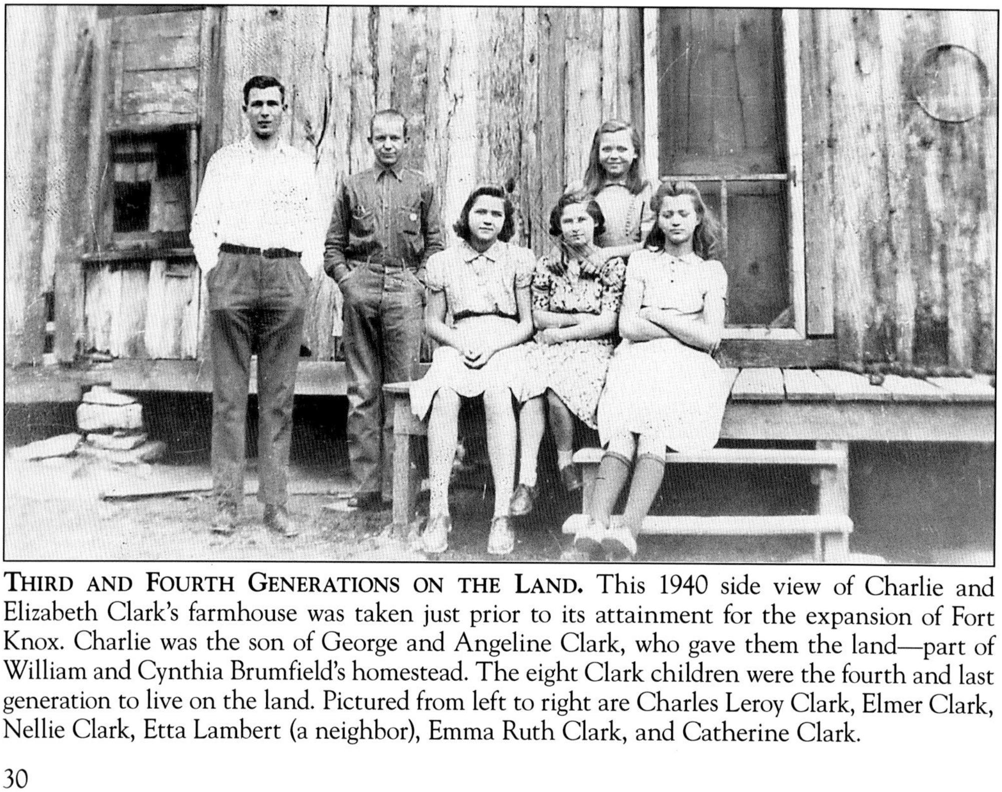

Third and Fourth Generations on the Land. This 1940 side view of Charlie and Elizabeth Clark's farmhouse was taken just prior to its attainment for the expansion of Fort Knox. Charlie was the son of George and Angeline Clark, who gave them the land—part of William and Cynthia Brumfield's homestead. The eight Clark children were the fourth and last generation to live on the land. Pictured from left to right are Charles Leroy Clark, Elmer Clark, Nellie Clark, Etta Lambert (a neighbor), Emma Ruth Clark, and Catherine Clark.

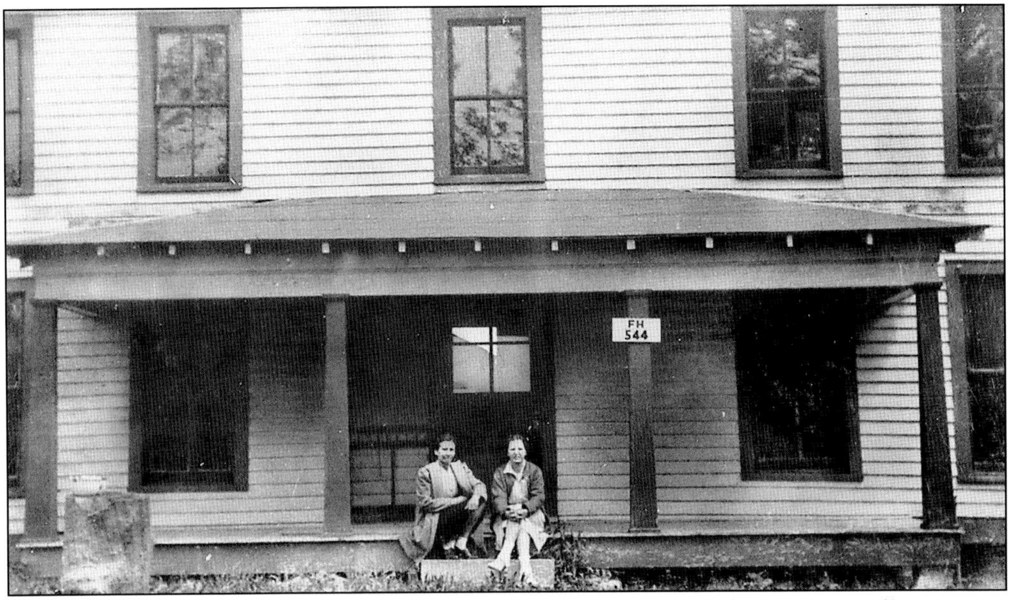

The Flats. Southeast of the confluence of the Rolling Fork and Salt Rivers in Bullitt County is an area known as the Flats. With some of the finest farmland in Kentucky, the area began to be settled in the early 19th century. In this 1941 view Hazel and Sadie Atcher sit on the porch of the empty Dawson farmhouse in the Flats. The Dawsons left when their farm was taken for the expansion of Fort Knox. Note the white sign on the porch post with the black letters FM 544. Every occupied building condemned for expansion of Fort Knox had such a sign, with a distinct number. An official letter followed in the mail notifying the occupants of the action.

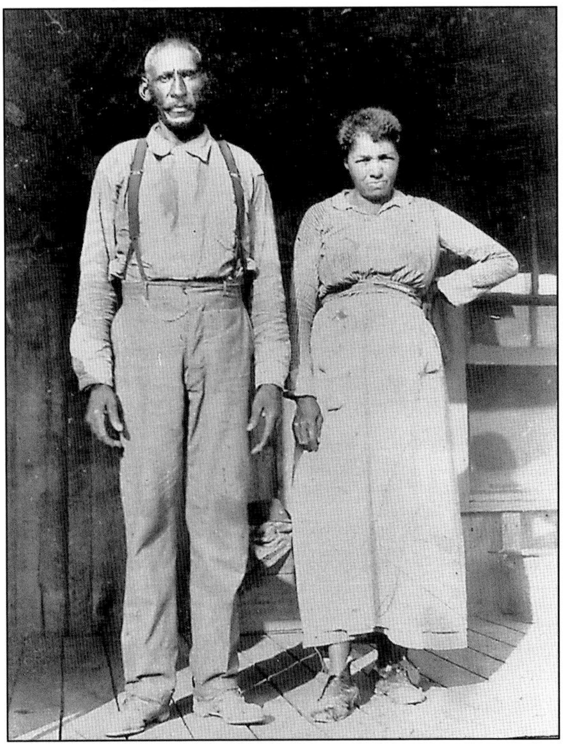

First Generation of Free African Americans. Tom and Molly Hill were tenant farmers on the Leonard Daugherty farm in the Flats. Just before the land was seized, the Hills moved to Pitts Point. Their home in Pitts Point was also taken. Tom, Molly, and their parents were born into slavery in the Flats. Molly was born on the Daugherty farm. The Leonard Daugherty "home place" was created when Leonard's father, Patrick Daugherty, married Rilla Stader, and they established a farm on the Stader property. Leonard married Mabel Ping, and they also established their farm on what was originally Stader land. Tom and Molly lived and worked on this farm.

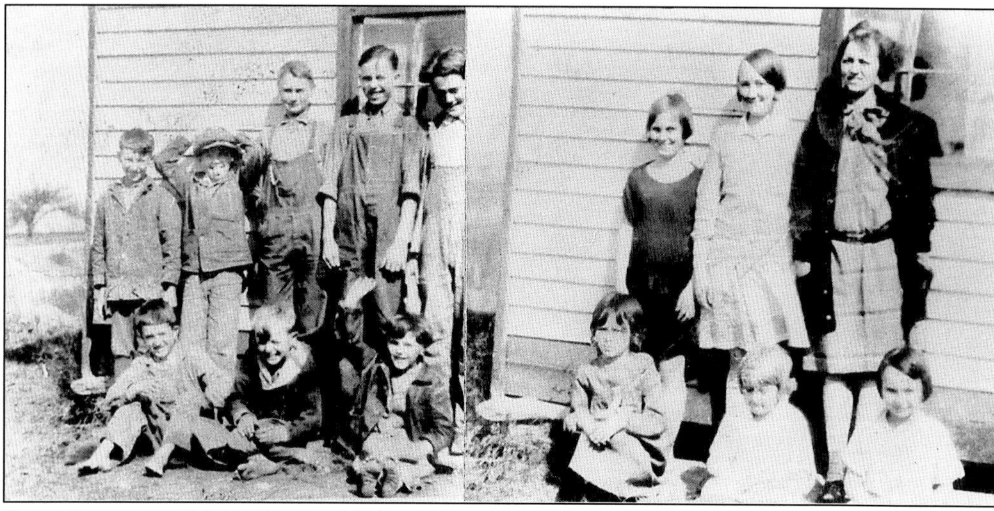

ZION SCHOOL, 1928. The establishment and expansion of Fort Knox consumed numerous schools in Hardin, Meade, and Bullitt Counties. Zion School was one such grade school in the Flats. Others were the Hays, Browns Run, and Beech Grove schools, all one-room schoolhouses attended by the local children. Students pictured from left to right, on the left, are (front row) Louis Gray, C.L. Ice, and Leo Newman; (back row) Raymond Coakley, Elmore Newman, Henry Lutes, Charles Conlin, and Raymond Hornback. Pictured from left to right, on the right, are (front row) Mary Conlin, Velma Lee Daugherty, and Louise Coakley; (back row) Dorothy Newman, Laverne Ice, and Louise Martin Bean (teacher).

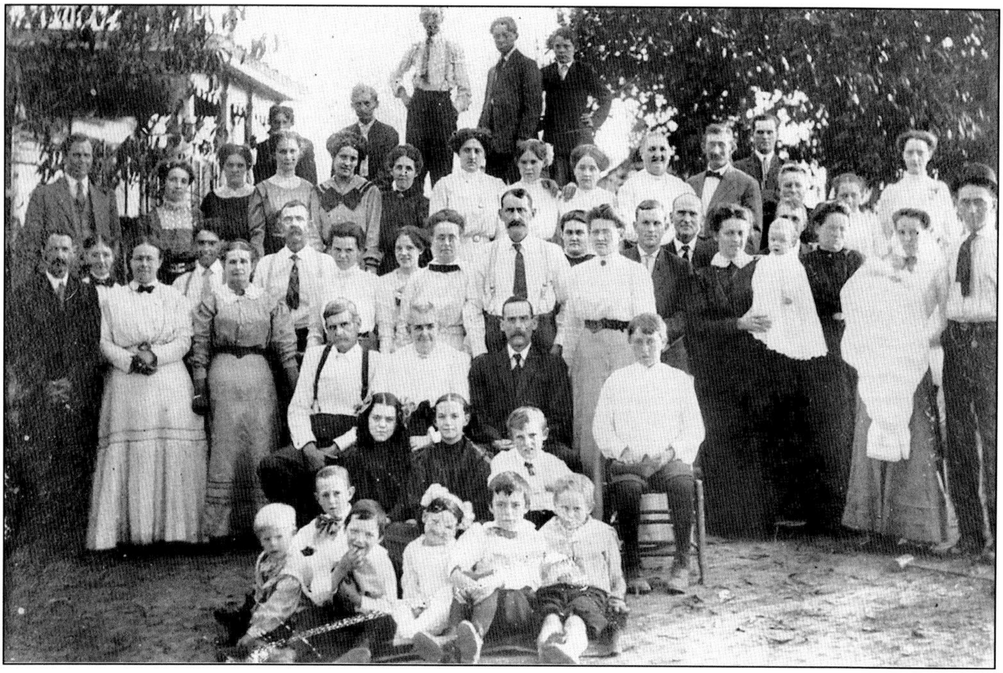

JAMES AND ELLA NEWMAN HOUSE IN THE FLATS, C. 1920. This is the last family gathering at the Newman house in the Flats; in March 1922, a fire destroyed the home. Perishing in the fire were Ella Stader Newman, her mother-in-law Mal Newman, the grandson of Ella Stader Newman, and Harry Newman, who died later from burns sustained while trying to rescue others.

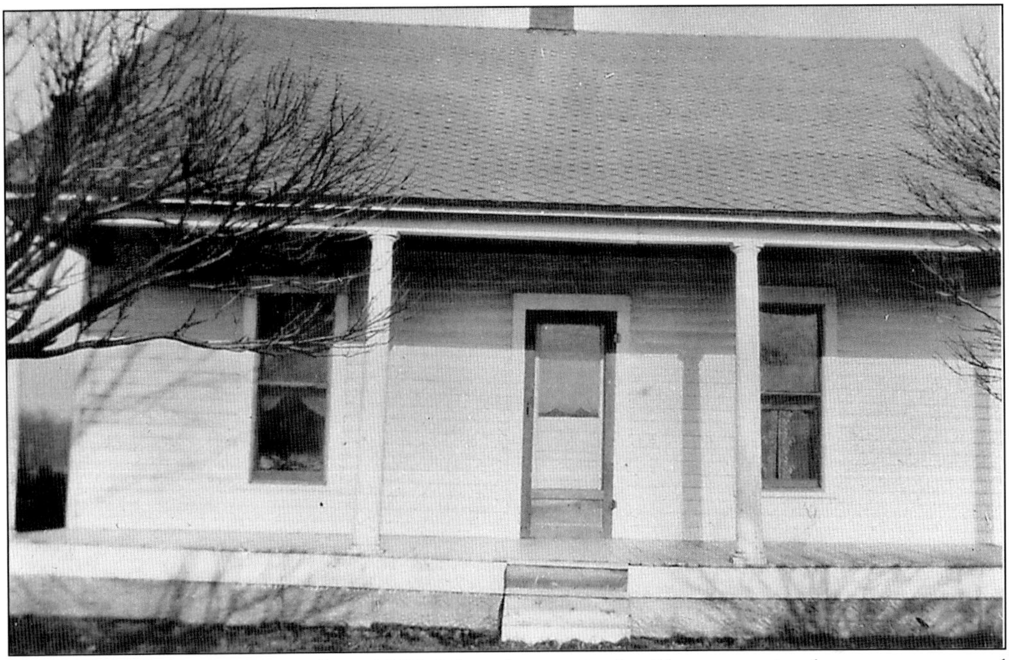

HOME OF LESLIE AND EDNA ICE, 1940. Many homes in the Flats were simple, one-story, wood frame homes, although some were two-story, and had long front porches with yards enclosed by picket fences. Remnants of earlier log homes often remained as outbuildings, slave quarters, or tenant homes. By the time the the land was taken, most of the farms were prosperous. The families had survived the Great Depression and had secured many of the material comforts commensurate with their efforts. Electricity and telephone service had just come to the area.

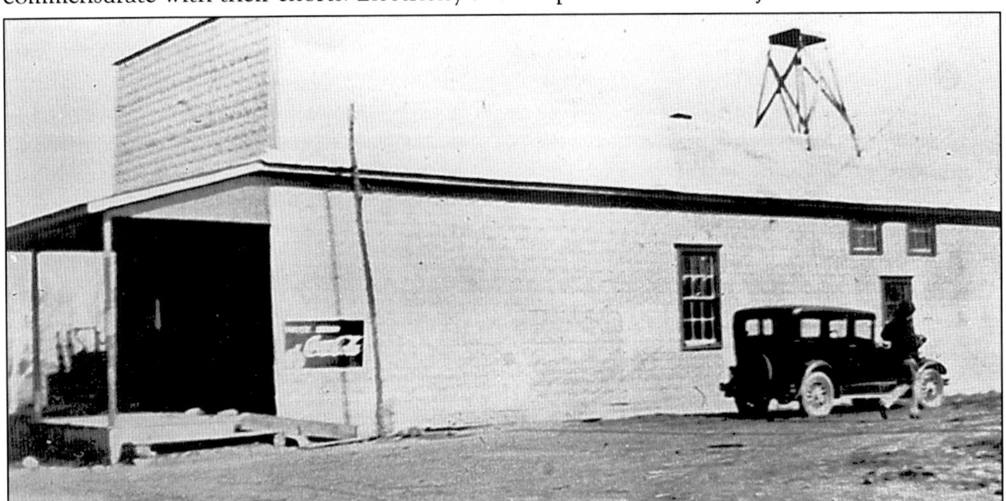

ELGY MASDEN STORE, 1942. The Masden store on Wooldridge Ferry Road near the intersection of Highway 251 served an area of Hardin County as well as Flats residents who crossed the Rolling Fork River on the Wooldridge Ferry Bridge into Hardin County. The store had a piano and was a place of congregation and entertainment for the "younger folks." The Hill Store, run by Claude Hill, was a smaller store on Belmont Road halfway between the Wooldridge Ferry Road and Belmont in Bullitt County. It served the Flats and was a favorite place for the "older" segment of the Flats population.

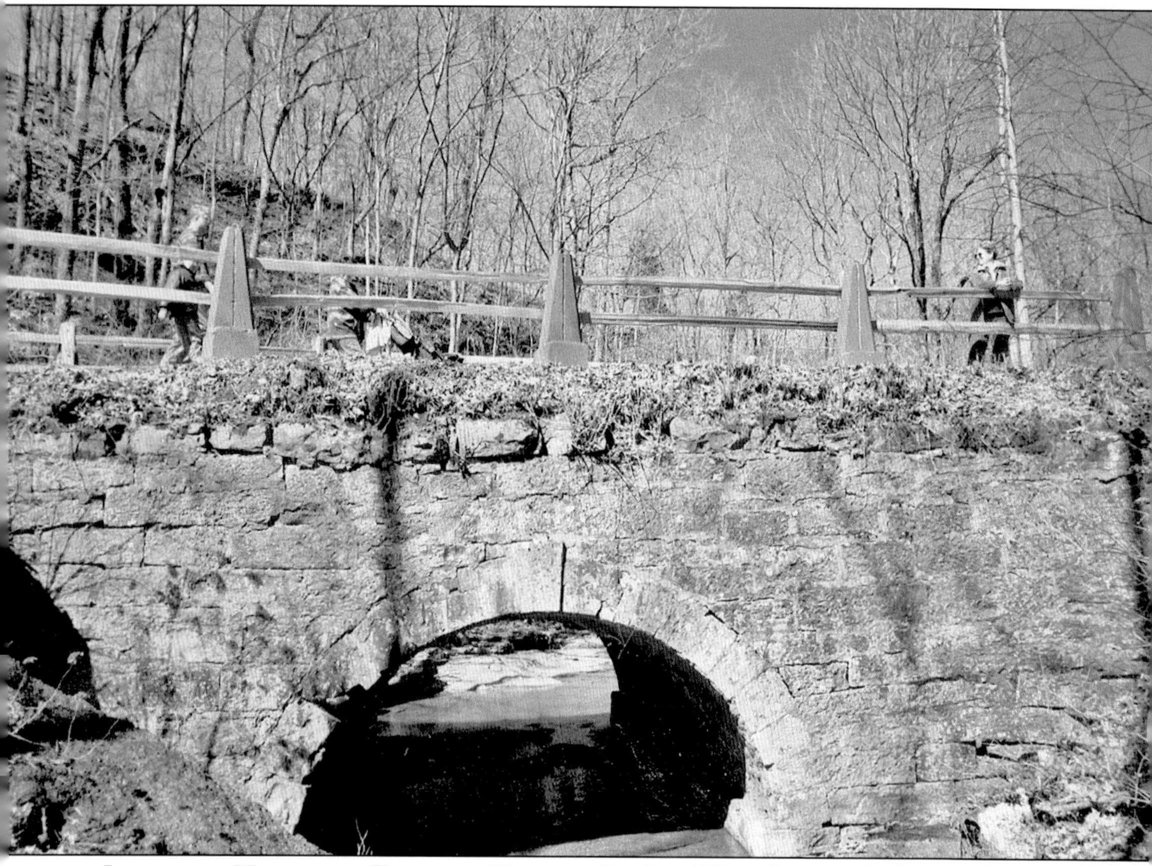

LOUISVILLE-NASHVILLE TURNPIKE BRIDGE. By the 1830s the area had numerous farms, churches, one-room schoolhouses, water-powered mills, country stores, and other such amenities of a prosperous rural area. The towns of West Point to the north and Elizabethtown to the south were prosperous and growing. Post offices were appearing, and clusters of homes and businesses were taking on the characteristics of towns. Grahampton and Garnettsville in Meade County and Stithton in Hardin County were sprouting. Impetus was given to the development and growth of towns in the 1830s with the construction of the Louisville and Nashville Turnpike that was to connect Louisville and Nashville. The Kentucky State Legislature first chartered the turnpike in 1829. Turnpike commissioners in this area included James Young, Henry Ditto, John Stockman, Horatio G. Wintersmith, and James Crutcher. The company was re-chartered in 1833 and again in 1837. The section of road between West Point and Elizabethtown was completed in 1838, and a section ran through the area that became Fort Knox. Thousands of Civil War soldiers passed over this bridge before the arrival of Fort Knox soldiers. For over 100 years the turnpike, later to become a state highway, carried vehicles from Louisville to Nashville. First stagecoaches, then automobiles, and finally Fort Knox soldiers with their tanks and other military vehicles traveled the road that crossed this bridge and the two other similar stone bridges that were part of the turnpike. This section of the turnpike later became Wilson Road. A one-mile section of the turnpike road has been preserved much as it was 150 years ago and is a popular hiking trail on Fort Knox that is open to the public. The three stone bridges, within one mile of each other, are popular attractions.

SPRING CAVE ON THE TURNPIKE. Two spring caves alongside the turnpike remain today much as they were over 150 years ago. These caves are within 200 yards of each other, and the cool water coming from them provided refreshment to the turnpike travelers. Farmers atop the ridges on either side of the turnpike placed milk and produce in these cool caves to keep them fresh for delivery to markets. In the late 19th and early 20th centuries various local celebrations and get-togethers were held at the spring cave. Because of the coolness of the valley through which the turnpike traveled and the fresh cool water from the spring, the area was popular. Many Fourth of July celebrations took place at the spring cave, as did family reunions and church picnics.

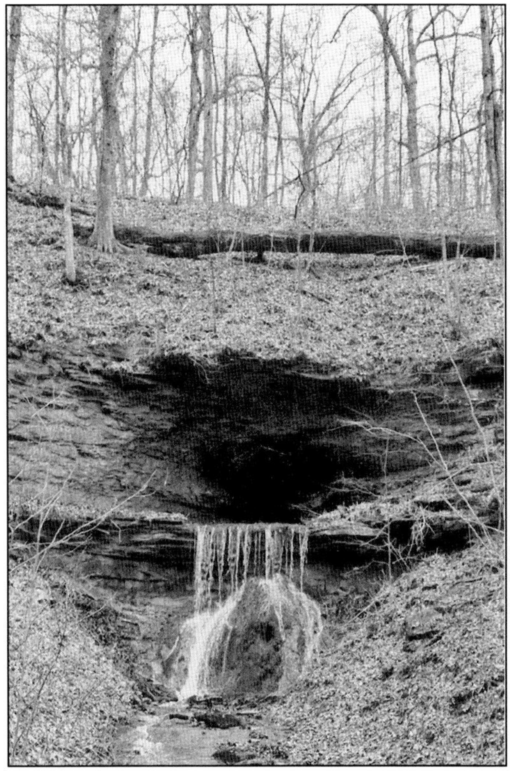

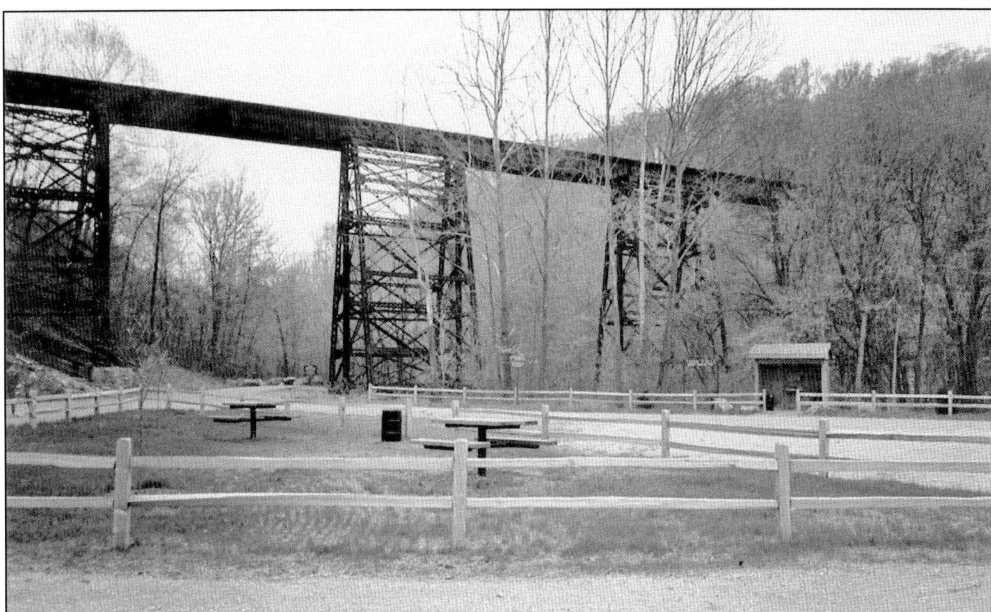

TRAIN TRESTLE BRIDGE BUILT IN 1873. At the parking area provided for visitors to the "Bridges to the Past" hiking trail (a preserved portion of the L&N Turnpike) is a high train trestle bridge that still carries trains over the valley. The parking area is also the entrance to Tioga Falls hiking trail, which follows the route of a 19th century road that led to the base of a 130-foot water fall.

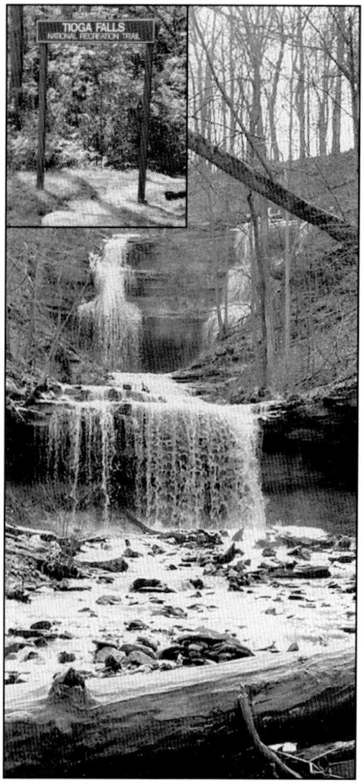

TIOGA FALLS. The Tioga Falls Trail leads to a waterfall that drops 130 feet down the face of Muldraugh Hill. Prior to the Civil War, Southern plantation owners sent their families to a popular resort hotel resting atop the falls during the malaria season in order for them to escape the possibility of infection. The hotel operated until the 1930s, although its popularity had declined. Later years saw the hotel used as a residence. At one time, a train station rested along the railroad tracks that cross the hiking trail. The station served visitors to the hotel who then completed their journey to the hotel by stagecoach. All is now gone except for the train tracks and bridges. The expansion of Fort Knox took the land.

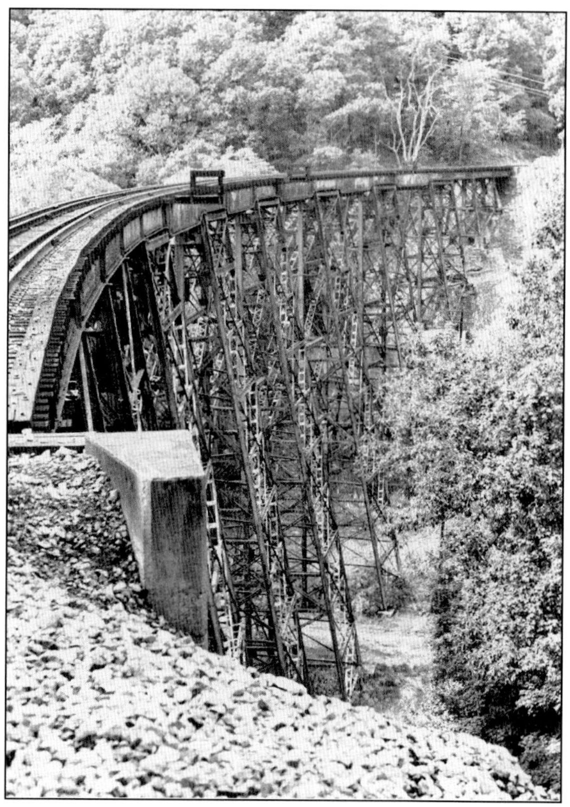

BRIDGE ACROSS TIOGA CREEK VALLEY. A train trestle bridge crosses the west fork of Tioga Creek Valley. This bridge is 130 feet high and 707 feet long, much larger than the trestle bridge at the trail parking area. The bridge still carries trains over the valley. Hikers encounter this bridge as they walk atop the ridge of the valley on the way to Tioga Falls, and again as they pass under the bridge on the portion of the hike that follows Tioga Creek in its valley. The bridge was built over 100 years ago, and at one time Dixie Highway, before construction of Highway 31 West in the 1940s, passed under this bridge. Today the road is clearly visible as it runs under the bridge and up the hill.

Two

CAMP YOUNG
The Precursor to Fort Knox

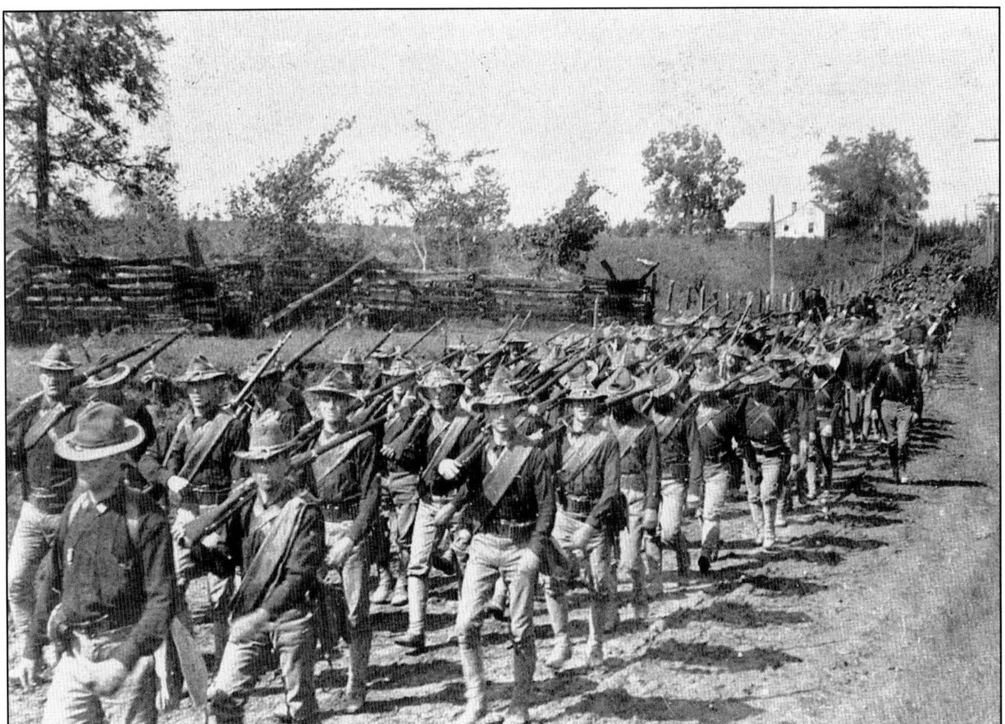

MILITARY MANEUVERS AROUND WEST POINT, 1903. The government considered the Hardin County area that is now occupied by Fort Knox as the site for a military post as early as 1903. In that same year the U.S. Army held large-scale maneuvers in the area, particularly in and around the small agricultural/river port village of West Point. The headquarters for these maneuvers was called Camp Young. The drills took place on several thousand acres of leased land, though not one farmer or landowner charged the government for use of the land. Allowing use of the land was regarded as a patriotic duty. Landowners asked only that the government reimburse them for any damage to property or crops that resulted from the military activity.

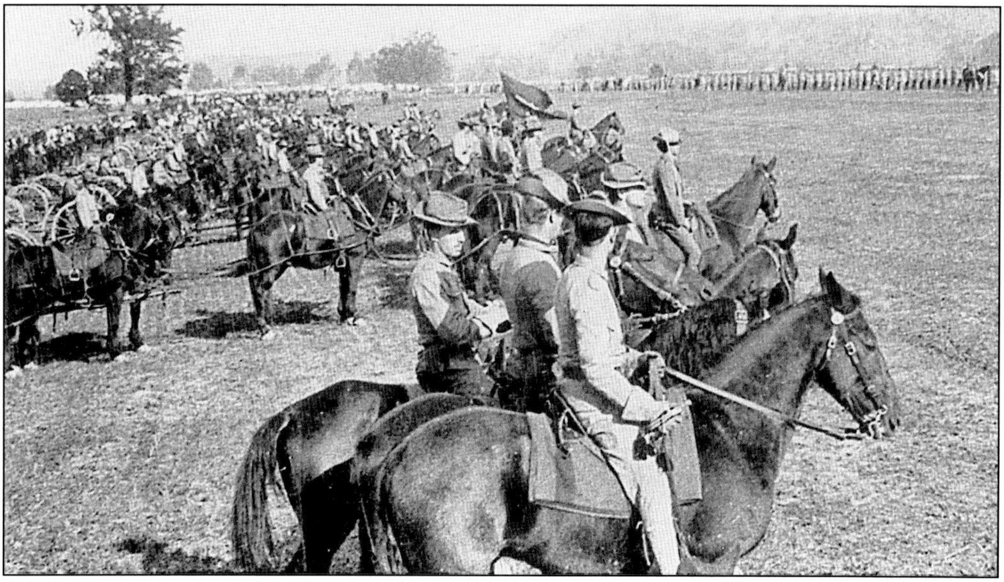

CAMP YOUNG, 1903. This photograph was taken in the vicinity of what is now 14th and Elm Streets in West Point. The horse stables used during these military exercises were in the area of current 1408 Elm Street. At the time of these maneuvers, the United States military was driven mostly by horsepower. The gasoline and diesel power of machines was just beginning to replace the hay and oat power of the horse and mule.

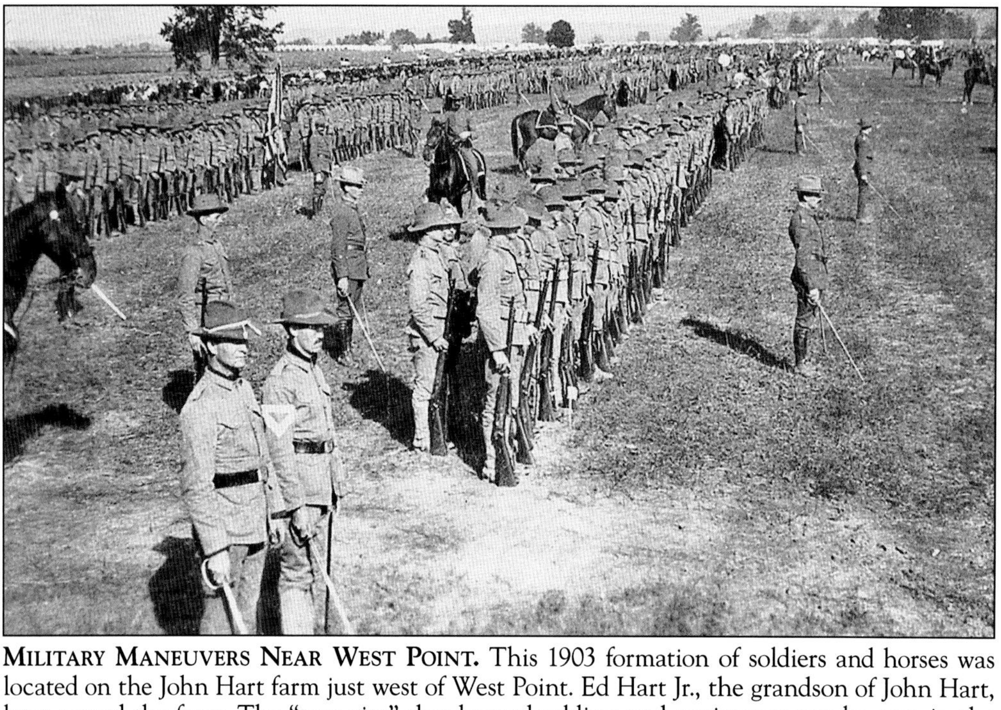

MILITARY MANEUVERS NEAR WEST POINT. This 1903 formation of soldiers and horses was located on the John Hart farm just west of West Point. Ed Hart Jr., the grandson of John Hart, later owned the farm. The "tent city" that housed soldiers and equipment can be seen in the background. Speculation abounded regarding when a permanent military installation would be established in the area. Prior to 1918 almost everyone believed the nucleus for the installation would be at West Point.

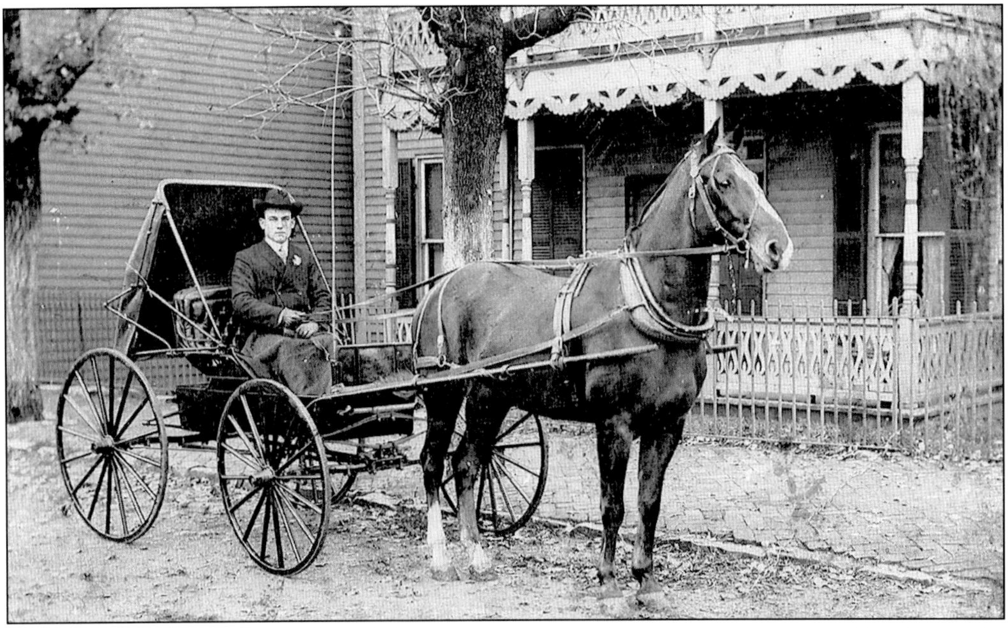

West Point, 1903. Ernest David Applegate poses at the corner of 4th and Elm Streets in West Point, which was at one time a thriving river port town. Samuel Pearman and James Young founded the town in 1798. The James Young Inn and James Young's home still stand today. The Louisville-Nashville Turnpike passed through in the 1830s, and the railroad arrived later. Thomas Lincoln, father of our 16th President, also passed though, as did Lewis and Clark, thousands of Civil War soldiers, and many river, highway, and railroad travelers.

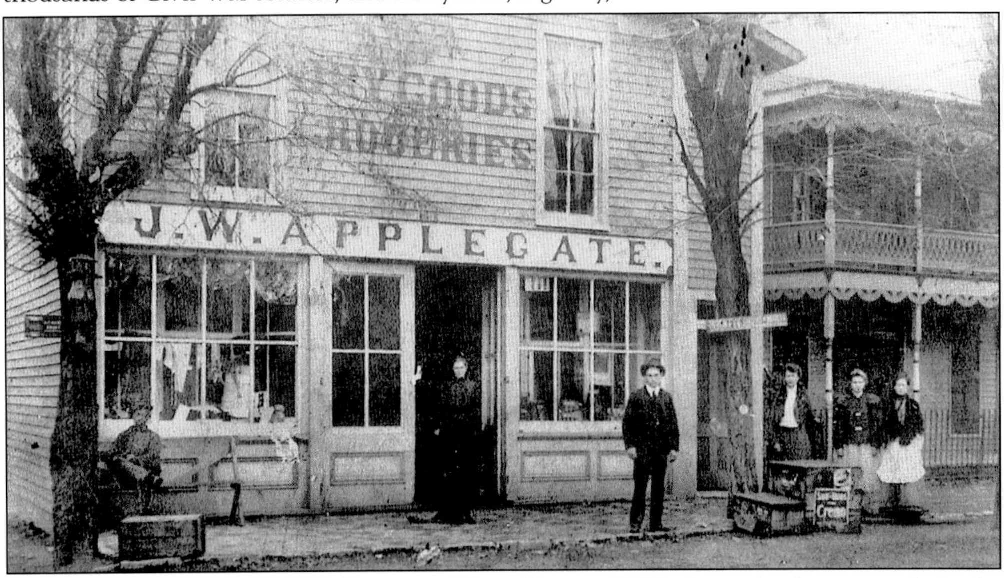

John and Anna Applegate Store in West Point, 1903. Anna Applegate stands in the doorway, and Ernest David Applegate is in the suit outside. In 1903 West Point was clearly a quiet, pristine, and prosperous town, though no longer an expanding river port town with travelers, tradesmen, craftsmen building boats, and warehouses full of goods. The town would soon be challenged when thousands of army troops arrived to participate in extensive military training in the countryside around the town.

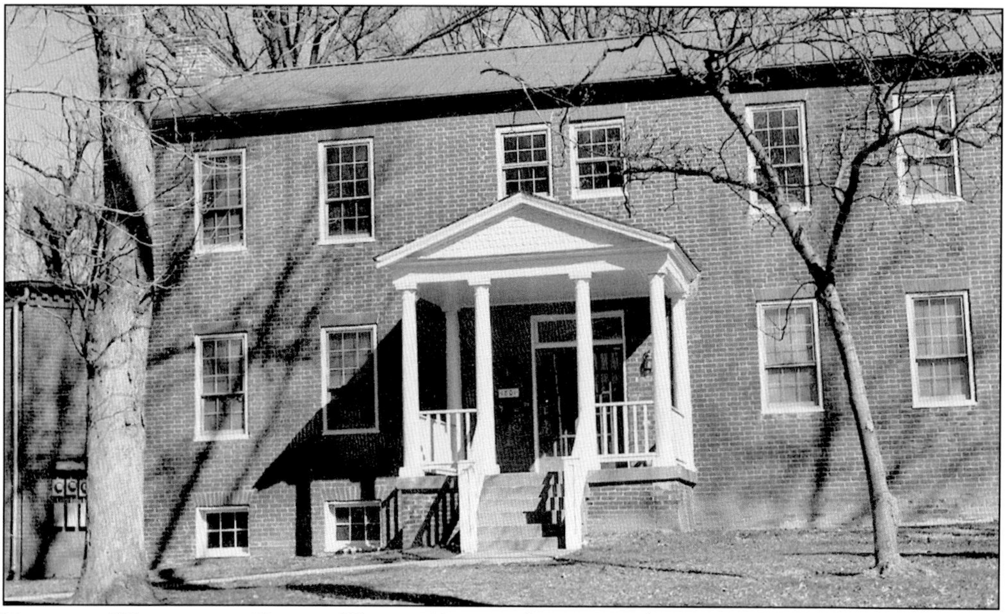

Bennett Henderson Young House. During the 1903 military training within and around West Point, soldiers camped and maneuvered on land once owned by James Young, co-founder of West Point. However, the military maneuvers named Camp Young was not named in honor of James Young but in honor of Confederate soldier Bennett Henderson Young. Born in 1843 in Nicholasville, Kentucky, Bennett joined John Hunt Morgan's cavalry at age 18. He led a raid from within Canada into St. Albans, Vermont, where he robbed three banks. The raid terrified Union states and was the northern-most Confederate engagement of the Civil War.

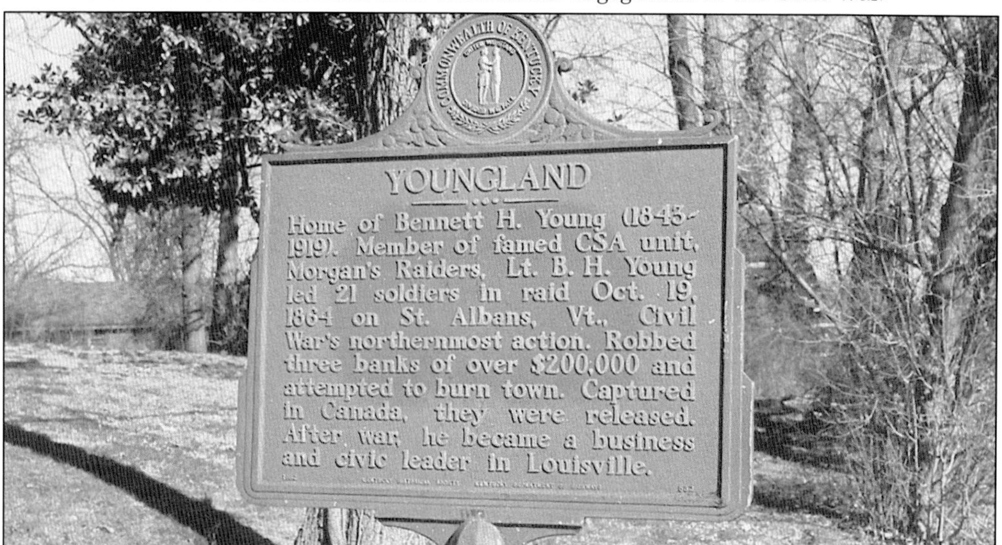

Bennett Henderson Young Historic Marker. In 1868, following his war service and study abroad in Europe, Bennett settled in Louisville and became one of the city's foremost courtroom attorneys, an entrepreneur, and a respected civic leader. He wrote books and articles on the Civil War, agriculture, and religion. His home still stands on the northwest corner of Dixie Highway (Highway 31 West) and Youngland Road in Shively, Kentucky. A Kentucky Historic Site marker stands in front of the house.

Three

ESTABLISHMENT OF CAMP KNOX

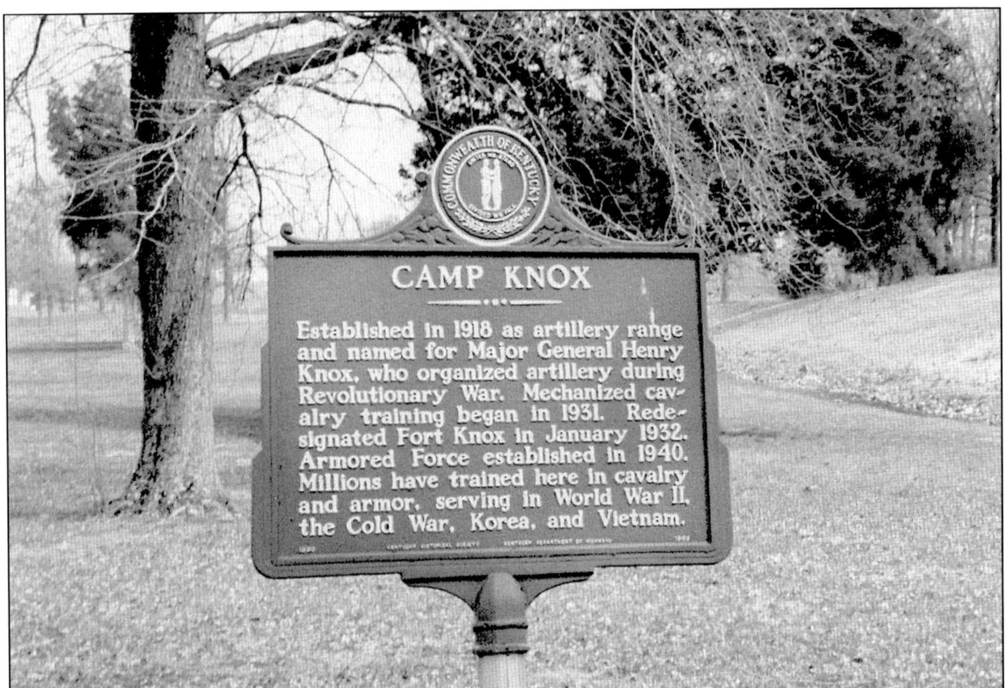

CAMP KNOX HISTORIC MARKER. The military maneuvers of 1903 demonstrated the suitability of the area for a military installation. In 1918 the government condemned and purchased land in Hardin County and a small portion of Meade County for a permanent military base. The base was to be called Camp Knox in honor of Maj. Gen. Henry Knox, chief of artillery for the Continental Army during the American Revolution and later the nation's first secretary of war. Using the experience of the 1903 maneuvers, most of the activity of the new military installation was around the town of West Point. This area proved unacceptable because of the problem of flooding from the Ohio River. The center of activity for Camp Knox came to be centered in and around the town of Stithton.

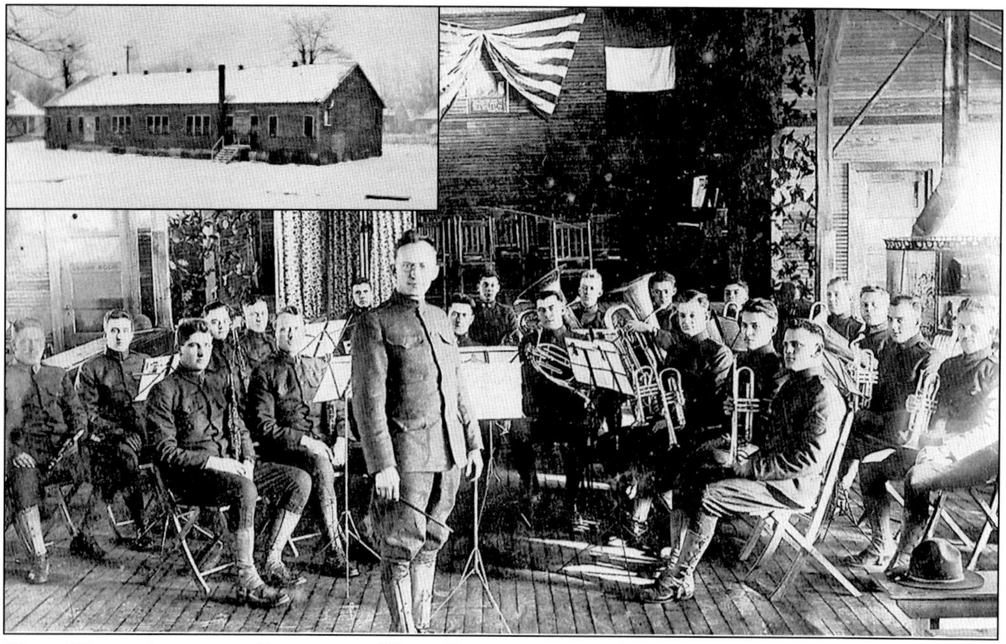

CAMP KNOX ACTIVITY CENTER IN WEST POINT. In its earliest years the center for Camp Knox operations was in West Point. The military used what available resources the town afforded until permanent structures could be provided on installation land. Seen here is the Camp Knox Army Band in concert in an activity center constructed for soldiers. This was one of the only permanent structures built by the army within West Point. The building is shown on the inset. When the army moved into newly constructed facilities in and around the town of Stithton, the building was relocated and used by West Point as a school gymnasium.

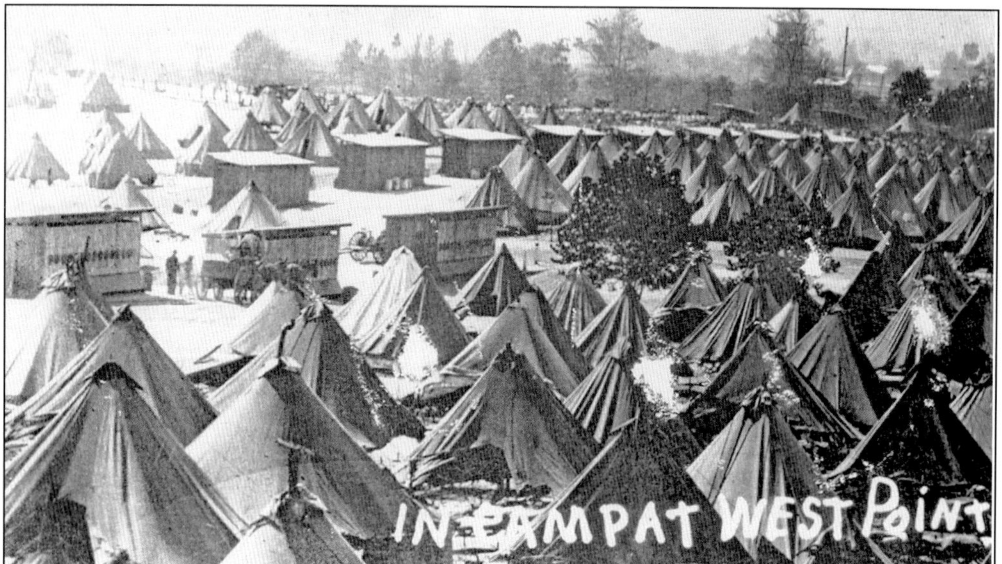

CAMP KNOX "TENT CITY." A Camp Knox training site, called a field artillery remount station, was located at the West Point brickyard, just south of the Rolling Fork River and east of West Point. Remnants of the brickyard are still visible today. Until permanent facilities could be constructed, tents served as housing, classrooms, mess halls, and medical centers.

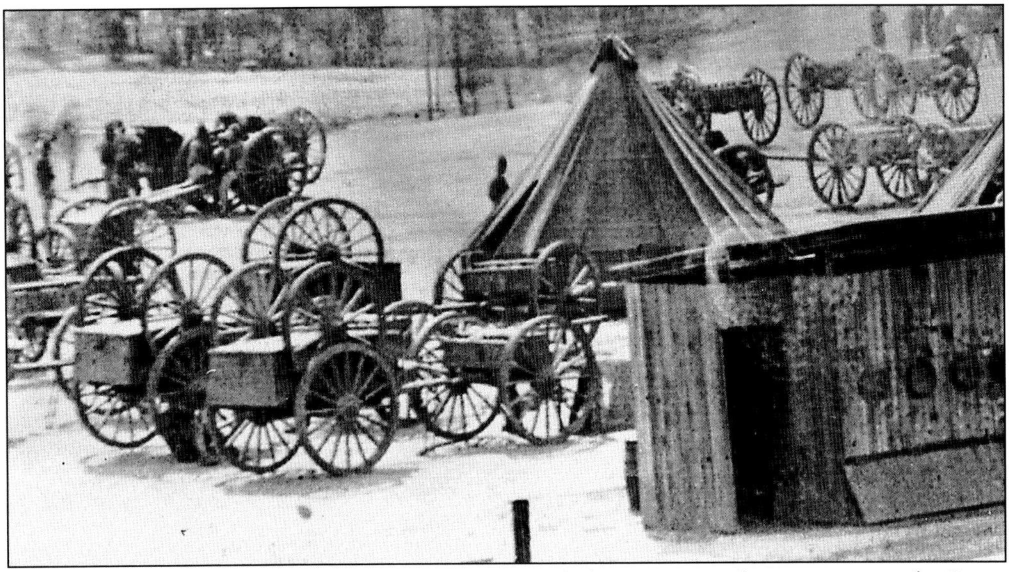

CAMP KNOX, 1918. Tents, temporary latrines, and showers greeted trainees to early Camp Knox. Pictured are wheeled carriers, called limbers, carrying material necessary for the firing and maintenance of field artillery pieces. The remains of some of these limbers can still be seen in Fort Knox training areas—remnants of bygone times.

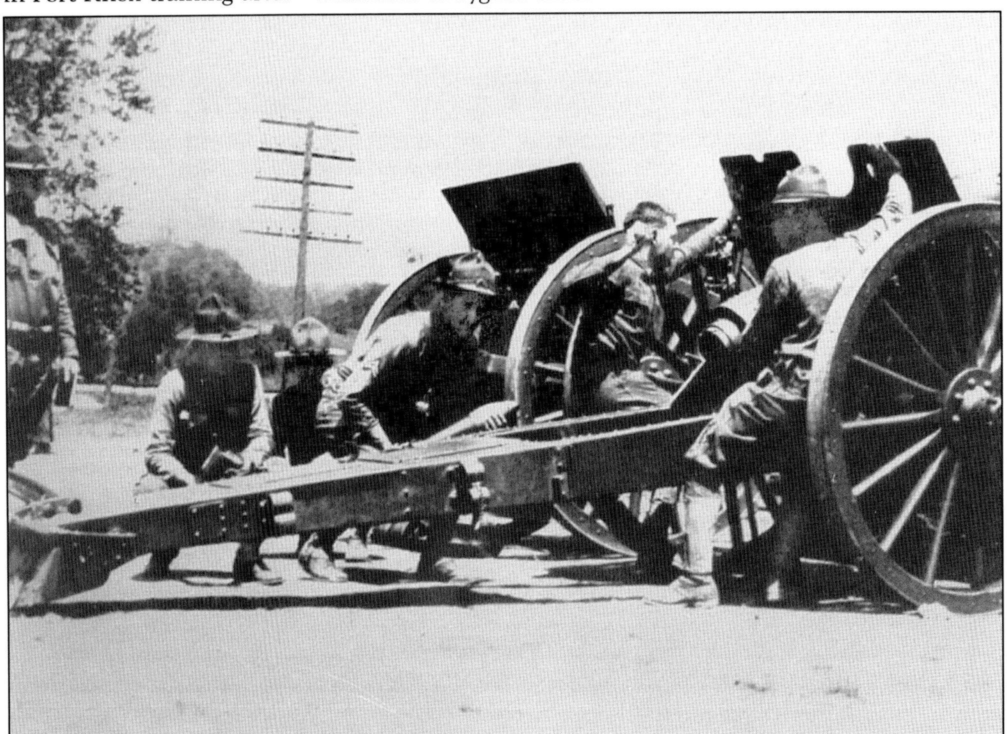

CAMP KNOX FIELD ARTILLERY TRAINING. This is a view of trainees outside West Point working their field artillery pieces. Limbers pulled by horses or mules carried the ammunition and items needed to fire these guns. For many years Camp Knox maintained numerous stables and veterinary offices to care for the hundreds of animals that moved army men and materials.

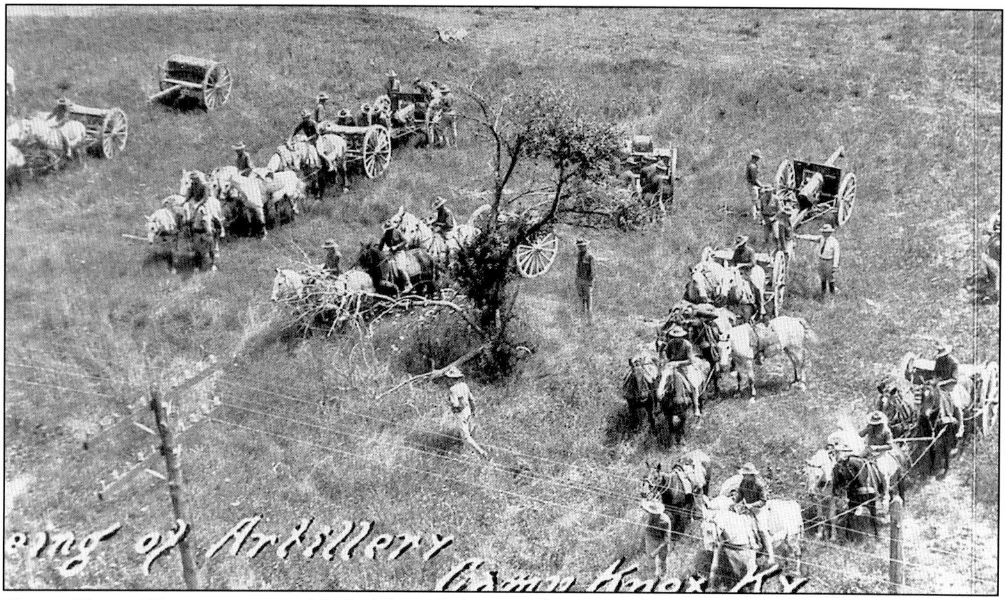

CAMP KNOX HORSEPOWER, 1919. Though horses dominated the field in 1918, it would not be long before gasoline- and diesel-powered vehicles replaced the horse and mule. Not until the 1930s did the remaining advocates of a horse cavalry surrender their position and the last horse cavalry disappear. Fort Knox had the distinction of having the last horse mounted, army band. The Kentucky National Guard, 123rd Cavalry Mounted Marching Band, with 26 members, served on Fort Knox and was deactivated on January 6, 1941. In 1918 the machine was just beginning to replace the horse. Residents within and around West Point were given an almost daily dose of thunder as the artillery pieces fired during training exercises. The streets in West Point would come to be lined with the spent cartridges from artillery shells that residents had picked up in the training areas.

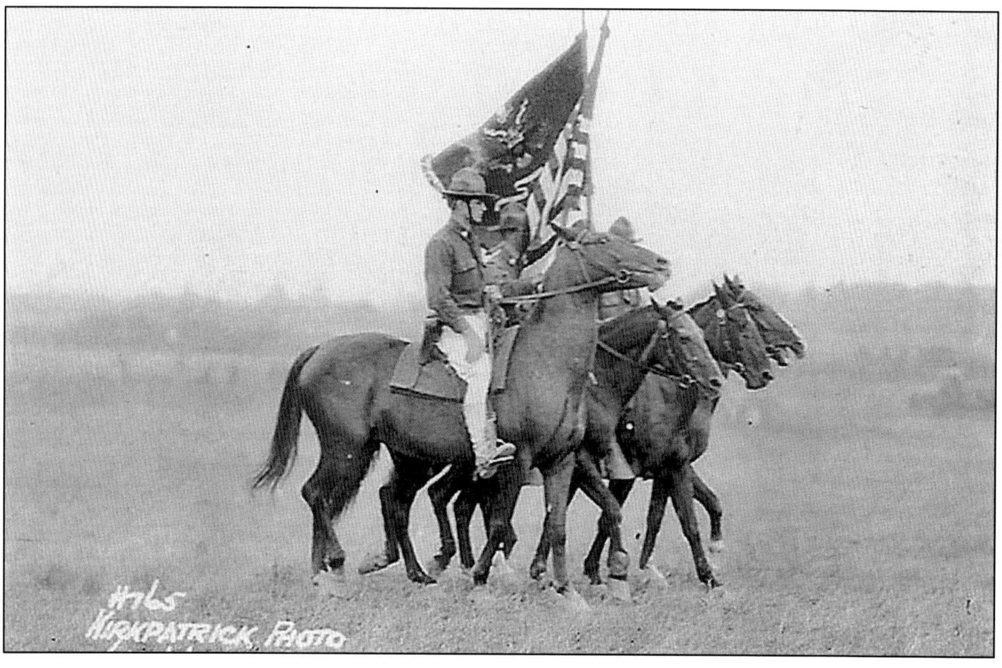

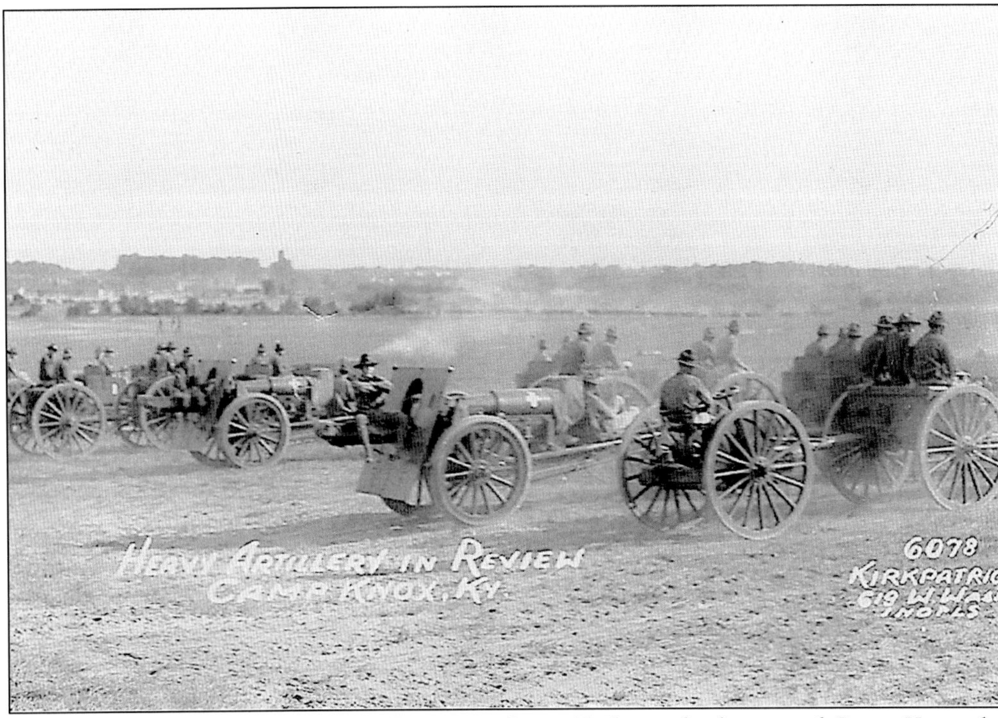

GASOLINE AND DIESEL REPLACE HAY AND OATS. Early in the history of Camp Knox the machine began to spell the demise of the horse and mule as the prime mover of men and materials on the training and battlefields. In the same year that horse-mounted soldiers carried the flags during the review of troops, motorized machines carried soldiers who performed the same task. The horse as a primary mover and instrument of cavalry operations was not completely replaced by motorized vehicles until the 1930s.

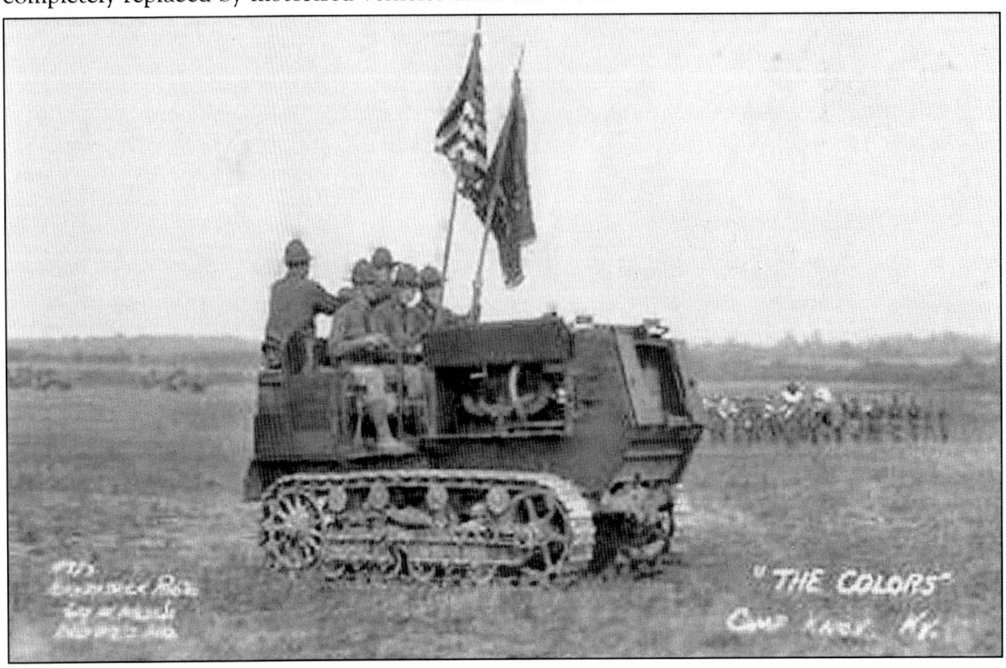

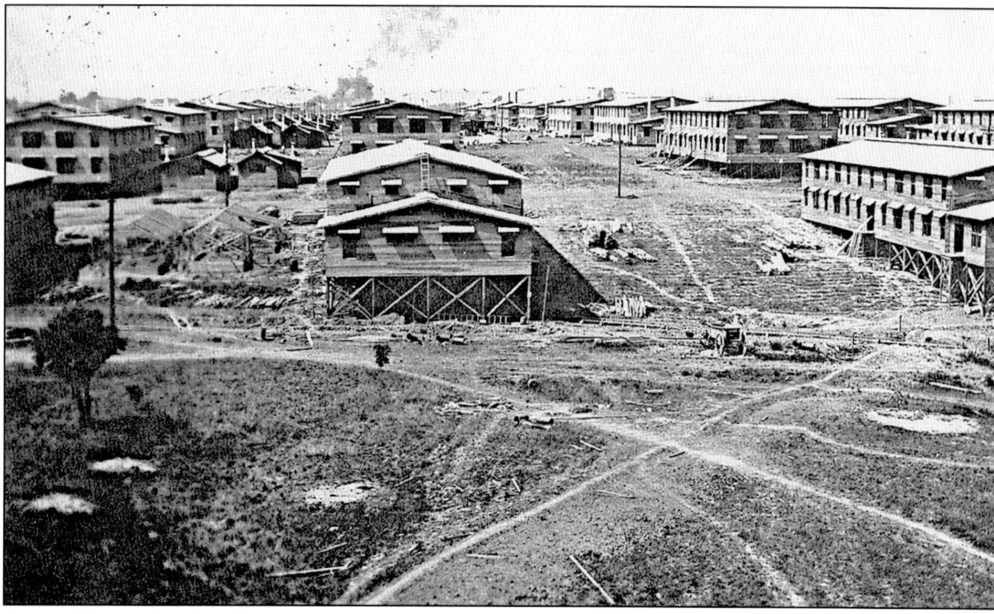

CAMP KNOX, 1918. While trainers and trainees were housed in tents in the area around West Point, the building of permanent quarters and training facilities was moving along at a rapid pace around the rural farming community of Stithton. Many of these buildings were later used as warehouses, training facilities, and offices. Some of these buildings remain today, but most have been demolished and replaced.

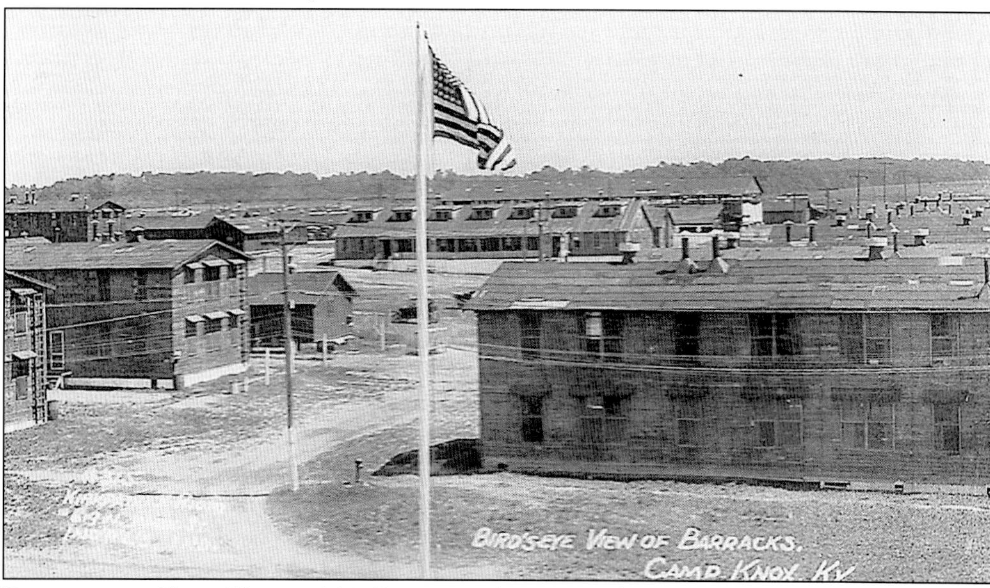

BARRACKS AT CAMP KNOX, 1920. Permanent housing and training facilities were constructed in and around the town of Stithton. Originally Stithton was to be left intact, completely surrounded by the Camp Knox military installation. The banks, stores, hotels, railroad depot, and restaurants were to serve the military community. Within a very short time it was discovered that a small town surrounded completely by a military installation was not a good idea. In 1919 Congress appropriated additional money for the purchase of Stithton. Soon this prosperous town was no more.

Four

LAND ACQUISITIONS OF 1918–1919

Stithton, Pleasant View, Tip Top, and Easy Gap

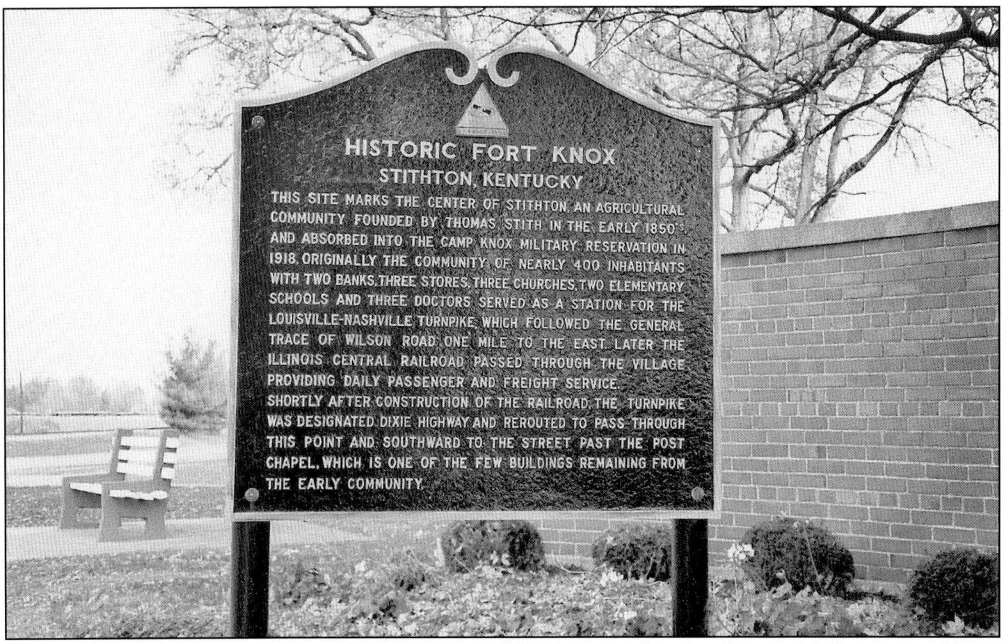

STITHTON. Stithton was the most prosperous of the towns taken by the establishment and later expansion of Fort Knox. Like so many of the towns that appeared on maps of the 19th and early 20th centuries, Stithton was never incorporated. Its identity depended on its name as a railroad station and service provider for farmers of the rural countryside. Still, Stithton was well-defined in the public eye as a "town." When the government took possession of the town in 1919, many of the businesses moved to an area just two miles southeast and rebuilt on the east and west side of the Louisville-Nashville Turnpike (now Wilson Road) in the area of the Anderson Golf Course. This became the community of New Stithton that did incorporate as a town and elect a mayor. The choice for relocation for their new community would surely have been different had they known that Fort Knox would expand 22 years later. New Stithton would be taken and become an extinct town, as did Stithton.

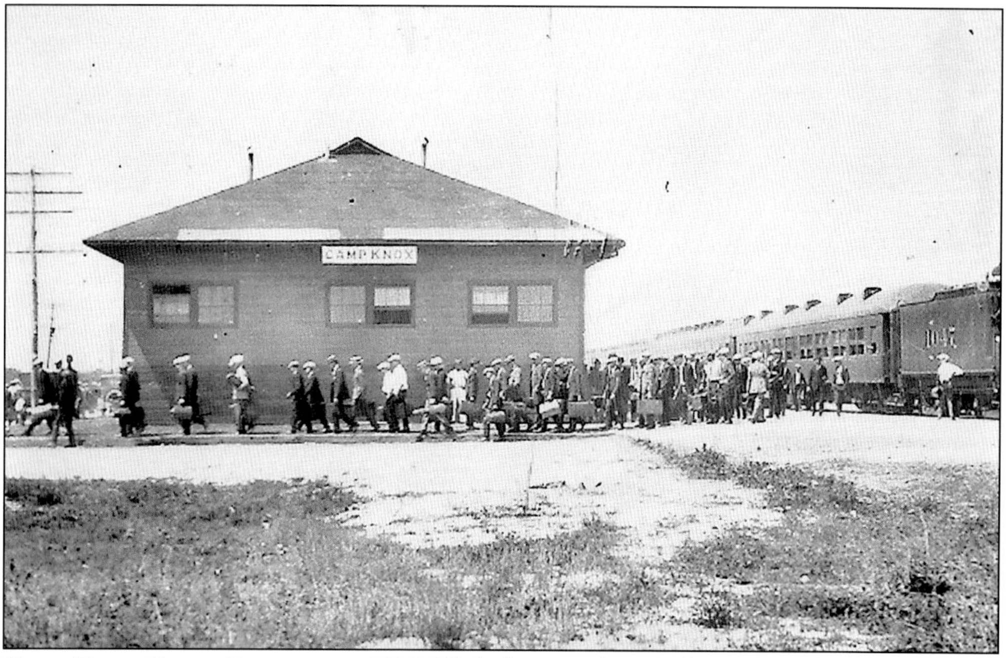

CAMP KNOX TRAIN STATION, C. 1926. With the completion of permanent structures in and around the town of Stithton, arrivals at Camp Knox could now arrive and depart at a new and larger train station in the cantonment area, which included the entire town of Stithton. Many of the Stithton buildings remained and served as housing and business facilities for Camp Knox. Other businesses and many residents relocated when the government took the town in 1919 just a couple miles to the southeast, where they established the town of New Stithton. It grew and prospered until it was taken in 1941 for the expansion of Fort Knox.

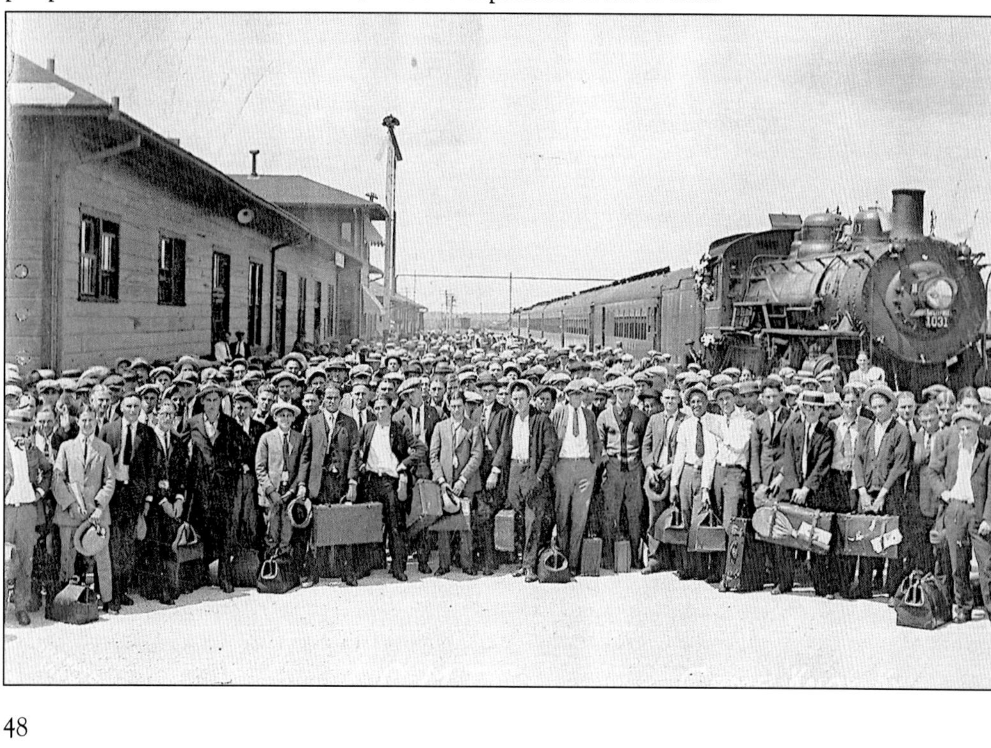

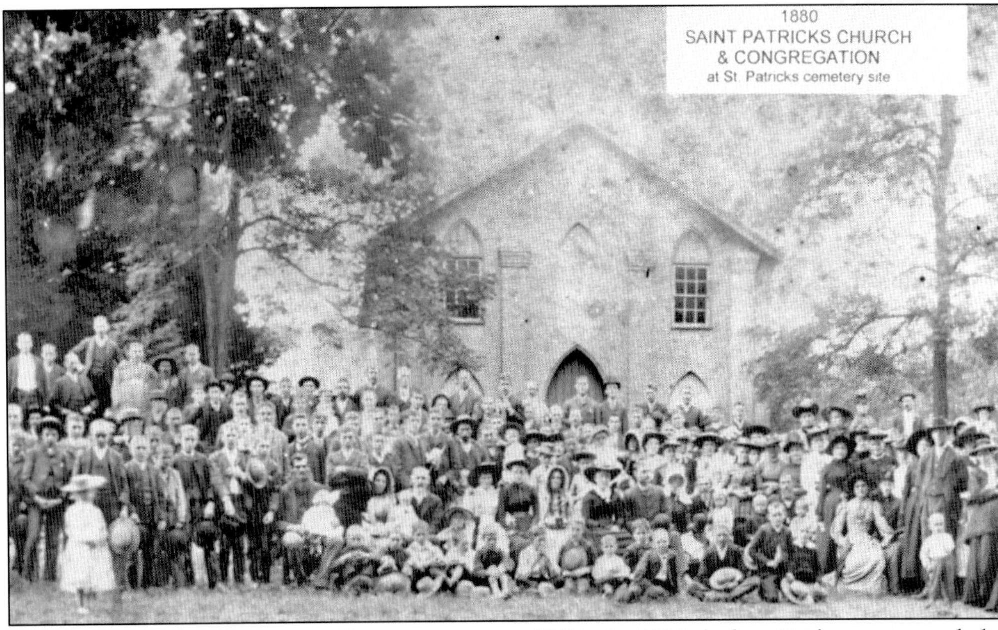

St. Patrick's Church and Congregation, 1880. In 1832, before Stithton assumed the characteristics of a town, construction of St. Patrick's Church was begun to serve the Catholic population. The church building is long gone, but the cemetery that surrounded the church on three sides is still active and maintained by Fort Knox. Rev. Charles Ignatius Coomes was the first priest at St. Patrick's Church and served for 38 years. Built of brick and completed in 1847, the church was 65 feet long and 30 feet wide. The building was abandoned when a new church was constructed about one mile to the east within the town of Stithton in 1900.

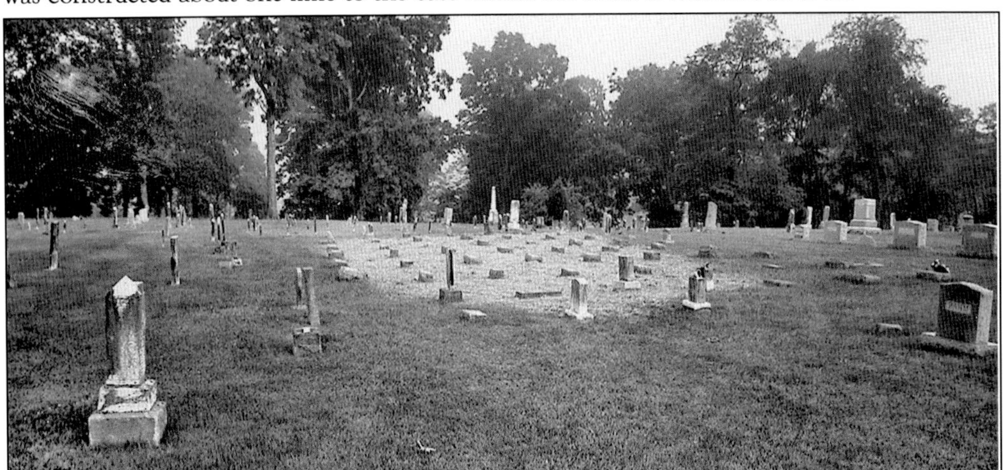

St. Patrick's Cemetery. In 1900 the new Catholic church in Stithton opened its doors, and shortly thereafter the old church was demolished. Stones from the old foundation were used in the wall around the adjacent Post Cemetery. The demolition of the old church left a large space in the cemetery that had surrounded the church on three sides. From the 1950s to the 1970s, the Catholic church consented to this area becoming the burial place for deceased infant children of soldiers stationed at Fort Knox. With its small, ground-level gravestones, the area now delineates the space where the church once stood. The cemetery was started in 1831 with the burial of Ann Carico and is still active today.

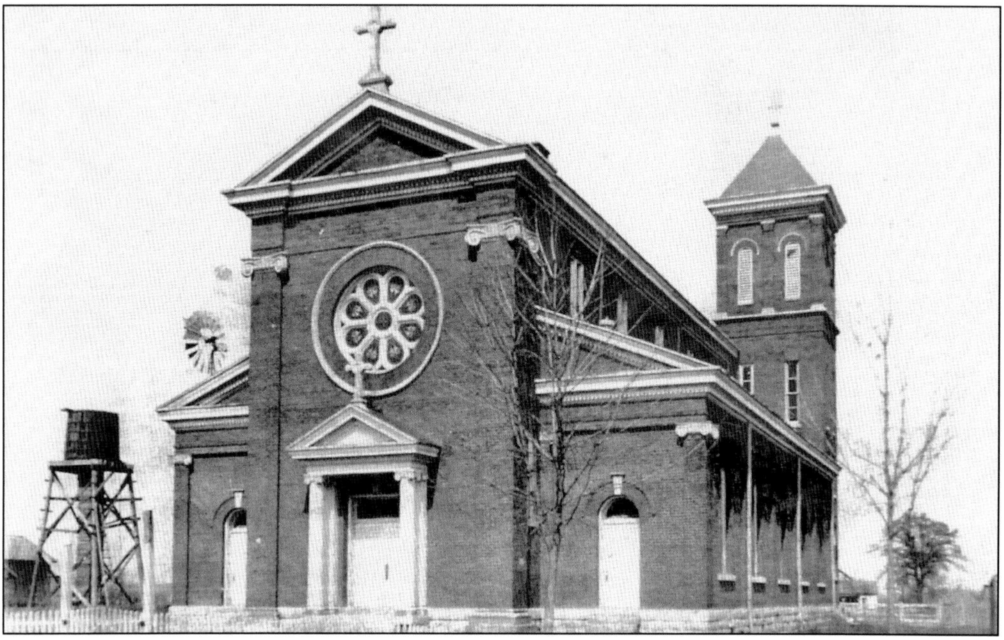

ST. PATRICK'S CHURCH IN STITHTON, 1905. St. Patrick's Church began in Plain Dealing on Otter Creek. For a time parishioners met in homes. A permanent church was completed in 1847 on land that is now St. Patrick's Cemetery on Fort Knox. Rev. James L. Whelan saw to the erection of the church in Stithton, which stands today as the Main Post Chapel. Parishioners built the church with supplies they furnished. An on-site kiln fired the bricks. On August 4, 1899, the cornerstone was blessed, and the church opened for services in late 1900. It served its flock until 1919, when Stithton was acquired for the establishment of Camp Knox.

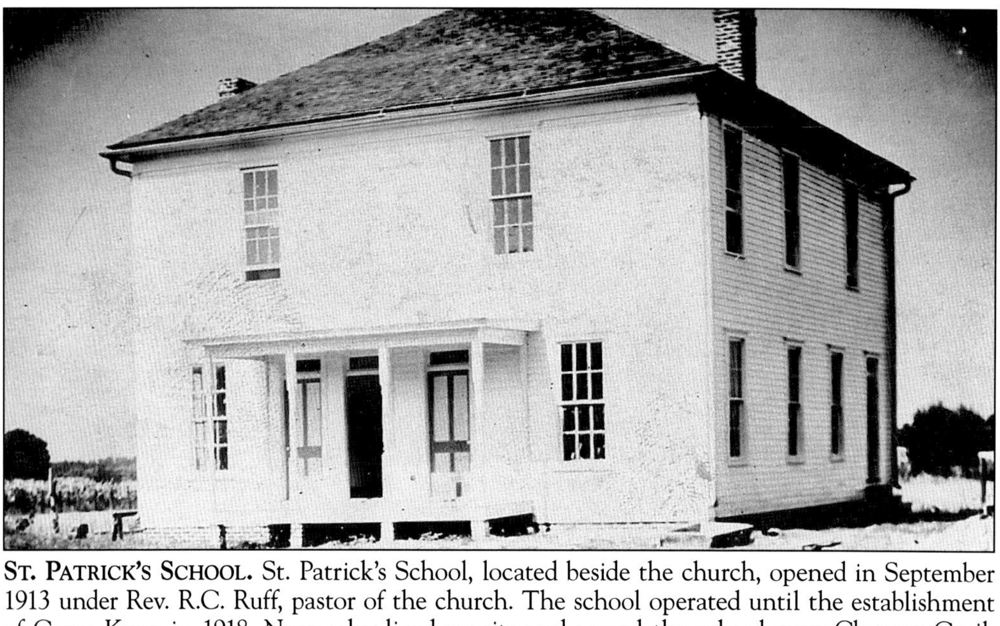

ST. PATRICK'S SCHOOL. St. Patrick's School, located beside the church, opened in September 1913 under Rev. R.C. Ruff, pastor of the church. The school operated until the establishment of Camp Knox in 1918. Nuns who lived on site and served the school were Clement Cecil, Stanislaus Hagan, Wilhelmina Pike, Merici Payne, Bernadine Howard, Rose Marie Thompson, Augustine Wethington, and Monica Aud.

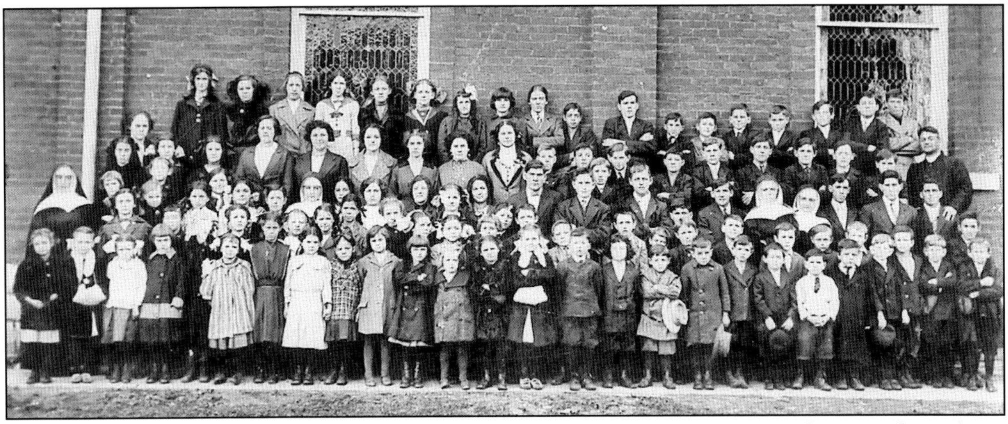

ST. PATRICK'S CHURCH SCHOOL STUDENTS AND TEACHERS, 1913. Students and teachers, from left to right, are (first row) J. Ray, R. Miller, unidentified, Sr. Sylvester Marie, P. Campbell, L. Ray, M. Castile, G. Ray, M. Newton, T. Newton, ? Barker, N. Miller, T. Ray, F. Cecil, A. Campbell, A. Pike, C. Plyman, R. Peak, ? Ray, unidentified, R. Wiseman, ? Marcum, E. Ray, and ? Ray; (second row) Sr. S. Hagan O.S.U., N.Barker, T. Barker, G. Ray, E. Bryan, J. Campbell, K. Plyman, M. Bryan, C. Ray, ? Shircliff, E. Ray, unidentified, E. Mash, ? Ray, ? Campbell, C. Campbell, M. Byerly, ? Ray, unidentified, and ? Campbell; (third row) F. Aubrey, G. Castile, T. Plyman, ? Shircliff, M. Mash, Sr. B. Howard O.S.U., E. Osborne, N. Ray, M. Cecil, ? Barker, N. Osborne, D. Shircliff, A. Ray (Trinitarian priest), J. Barker, M. Pike, Sr. M.C. Cecil O.S.U., Sr. W. Pike O.S.U., R. Ray, K. Ray, and ? Ray; (fourth row) M. Cecil, G. Buzzard, ? Barker, N. Hager, A. Payne, Sr. Mary Rudolph S.C.N., F. Hardesty, P.Hardesty, G. Ray, M. Ray, B. Fisher, E. Hardesty, ? Payne, C. Campbell, M. Buzzard, C. Campbell, ? Hardesty, ? Bryan, two unidentified, and Fr. R.C. Ruff; (fifth row) R. Ray, G. Aubrey, Sr. Mary Rudolph O.S.U., L. Fisher, E. Todd, E. Castile, Sr. Generose O.S.U., N. Osborne, B. Ray, J. Plyman, K. Cecil, unidentified, and C. Bryan.

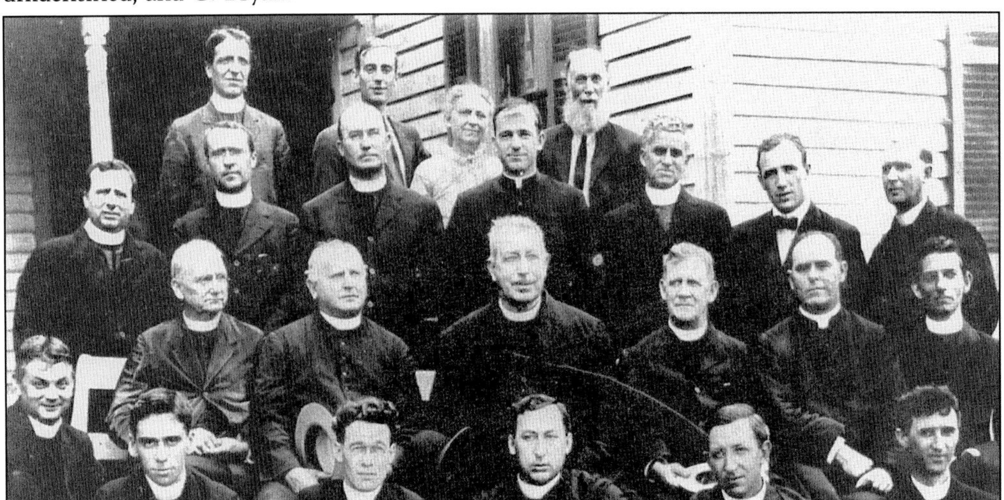

NEWLY ORDAINED REV. JACOB RAHM. The religious community attends the first mass presented by newly ordained Rev. Jacob Rahm at St. Patrick's Church in 1915. From left to right are (front row) Rev. Rudolph C. Ruff, ? Thompson, ? Fallon, Charles Rahm, John M. Abell, and ? Keller; (second row) J.J. Pike, J.S. Henry, J.J. Abell, Joseph Hogarty, ? Kalaher, and ? Frederick; (third row) Reverend Norman, ? Beruatto, ? Brey, Jacob Rahm, ? Doherty, ? Martin, and ? Clemons; (fourth row) Rev. Delphine Autherman, Dr. Rahm, Mrs. Rahm, and Mr. Rahm.

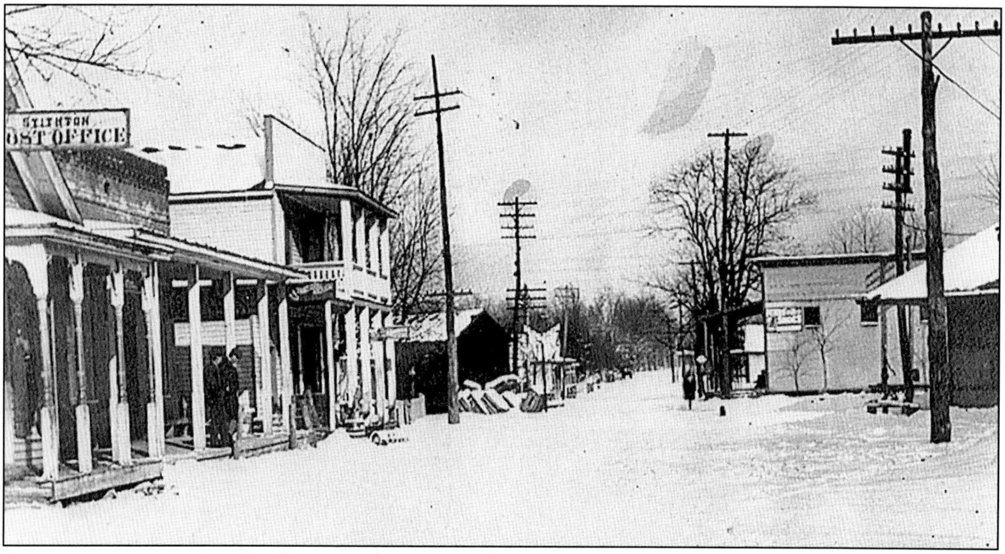

STITHTON, 1910. With the completion of the Louisville-Nashville Turnpike (now Wilson Road), the population of the area atop Muldraugh Hill between Elizabethtown and West Point grew. The arrival of the Elizabeth & Paducah Railroad in 1873 accelerated growth. Along the railroad, on land now occupied by the Fort Knox Chaffee Avenue traffic circle, Benjamin Jones built a hotel and applied for a license to open a post office in 1874. In 1877 Jones gave land for a train station across from his hotel. The nucleus of Stithton was now in place. This winter street scene looks east down Main Street (later Fifth Avenue in Fort Knox) and shows the post office, hotel, train station, and Mossbarger dry goods store.

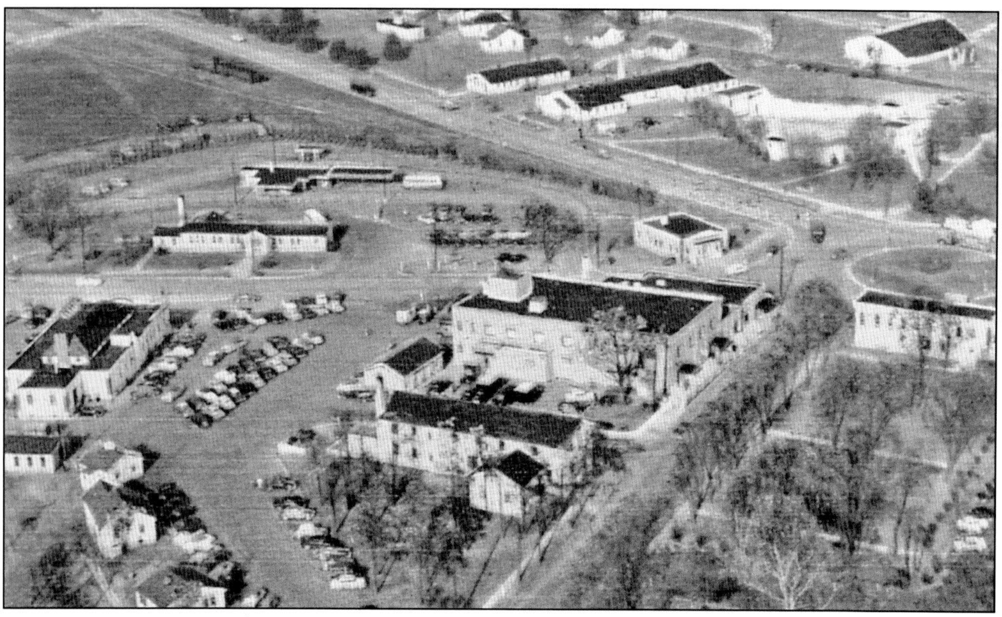

FORT KNOX, 1956. This area was once Stithton. The large building in the center is the approximate location of the Stithton post office and hotel. The Chaffee Avenue traffic circle can be seen on the right side. The two-story, rectangular building below the traffic circle is the remnants of the Wiseman dry goods store that has undergone considerable renovation since 1919 and remains today as building #1224 on Fort Knox.

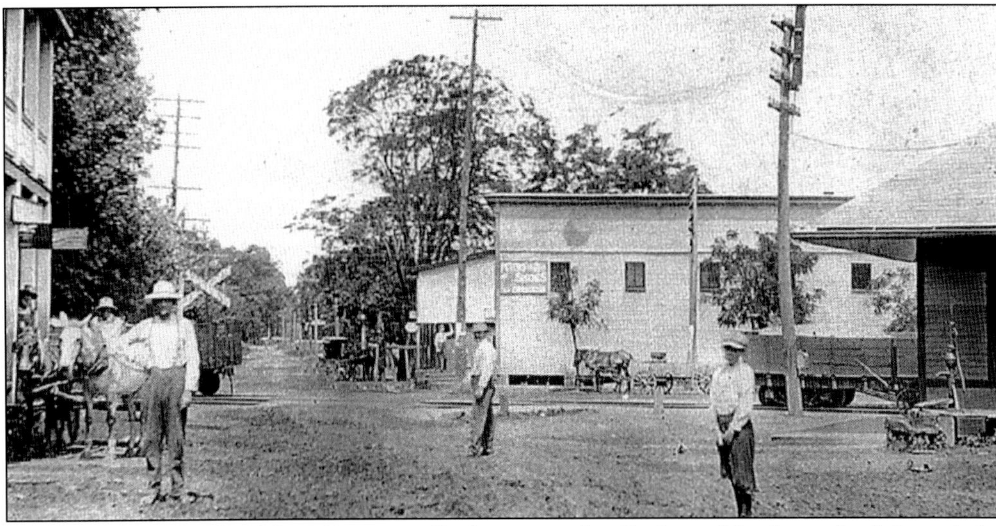

STITHTON, 1895. On Main Street in Stithton are the Stithton Hotel on the left and the train station and town well (with community pump) on the right. Just past the station is the Mossbarger store. Further down the street are residential homes and businesses, and at the end was the Patterson farmhouse, near the present commanding general's house, Quarters 1. Across from the farmhouse was the Stithton school and Baptist church. The train depot was on the southwest corner of Main and Ray Streets (now Fifth Avenue and Dixie Street). The Mossbarger store was on the southeast corner of Main and Ray Streets.

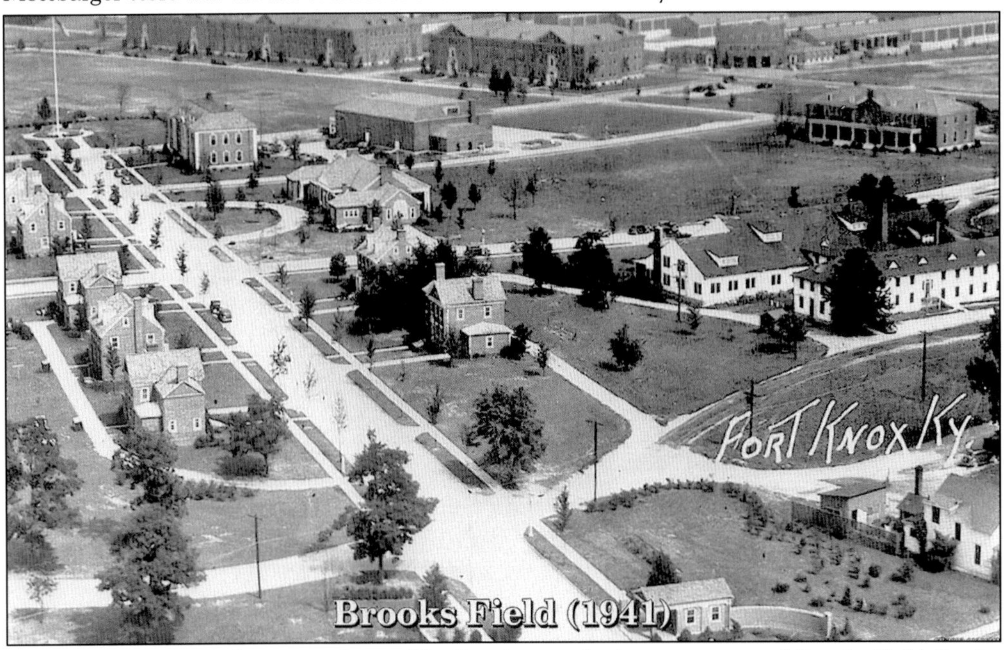

FORT KNOX, 1941. This scene shows Chaffee Avenue looking east toward Brooks Field. In the background, right side, are the First Cavalry Barracks, now Buildings #1109 and #1110 on Sixth Avenue and presently used as office buildings. The remnants of Stithton's Main Street are seen as Fifth Avenue arches off to the left from Chaffee Avenue. Brooks Field, the Main Post Parade field, is on land once owned by B.A. Hunter (13 acres), M.A. Campbell (14 acres), and H.J. Allen (20 acres). One of the last homes from Stithton is in the lower left corner.

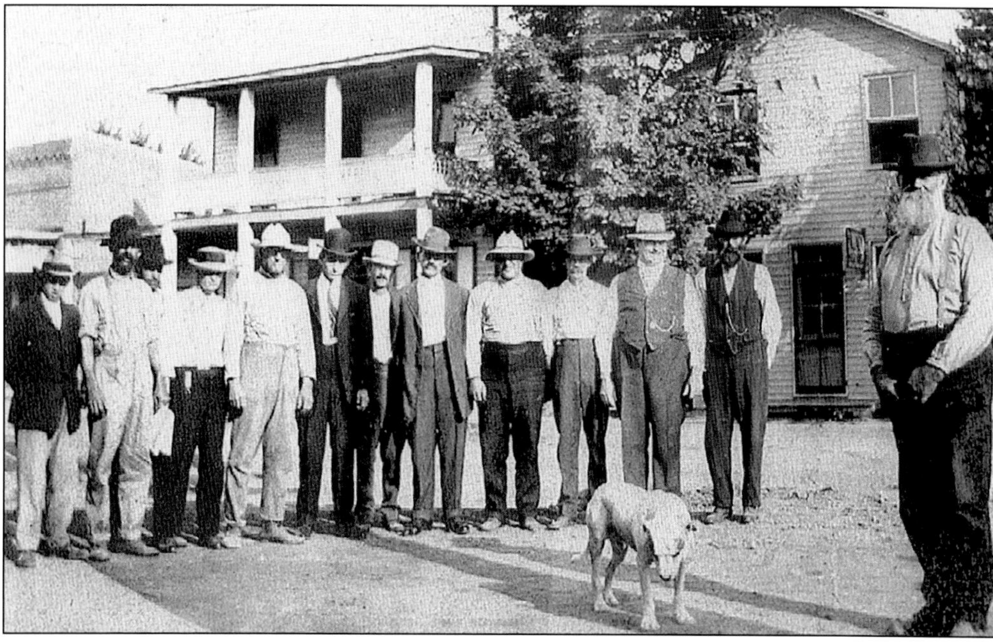

Stithton, 1899. A group of Stithton gentlemen pose for a photograph on Main Street. The Stithton Hotel can be seen in the background. The man to the far right in the foreground is Charles Ignatius Corbett (September 30, 1846–January 13, 1917). The son of James and Nancy Corbett and the husband of Catherine Elizabeth Buckman, he lived to see the beginning of the end of Stithton. He is buried in St. Patrick's Cemetery where St. Patrick's Church once stood.

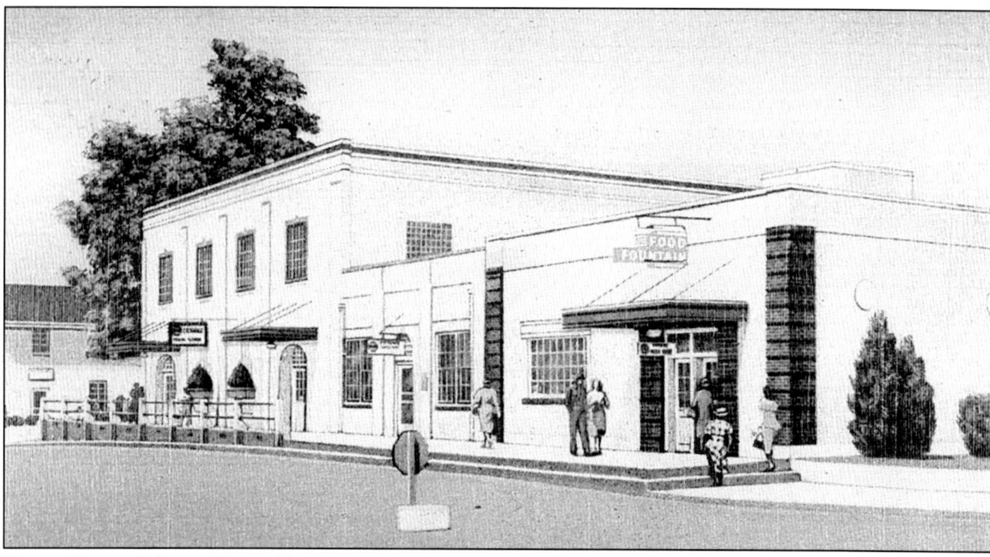

Fort Knox Main Post Exchange, 1956. With the establishment of Camp Knox in 1918, Stithton was to be left intact to provide banking, retail, and other services to soldiers on the installation surrounding the town. This proved to be a bad idea, and in 1919 Congress appropriated money to purchase Stithton. Many buildings and homes remained for years. However, by the late 1960s, only St. Patrick's Church and a greatly renovated Wiseman store remained from the town. The Main Post Exchange was located approximately where the Stithton Hotel and post office once stood.

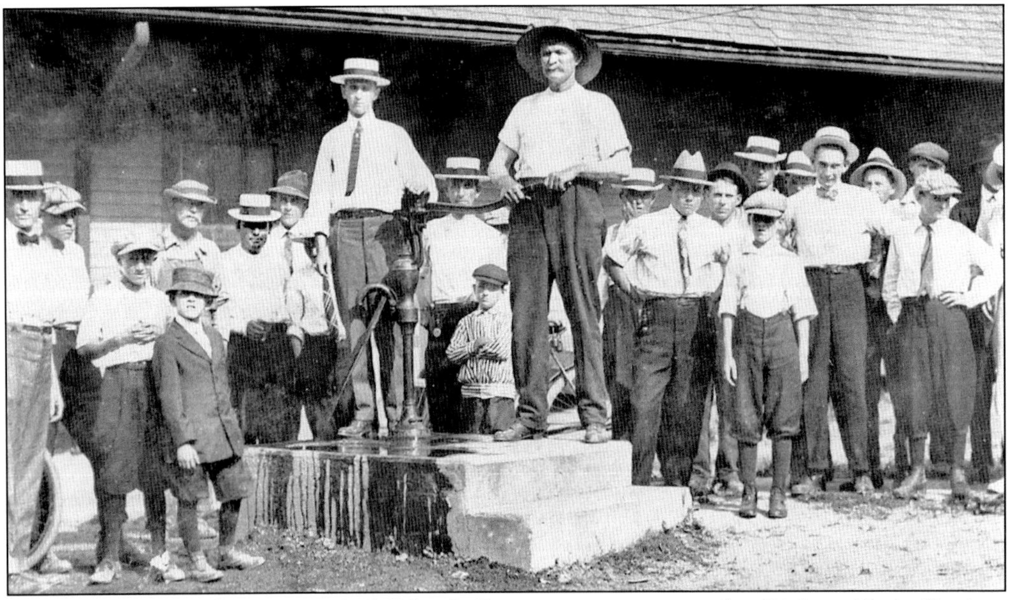

STITHTON TRAIN STATION, 1915. John J. Davis pumps water at the Stithton Train Station. John had lost a bet related to the outcome of a local election and as a consequence was required to pump water for a period of hours. Many of the local citizens were on hand to watch him pay off his bet. In places like Stithton, almost everyone in town knew everyone else. Few events of any consequence went unnoticed by the populace. If there was a photo opportunity, everyone who could turn out did so.

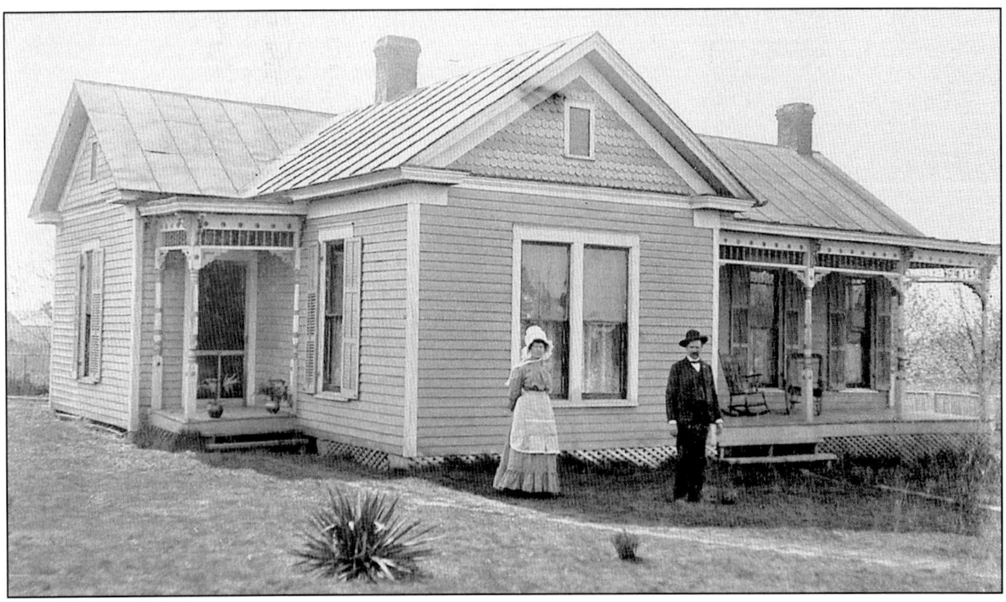

DR. ALLEN AND HIS WIFE, NORA, 1895. Dr. M.S. Allen and his wife, Nora Brian, are pictured in front of their home in Stithton. St. Patrick's Church was built across the street from their home in 1900. Dr. Allen began his medical practice in the town of Pitts Point and later moved to Stithton, unaware that Stithton would be acquired for the establishment of Camp Knox in 1919. The town of Pitts Point, where he began his practice, was taken for the expansion of Fort Knox in 1941. Mrs. Nora Allen died of "complication of diseases" in this home in 1902.

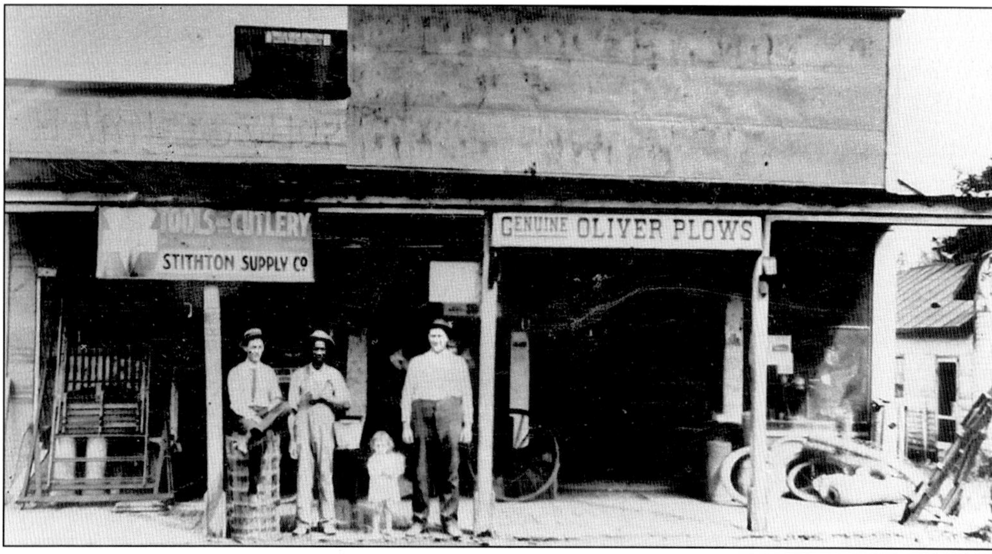

CORBETT HARDWARE STORE IN STITHTON, 1913. This store was on the north side of Main Street, east of the railroad tracks. To the west was a warehouse for store goods, and to the east was the George and Laura Jones home and blacksmith shop. Across Main Street were the Mossbarger store and Dr. Ressor's office. Will Ray and A.C. "Conn" Corbett purchased the store, originally the Stithton Supply Company, in 1908. When they left, they loaded their stock on a freight car for shipment to Vine Grove. The car burned, and everything was lost. Pictured from left to right are two unidentified people, Jim Corbett (child), and Conn Corbett.

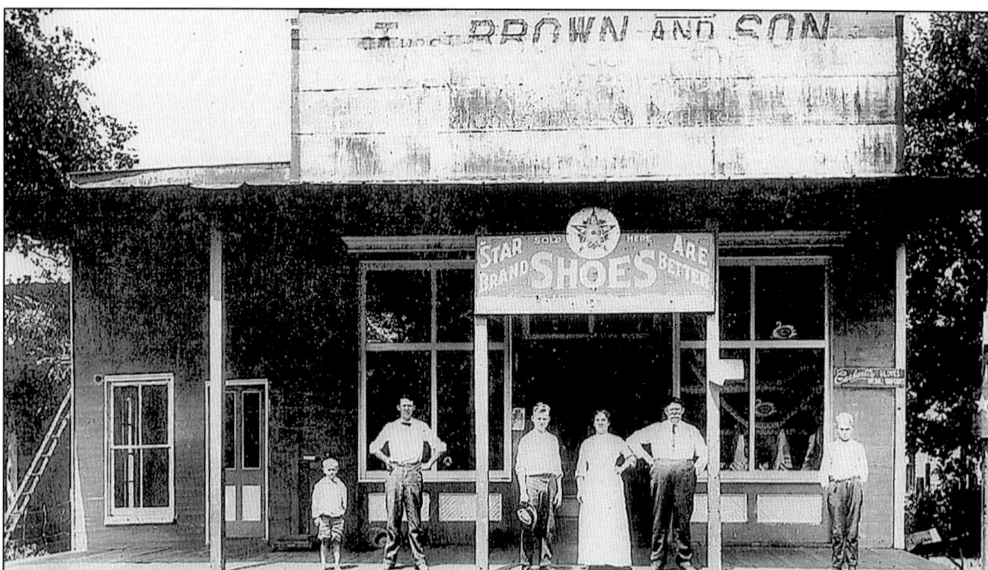

BROWN STORE IN STITHTON, 1910. This store sold mostly hardware items. Closing in 1920, it was one of the last businesses in Stithton to vacate for the establishment of Camp Knox. Pictured, from left to right, are William Harold Brown, William Martin Brown, Clyde Brown (brother of William Martin Brown), Sally Brown (wife of Thomas), Thomas Brown, and Claude Brown. Claude and Clyde were twin sons of Thomas and Sally Brown. The store was on the north side of Main Street and west of the railroad tracks. .

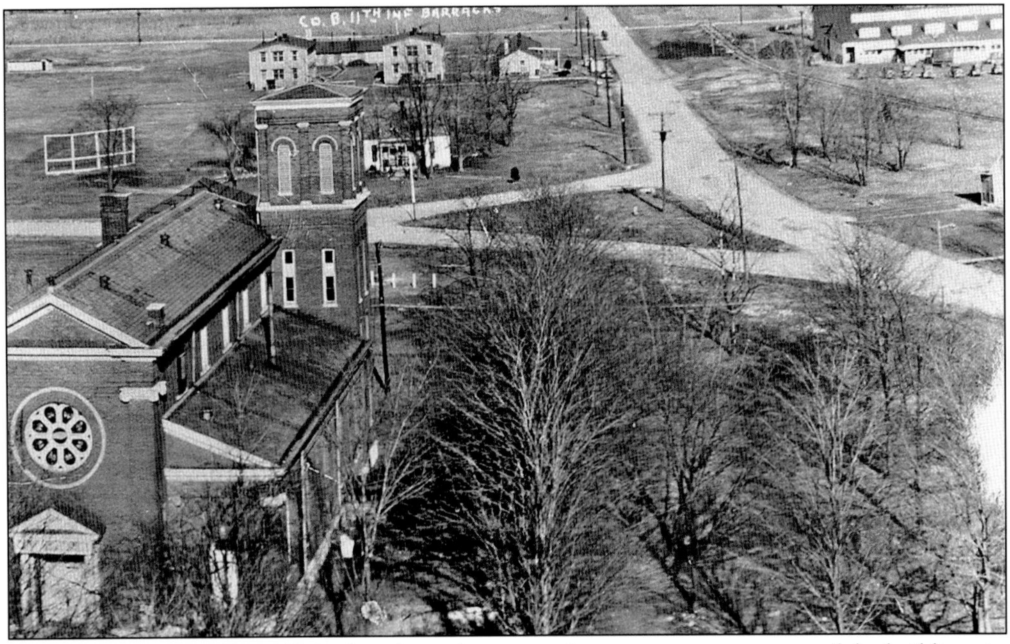

CAMP KNOX, 1932. By 1932 Stithton's residents were long gone, as were most of the buildings in the business district around the train station. However, many of the handsome, two-story, wood-frame houses remained and were used as quarters for army officers. Around this time the Fort Knox commanding general lived in a house just north of St. Patrick's Church. The street in front of the church was Ray Street in Stithton times and Dixie Street in Camp Knox times.

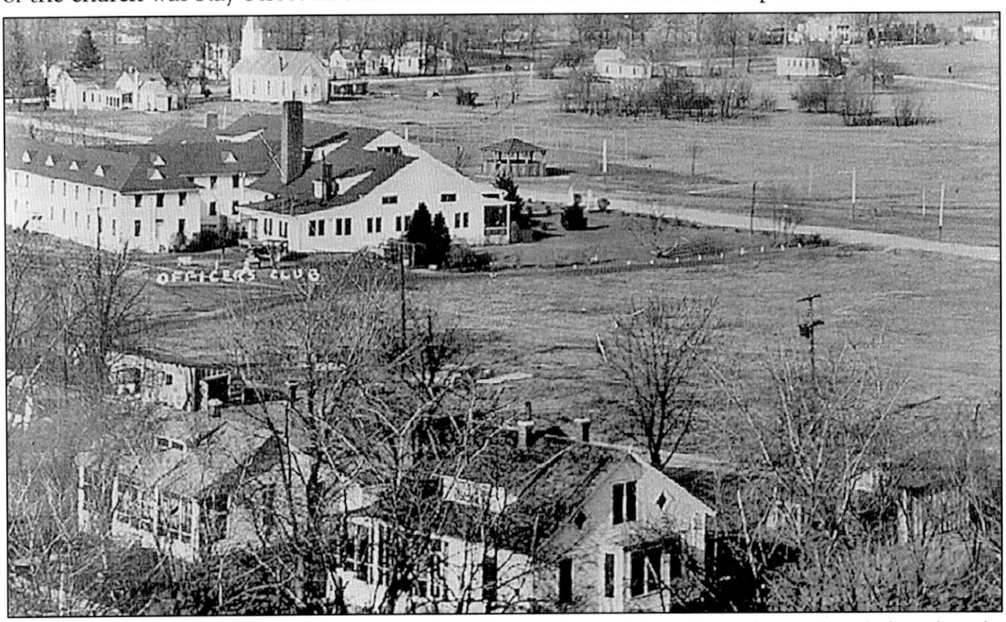

CAMP KNOX, 1932. Residences lined Ray Street (now Dixie Street) north of the church. An officers' club is behind the homes, and Fifth Avenue (Main Street in Stithton) is in the background. The building with the steeple on Main Street in the background of the photograph was the Stithton Baptist Church. Quarters 1, home of the Fort Knox commanding general, was later built across the street, east of the church. None of these buildings remain.

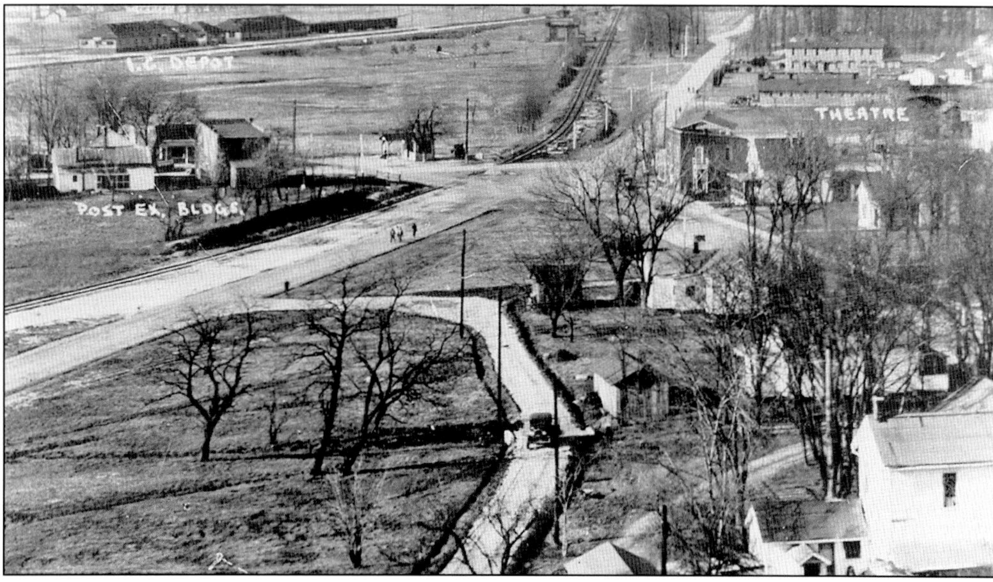

CAMP KNOX, 1932. In 1932 Camp Knox became Fort Knox. The intersection in the upper quarter of this photograph is Fifth Avenue (Main Street in Stithton) and Dixie Street (Ray Street in Stithton). The Chaffee Avenue traffic circle developed from this intersection. On its southwest corner is a two-story, rectangular building, which was the Wiseman store in Stithton. It has undergone renovation but remains today as building #1224. Until 1919 the Stithton Hotel, post office, drug store, and other businesses were located across from the Wiseman store.

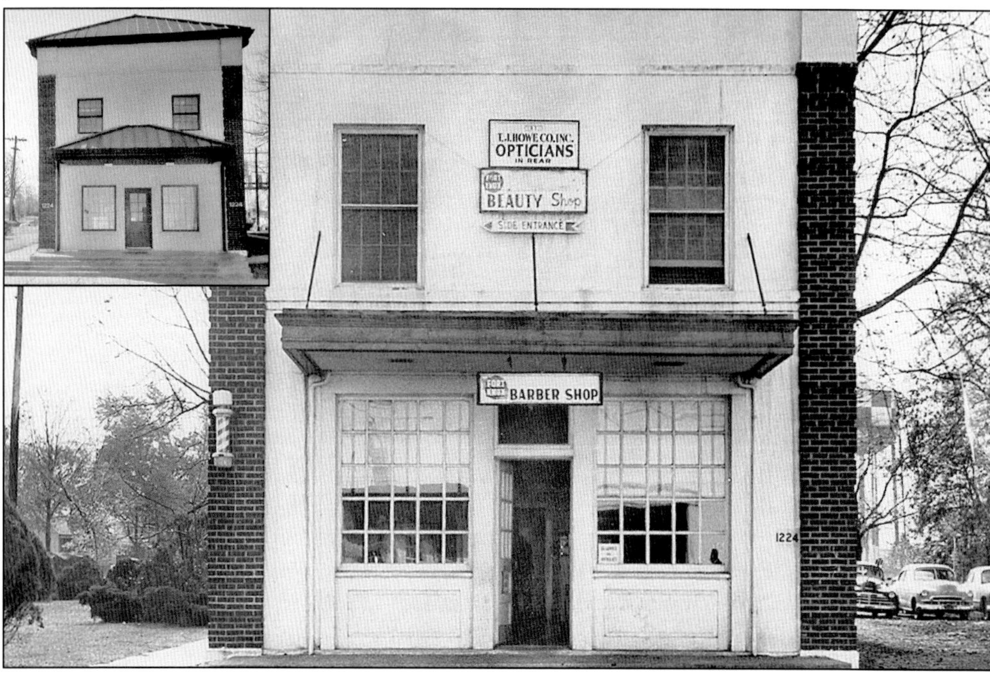

THE WISEMAN BUILDING, 1956 AND 2002 (INSET). The Wiseman Merchandise/Dry Goods Store served Stithton residents for many years. Having served many purposes since the acquisition by Fort Knox, it remains today as an office building. Now building #1224, it and St. Patrick's Church are the only surviving buildings from Stithton.

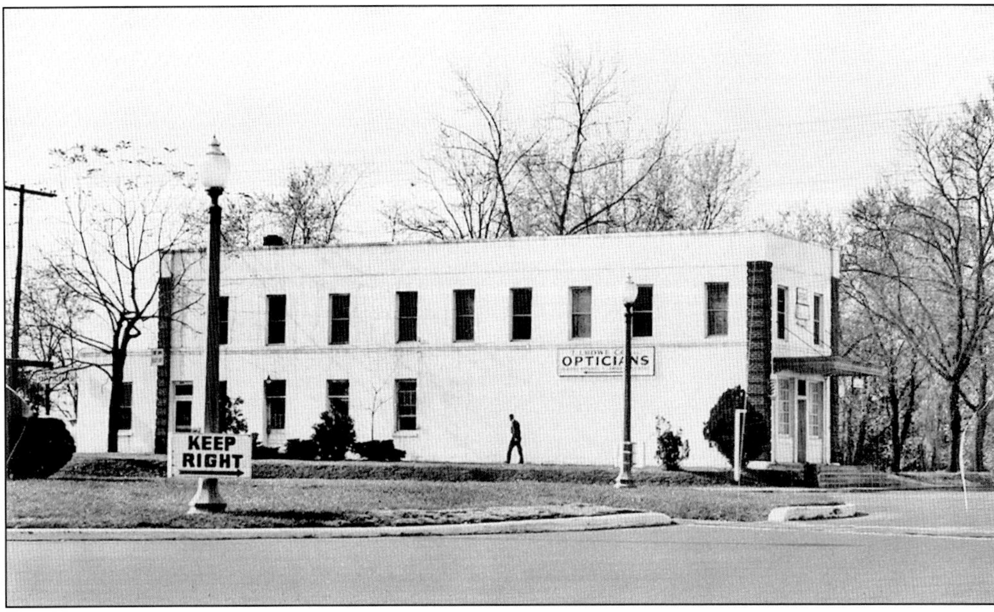

WISEMAN STORE BUILDING, 1956. Greatly renovated, the Wiseman store became building #1224 on Fort Knox. It was home of the local Masons who used the second floor of the store as the Masonic Hall. Alongside the Wiseman store (approximately where the "Keep Right" sign is in the photograph) was the town well with a pump, and adjacent to the well was the Stithton Train Station. Across the street (Main Street in Stithton) from the store were a post office, the Brown Store, Joyce Drug Store (once the Peoples Bank of Stithton), a dry goods store, and the Huff Deli. Further down Main Street (now Fifth Avenue) to the east were residences, and near the intersection of present Fifth Avenue and Old Ironsides Avenue were the Stithton Baptist Church, a paint and wallpaper shop, the residence of E.T. Carrico, and the Stithton school.

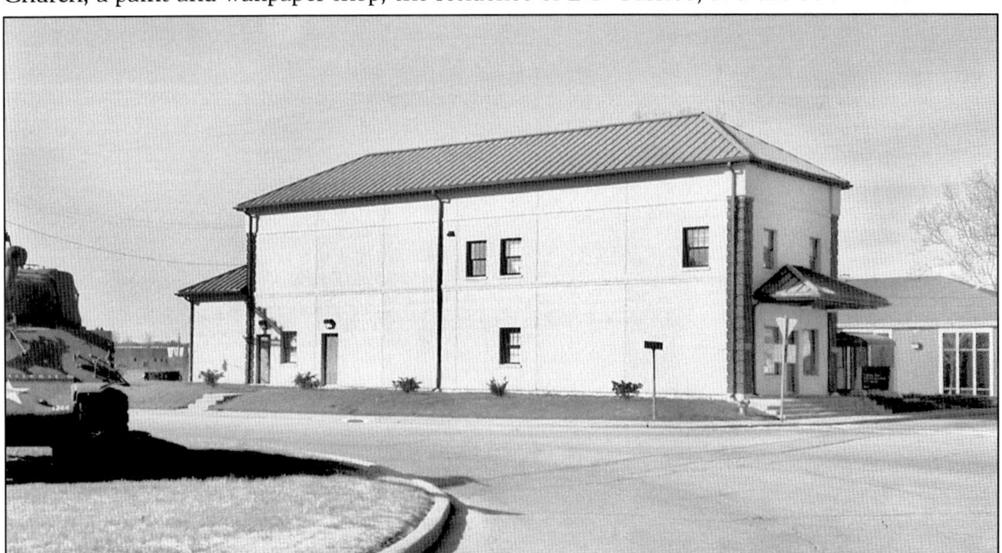

BUILDING #1224, 2002. In bygone Stithton times, behind the Wiseman store (now building #1224) on Ray Street (now Dixie Street) was a railroad tie yard, stock pens, public scale, livery stable, telephone exchange building, and Dr. Allen's home.

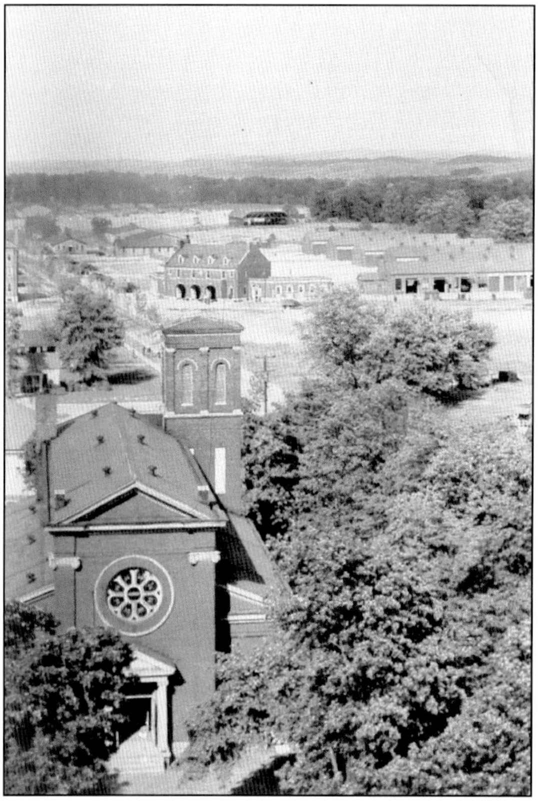

STITHTON, 1932. Six acres of land behind St. Patrick's Church was once owned by L.D. Calvin, and M.A. Campbell owned 14 acres. Old Ironsides Avenue came to cross these properties from east to west. Just south of St. Patrick's Church was Dewey Street in Stithton times. Dewey Street was extended and named Spearhead Division Avenue with the demise of Stithton. In 1934 a firehouse and guardhouse were constructed on the corner of Spearhead Division Avenue and Old Ironsides Avenue. The building can be seen in the background of the photograph and remains today as a fire station in building #469.

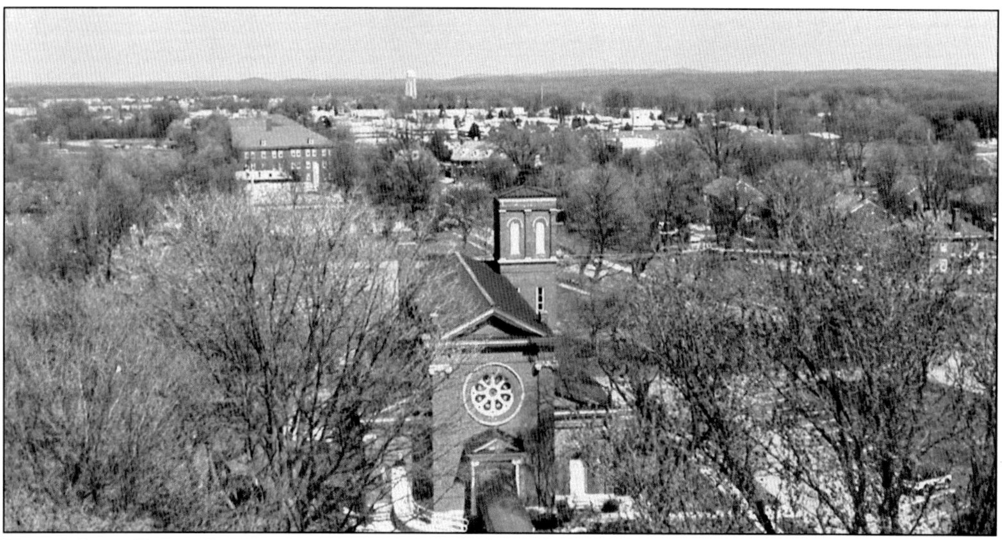

THE MAIN POST CHAPEL, 2002. St. Patrick's Church is currently used as the Main Post Chapel. Constructed as a Catholic church in 1899–1900, the chapel is the only intact building left from the town of Stithton. The steeple houses the original bell, inscribed "St. Patrick's Church 1904." Many of the stained glass windows are original, while others were added in 1938 to honor the units stationed at Fort Knox. Brick for the construction of the church was fired in a large brick kiln that was located behind the church. Catholic families from the area volunteered in 24-hour shifts to tend the kiln fires.

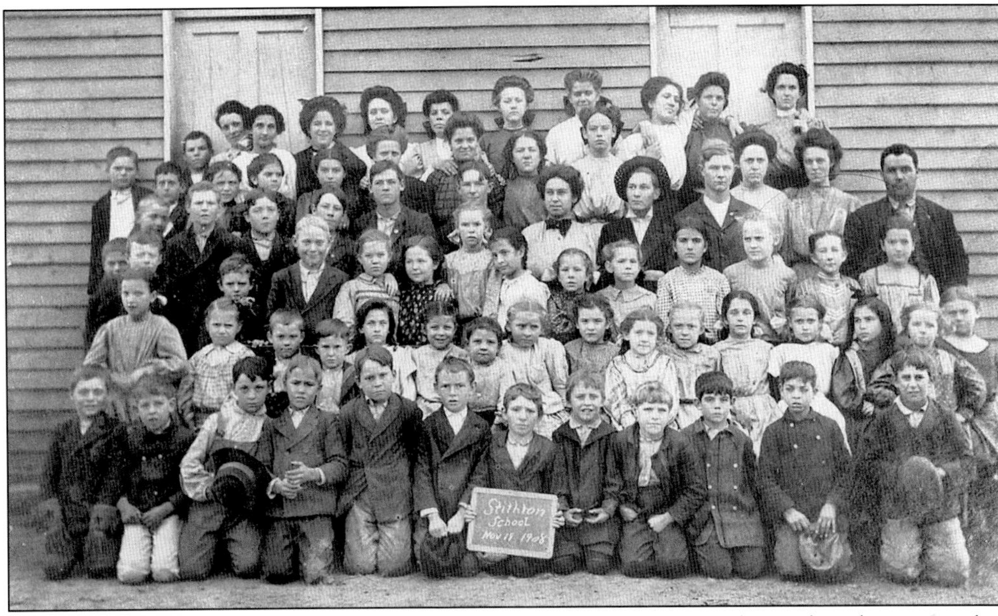

STITHTON PUBLIC SCHOOL, 1908. The Stithton public school was located at the east end of Main Street (now Fifth Avenue). To the west of the school were the home of E.T. Carrico, a paint and wallpaper shop, the residence of Rev. Ben Hunter, and the Baptist church. Across the street (north) from the school was the L.N. Patterson farmhouse. The farm was very progressive in having the first silo in the area and the first gasoline engine used to run a compressor to cool milk.

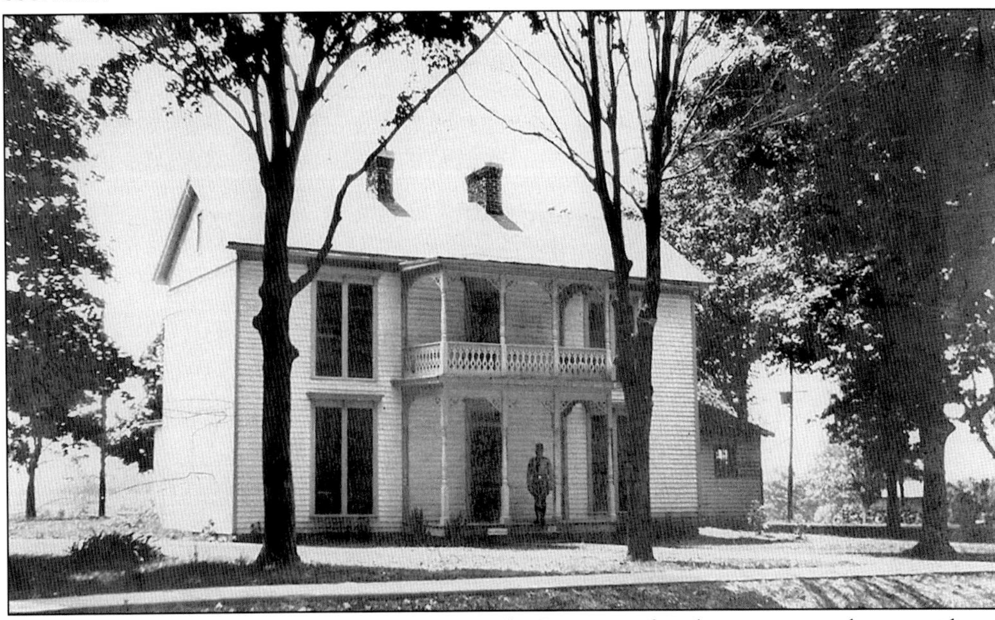

PATTERSON FARMHOUSE, C. 1919. For a time the Patterson farmhouse was used as a residence for the post commander. After the construction of permanent quarters for the commander west of the farmhouse, the building was used as a residence for Fort Knox schoolteachers. The farmhouse was demolished in the 1930s, when permanent, brick officers' quarters were built along Fifth Avenue.

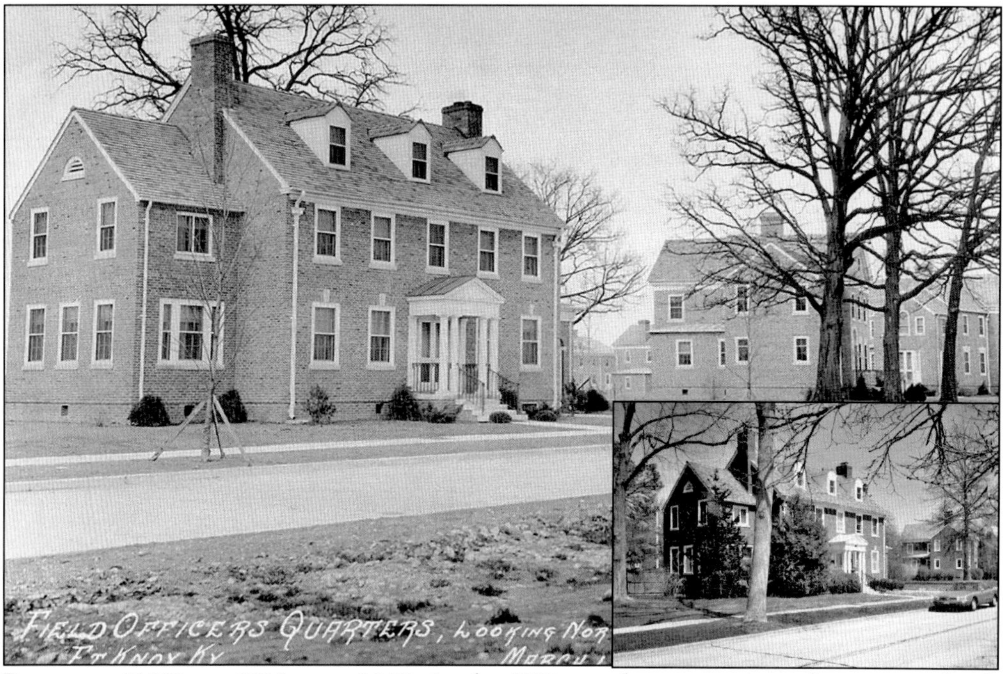

BUILDING #1403 IN 1935 AND 2002. In the 1930s much construction of permanent brick quarters and barracks was initiated. This construction established the architectural style of Fort Knox buildings well into the future. Building #1403 came to be built on the approximate location of the Patterson farmhouse that served Camp Knox as quarters for many years. Building #1403 is shown in the inset 67 years after its construction.

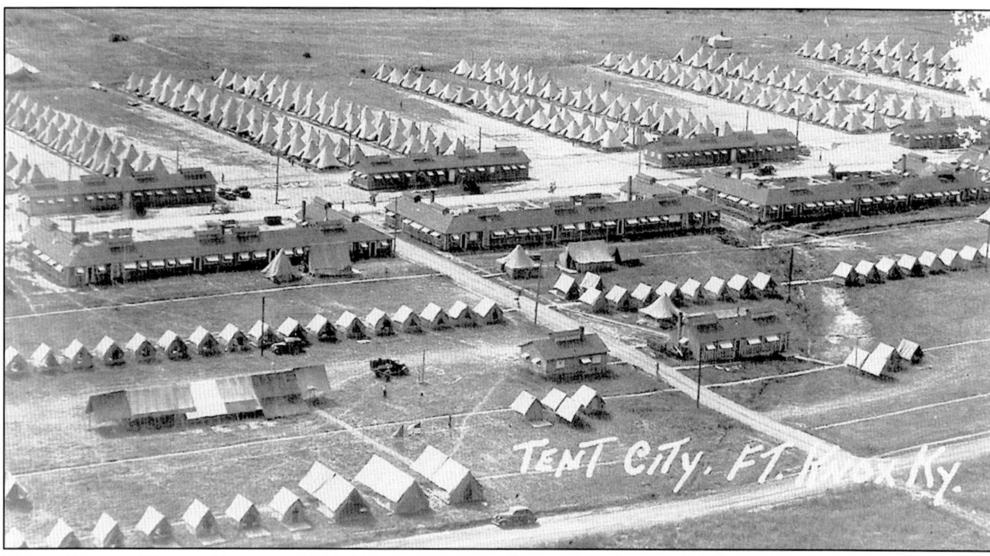

FORT KNOX TENT CITY, 1935. Construction of barracks, mess halls, and classrooms for Fort Knox soldiers could not keep pace with the considerable increase in their numbers. "Tent Cities" arose at numerous locations on the installation to accommodate the troops. This tent city was located behind the present site of Gaffee Hall (building #2369) and Harris Hall (building #2368). Some of the cement block structures in the photograph remain standing today, though remodeled; however, most have been demolished.

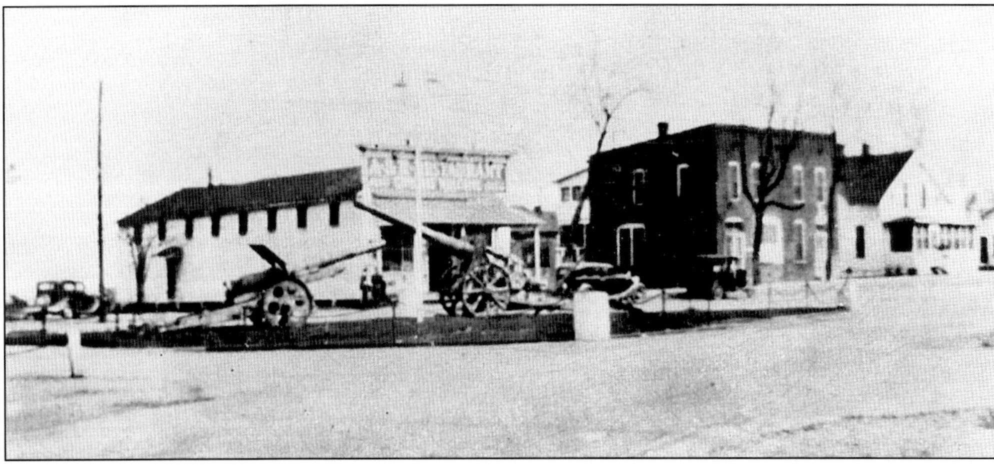

STITHTON CIRCLE, C. 1920. A year after the establishment of Camp Knox in 1918, the government appropriated funds for the purchase of Stithton. Through the early 1920s, most of Stithton's buildings—residential and commercial—still stood. Though owned by the government, buildings that housed businesses beneficial to Camp Knox operations could be leased by the previous owners to continue business operations. The artillery pieces in the picture rest on what would become the center of the Chaffee Avenue traffic circle. In 1979 the traffic circle was named Stithton Circle in a special ceremony, and a commemorative sign was placed. The buildings shown here are Mossbarger's store and the Union Bank of Stithton; both were on the southeast corner of Main and Ray Streets (present Fifth Avenue and Chaffee Avenue).

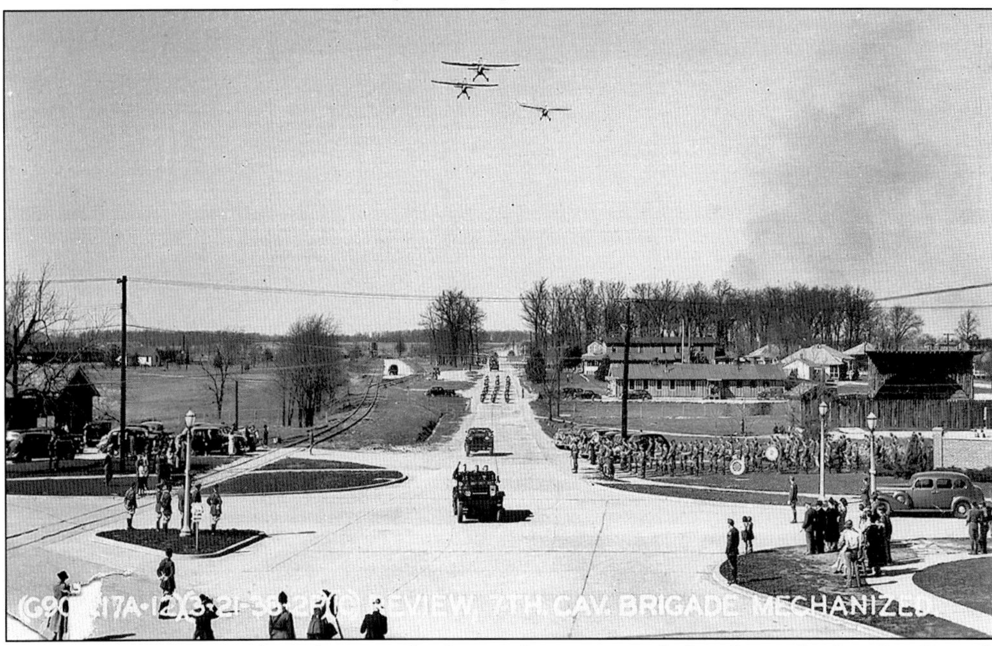

FORT KNOX, 1938. This photograph shows the review of the Seventh Cavalry Brigade Mechanized as they approach the traffic circle from the north on Knox Street. By 1938 Camp Knox had been renamed Fort Knox, and the Chaffee Avenue traffic circle was approaching its present configuration. The Mossbarger store and Union Bank of Stithton would have been on the southeast corner of the traffic circle (lower right corner of the photograph). Almost all of the buildings from the town of Stithton are gone at this time.

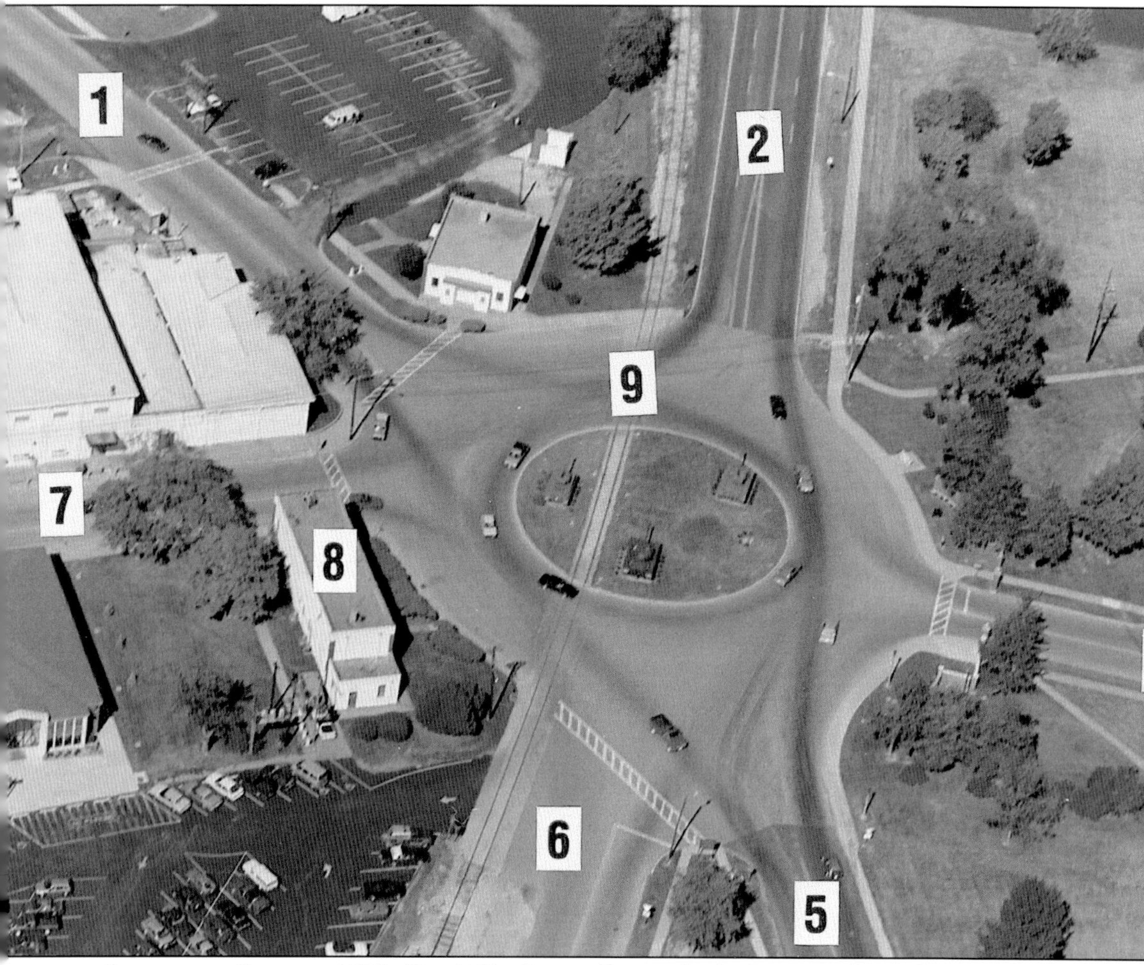

STITHTON CIRCLE, 1975. By 1975 the traffic circle had assumed much of its present configuration. The railroad tracks, which at this time still ran through the island in the traffic circle, follow the same right of way as the original Elizabethtown & Paducah railroad tracks that were constructed through Stithton in 1873, resulting in rapid growth and expansion of the town. The railroad changed hands and names numerous times and, in 1901, became the Illinois Central, and finally the Paducah & Louisville Railroad. The tracks no longer traverse the traffic circle. The following landmarks are numbered in this photograph: (1) Chaffee Avenue, (2) Knox Street, (3) Fifth Avenue (Main Street in Stithton), (4) Chaffee Avenue, (5) Dixie Street (Ray Street in Stithton), (6) Knox Street, (7) Vine Grove Road (Main Street in Stithton), (8) building #1224 (the Wiseman Store in Stithton), and (9) Paducah & Louisville Railroad tracks. The western third (left in the photograph) of the island within the Stithton Circle occupied the land that until 1919 held the Stithton train station.

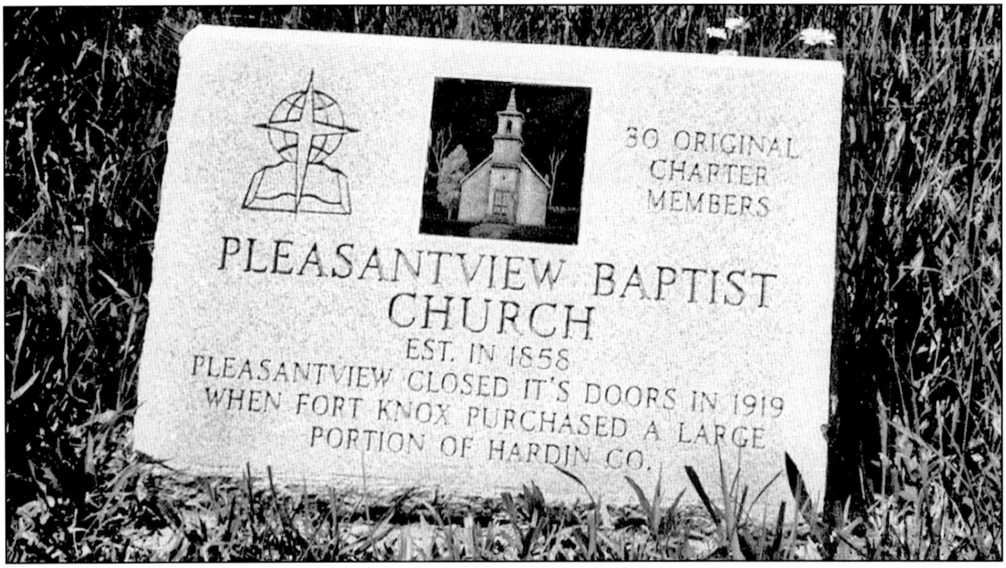

The Town of Pleasant View (Wigginton). In 1858, 22 charter members established the Pleasant View Baptist Church, and it was built on the east side of the Louisville-Nashville Turnpike, south of Dripping Springs Cave. Charter members were Arabel Davis, William Torrence, James Irwin, Mary Morrison, Susan Scanlon, Robert Scanlon, Albert Hubbard, Greenup King, William Kendall, Hannah King, Susan Hubbard, Thomas Kelly, Jane Harris Artimia Kelly, Ann Harris, John P. Hayes, Dabney Withers, Martha Hays, Elizabeth Davis, William Stephens, Jane Lane, and Jane Stephens. Rev. J.H. Jenkins offered the first prayer in the new building, and Rev. G.H. Hicks preached the first sermon from Matthew 5:13–16. A cemetery soon surrounded the church. A new building (the third) was constructed in 1905, and Reverend Kimball preached the first sermon on January 1, 1905, from Matthew. On May 27, 1996, a memorial stone was placed where the front steps of the church once stood in a memorial service conducted by Rev. Dexter Jones.

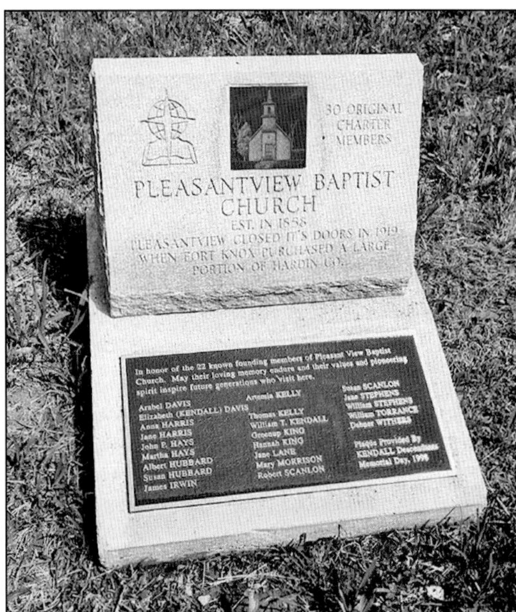

Pleasant View Baptist Church Monument. Three years following the placement of the Pleasant View Baptist Church monument, descendants of those buried in the church cemetery and descendants of church members placed a base beneath the monument with a brass plate that listed the charter members of the church.

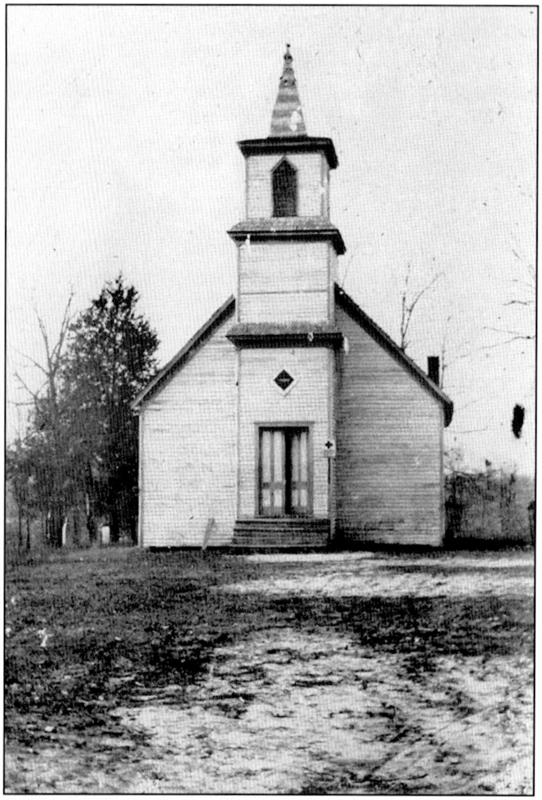

PLEASANT VIEW BAPTIST CHURCH, 1920. The first church building, constructed in 1858, was the site of a murder. No one knew the murderer (he escaped) or the man he killed; it is believed they were hoboes from the railroad. The murder left blood all over the church, both from the killing and from parishioners attempting to escape through glass windows. Unable to remove all of the blood, the church was greatly renovated. It later burned and was replaced. The last church building was constructed in 1905 and was taken by the government in 1918 for the establishment of Camp Knox. The church officially closed on July 11, 1920. The Pleasant View Baptist Church cemetery has 334 known burials. Many more are suspected but unrecorded. The first burial was that of Elizabeth Young on August 9, 1852, and the last burial was that of Lena Wigginton in October 1967. Salem Baptist Association records show that 25 pastors served the church in its 62 years of service.

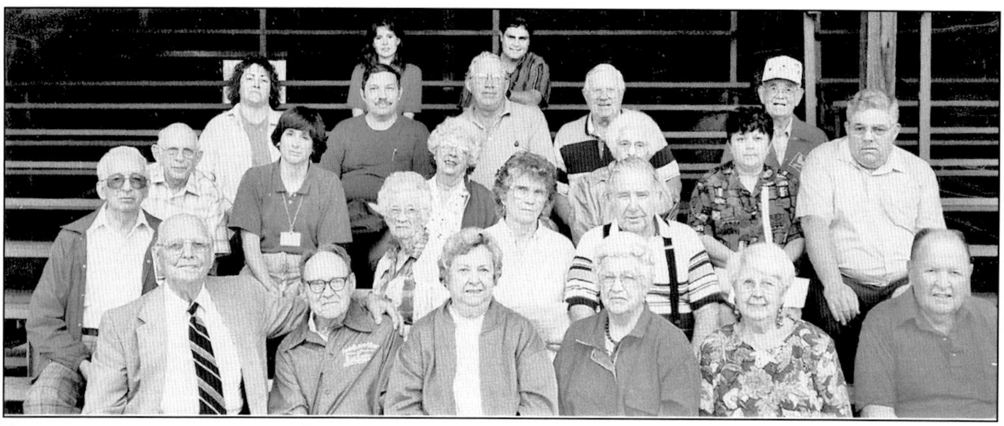

PARTICIPANTS IN THE 1996 PLEASANT VIEW CHURCH MEMORIAL SERVICE. On a chilly, rainy day, a group attended Pleasant View Church monument dedication. From left to right they are (first row) Rev. Dexter Jones, Russell L. Preston, Mary Preston, Katherine Miller Paulley, Doris E. Culver, and Clifford E. Culver Sr.; (second row) Lawrence Roeder, Agnes Rahm Rice (born near the cemetery where she lived with her family until 1919), Jackie Aikens, and James Aikens; (third row) Robert E. Goodman, Cynthia Eagles (*Courier-Journal* reporter), Jean Roeder, Dorothy Harris Brown, Mrs. Brown, and Robert Brown; (fourth row) Betty Warren, Paul Urbahns, John Carlberg, David Carlberg, and Clifford Paulley; (fifth row) Tara Marine and Dean Sprague. Present but not pictured were Gary Kempf, James E. Culver, Robert Ruff, Laureen Ruff, Marguerite Lewis, Lindsay Lewis, Sandy Urbahns, SSG J. Pope, Roosevelt Price, and Lillian Price.

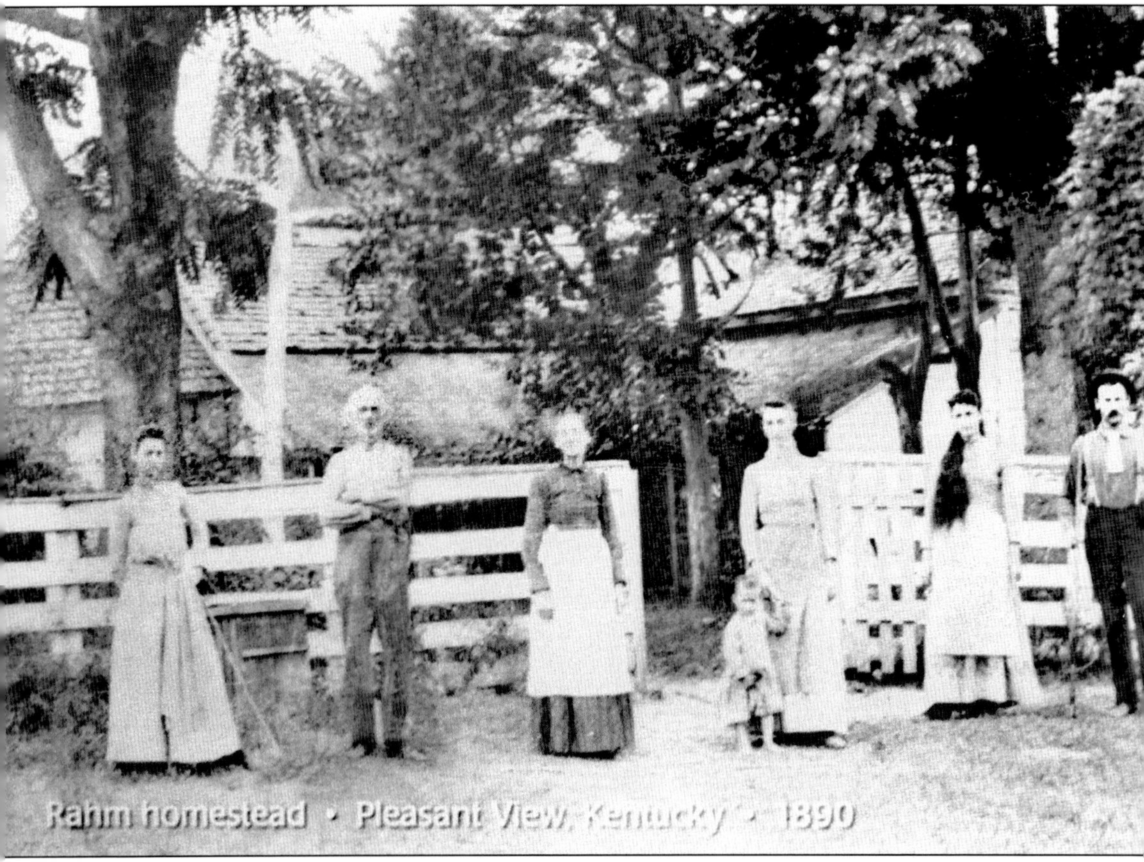

GEORGE RAHM HOME AND FAMILY, PLEASANT VIEW, 1890. Many of the early settlers in the area were veterans of the American Revolution who were given land grants for their war service. Documents for such land grants are common in courthouses throughout Kentucky. Most were signed by Patrick Henry or Thomas Jefferson, governors of Virginia. Gradually, first-generation European immigrants also settled in Kentucky. Johann Georg Rahm, such an immigrant, came from Beyreuth, Germany, and settled on a large tract of land north of Pleasant View. His son John Rahm is shown here in front of his home with the following people, from left to right: Minnie Rahm, John Rahm, Margaret Rahm, Paul Anshutz (child), Hattie Rahm Anshutz, Sophie Rahm, and Clarence Rahm. Common for the time and place, Johann gave a piece of his property to each of his sons, and they in turn gave property to each of their sons. (Daughters were often given land in the same manner.) Thus, four generations lived on land that was taken for the establishment of Camp Knox. Near the John Rahm home was a family cemetery. Known to have been buried within are Johann George Rahm, Anna Rahm (Johann's wife), Georgiann Missouria Rahm (grandchild), Francis Rahm, and an unidentified child, and there may have been others. This cemetery has not been located and is assumed to have been claimed by time and forever lost.

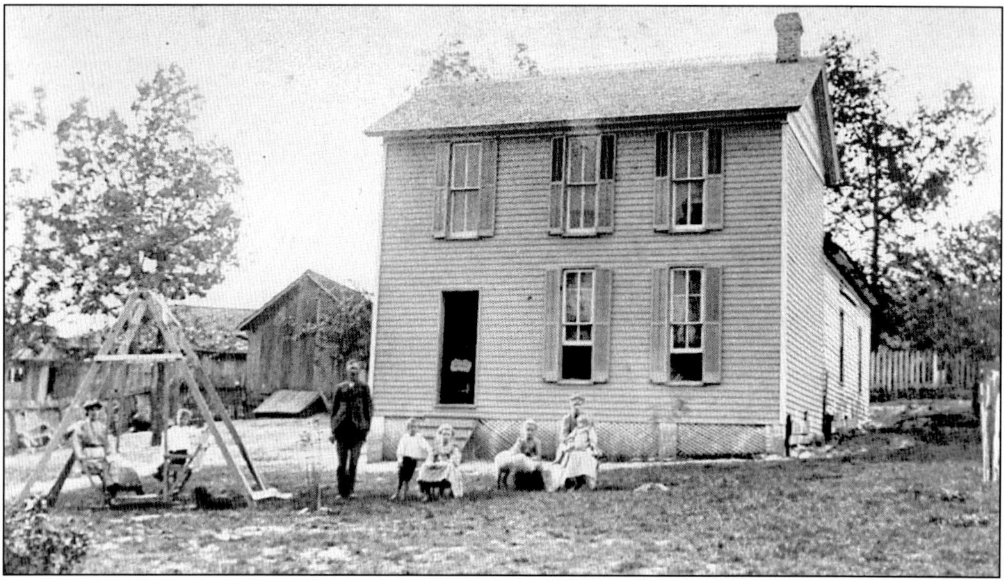

VICTOR RAHM HOME AT PLEASANT VIEW (WIGGINTON), 1903. The area around the Baptist church built in 1858 soon included a school, merchandise store, and post office. The first postmaster was Ben Wigginton, causing Pleasant View to appear on some maps as Wigginton. Many prosperous farms in the area had been in a particular family for three generations or more. The Victor Rahm farm was one such farm. Shown in front of the family home, from left to right, are Maybel and Elwood on the swing, Victor, John, Nell, Nora, and Betty Rahm with baby Agnes in her arms. Agnes celebrated her 103rd birthday in January 2004.

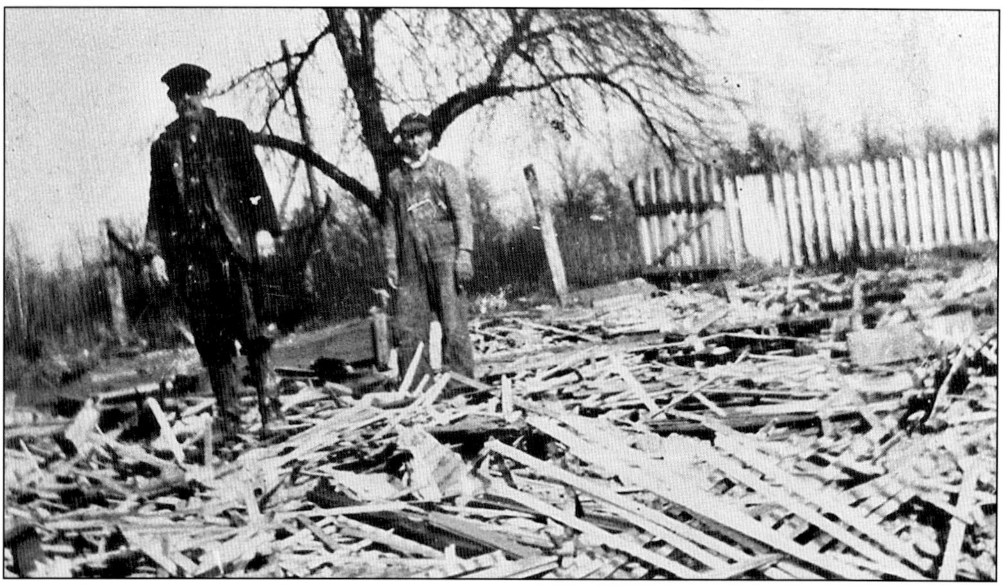

RAHM HOUSE IN RUINS. Shortly after his farm was seized for Camp Knox in 1918, Victor Rahm and Virgil Blakely returned to the site. The house had already been demolished to make room for army firing ranges and the maneuvering of men and machines (mostly horses at that time). Victor died two years after this photograph was taken. He was buried in St. Patrick's Cemetery in the Fort Knox cantonment area. Being Catholic, the Rahm family attended the St. Patrick's Church in Stithton rather than the Pleasant View Baptist Church.

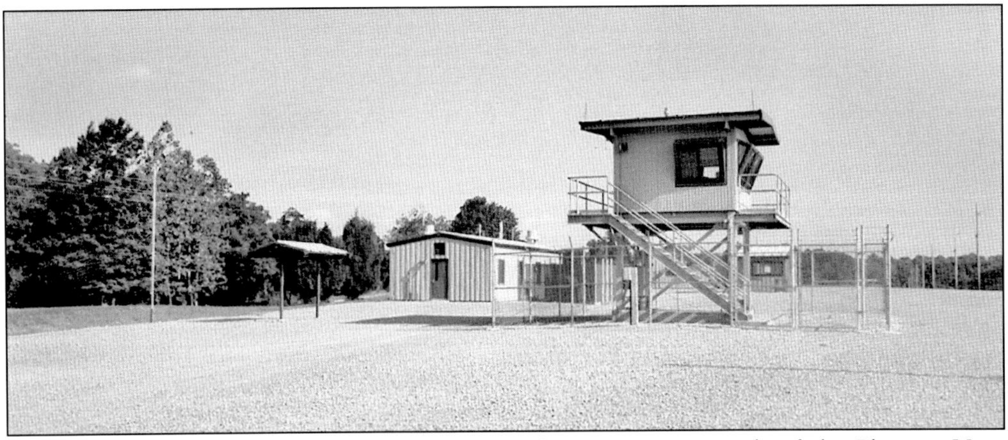

PELL FIRING RANGE. Although the Rahm farmhouse was just north of the Pleasant View Baptist Church and Cemetery, they were Catholic and therefore attended St. Patrick's Catholic Church in Stithton. Victor Rahm, as well as numerous relatives, was buried in the St. Patrick's Cemetery outside Stithton. Less than 100 yards north of where the Rahm home once stood is the Pell Firing Range control tower. The control tower sits where an orchard once stood.

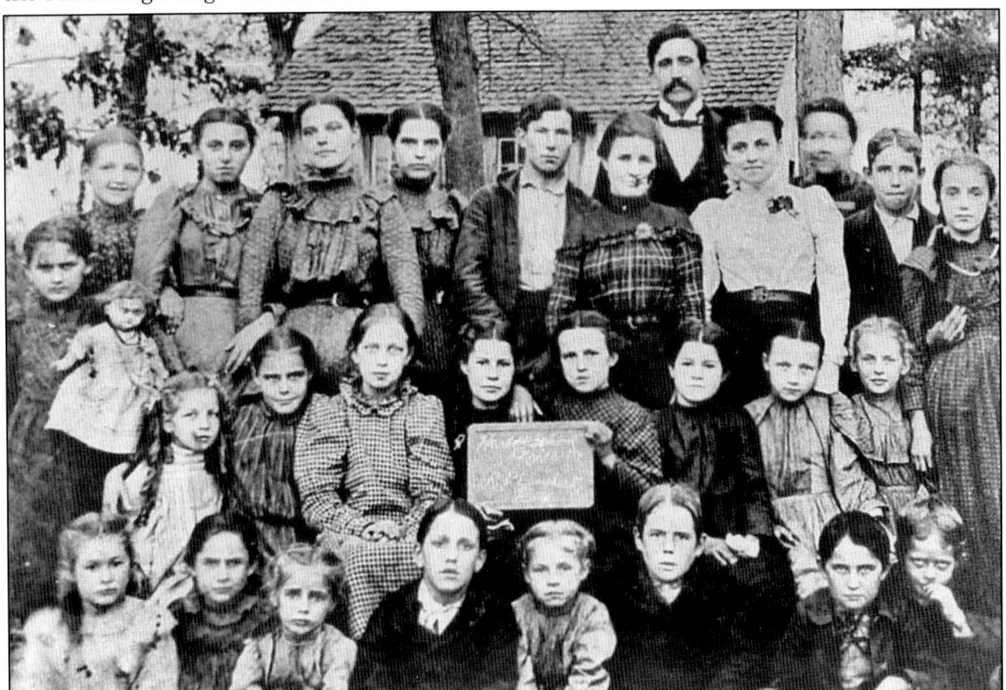

HARBOLDT SCHOOL, 1898. Behind and just east of the Rahm home was the Harboldt School, which was attended by all of the Rahm children and other children of the Pleasant View area. It was a one-room, wood-frame building. Students in 1898 and pictured from left to right are (front row) Verna Blevins, Alda Stevens, Nora Rahm, Jim Robinson, Pansy Ogle, Guy Ogle, Jim Stevens, Henry Robinson, and Guy Russel; (middle row) Nora Wigginton (with doll), Lottie Harris (with curls), Sylvia Wilkerson, Eula Robinson, Ethel Blevins, Della Harrison, Carrie Blevins, Carrie Harrison, and Nell Rahm; (back row) Linnie Harris, Martha Daugherty, Ella Wilkerson, Rhoda Wilkerson, Herman Ogle, Fannie Blevins, Bob Daugherty (teacher), Nora Harrison, Ella Tanner, Elmer Ogle, and Mabel Rahm.

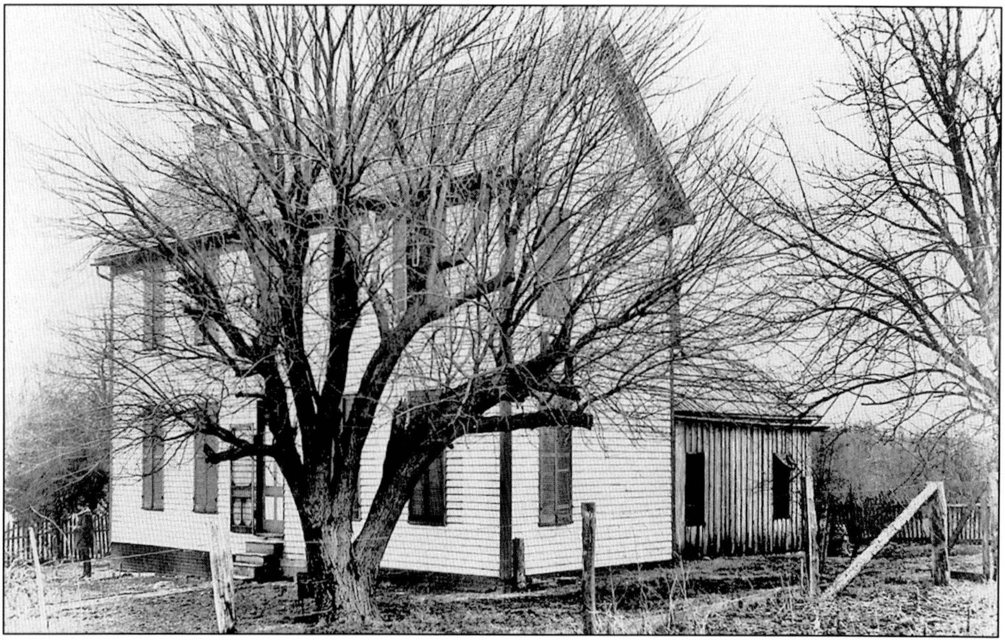

Stanton Harris Home outside Pleasant View, 1918. The Stanton Harris farm was southeast of the Victor Rahm farm, and the Harboldt School was on the southeast corner of the Harris farm. The Rahm children walked through the Harris property to reach the school. Of the Stanton's 14 children, three died in infancy and were buried in a fenced plot on the Davis farm with no markers. Thus, these graves are presumed forever lost. The Harris family, like the other farm families in the Pleasant View area, received mail through the Wigginton post office and purchased goods at the Robinson store, located behind and north of the Pleasant View Baptist Church on the east side of the Louisville-Nashville Turnpike (now Wilson Road).

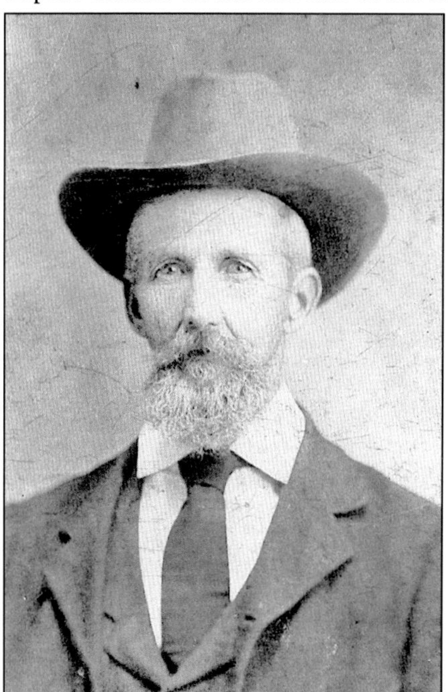

Stanton Harris, 1903. Stanton Harris raised hogs, chickens, and milk cows. He also raised bloodhounds. In a rare instance of a burglary, someone broke into the home of Stanton's neighbor, Jack Shipley. Stanton was called upon to use his hounds in an attempt to track the burglar. The attempt failed and the burglar was never found. In 1900 tragedy struck the Harris family when son James William Harris was accidentally shot to death by his brother Benjamin Felix Harris. Neighbor Victor Rahm was one of the first on the tragic scene to observe the body. He reported that James must have been walking with his arms folded across his chest when the fatal bullet struck as that was the way he lay, on his back with his arms folded across his chest.

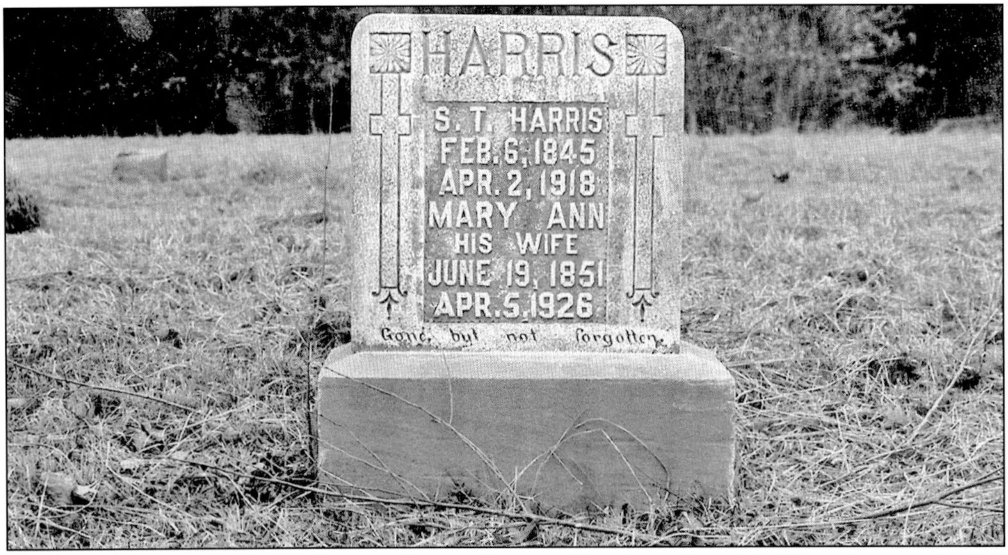

STANTON AND MARY ANN HARRIS GRAVE. Stanton Harris and his wife, Mary Ann, are buried in the Pleasant View Baptist Church Cemetery. Others from the Pleasant View (Wigginton) area are buried in this large cemetery. The earliest burial in the cemetery was that of Elizabeth Young on August 9, 1852. Many never had a gravestone, the gravestone surrendered to time and elements, or perhaps it was destroyed by acts of man. Many of those listed as buried are based upon obituaries and other documents rather than gravestones. Such is the case with many of the other cemeteries on Fort Knox.

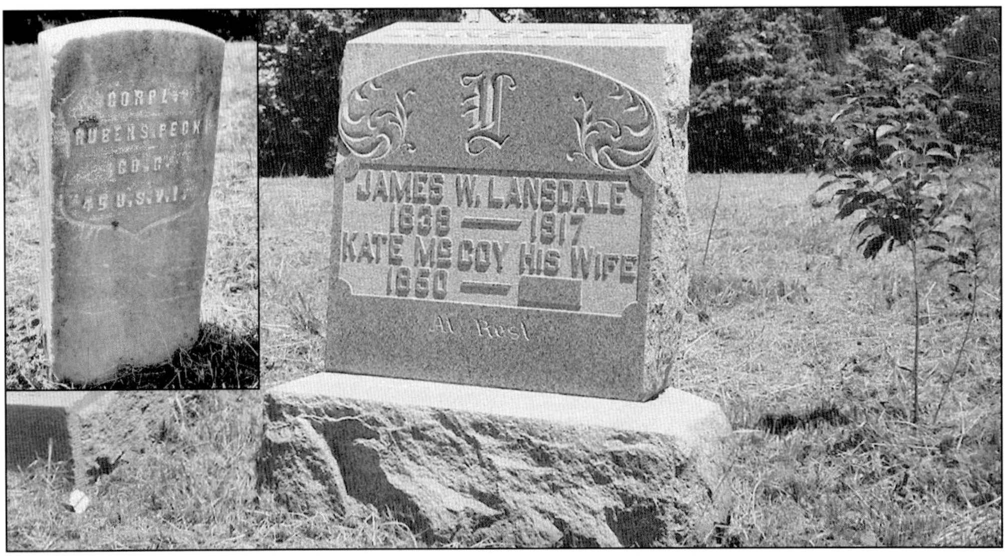

NORTH AND SOUTH CIVIL WAR SOLDIERS. The area behind the Pleasant View cemetery was heavily forested and during the Civil War was a stronghold for Southern guerrillas and raiders. The well-known, self-proclaimed Confederate general Ben Wigginton operated here and once laid siege to West Point. The area was called Wigginton Woods, and few ventured into the area. Union and Confederate soldiers, once neighbors and friends, are buried in the cemetery. Confederate James Lansdale is buried near Union soldier Ruben S. Peck. While off fighting for the Confederate cause, Union soldiers camped on Lansdale's farm during the construction of Fort Duffield.

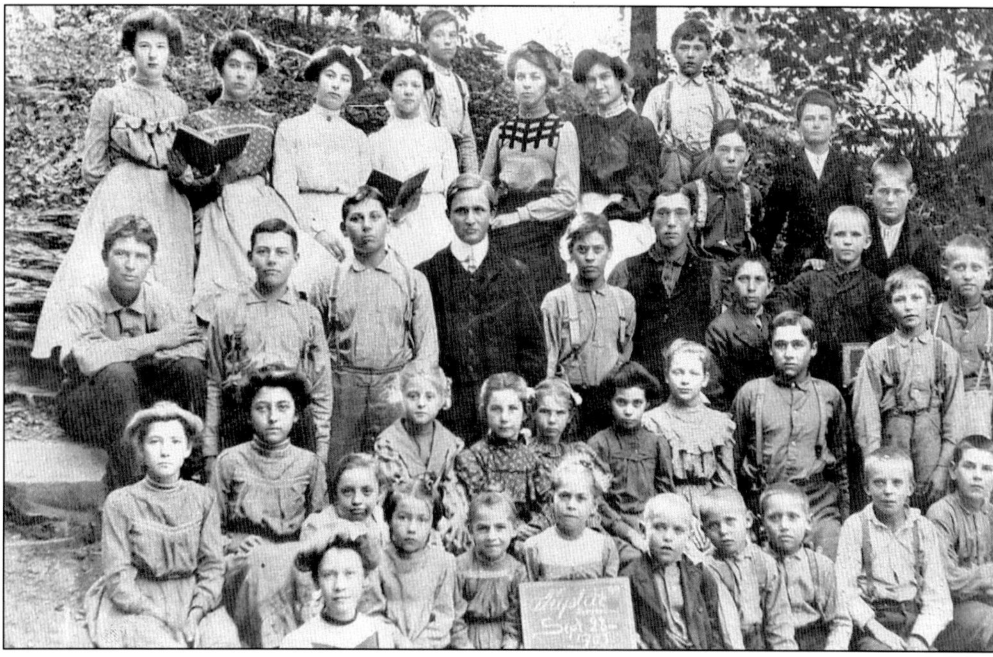

TRIPLETT SCHOOL STUDENTS, 1903. About a 1.5 miles south of the Harboldt School was the Triplett School. From left to right are (first row) F. Wise, R. Wise, M. Wise, A. Wise (holding slate), J. Preston, V. Preston, H. Stith, H. Wigginton, and C. Reesor; (second row) E. Lovell, A. Lovell, B. Preston, I. Sallee, V. Spalding, H. Spalding, D. Wise, L. Calvin, H. Stith, G. Hibbs, and P. Stith; (third row) H. Carrico, J. Wise, E. Wise, unidentified teacher, C. Wise, J. Lee, S. Grubb, H. Wigginton, and J. Numier; (fourth row) E. Calvin, S. Calvin, J. Kendall, M. Calvin, L. Kendall, L. Calvin, G. Hubbard, L. Hibbs, B. Lee, and R. Munier.

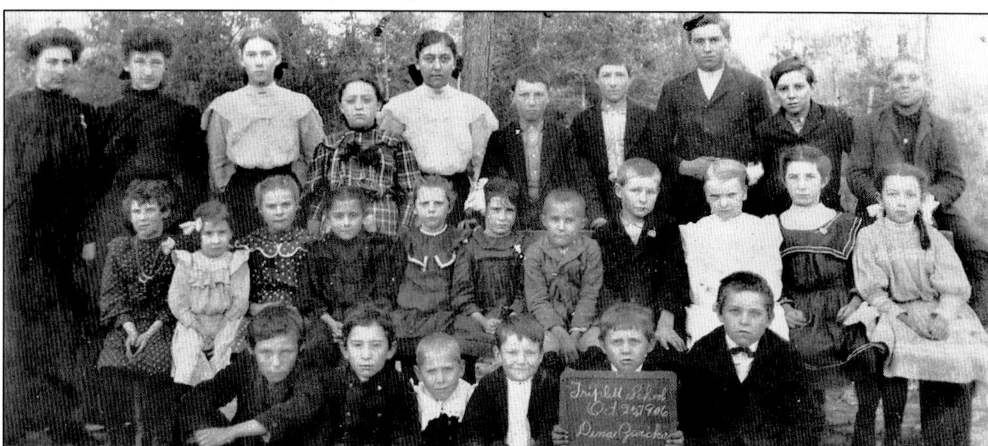

TRIPLETT SCHOOL STUDENTS, 1906. The land purchases of 1918 took the Harboldt and Triplett Schools, as well as the Highland, Chappel Ridge, Shady Grove, Cedar Grove, Stithton, St. Patrick's, and Liberty Hall schools. From left to right are (front row) E. Kendall, W. Connell, C. Connell, E. Hawkins, V. Preston (holding the chalkboard), and J. Preston; (middle row) H. Spalding, M. Shircliff, L. Jeffries, A. Connell, E.R. Brown, I. Spalding, J.O. Lovell, G. Hawkins, B. Bohannon, V. Spalding, and R. Wise; (back row) D. Zuriker (teacher), L. Zuriker, E. Lovell, B. Preston, A. Lovell, W. Wise, C. Hawkins, H. Stith, H. Miller, and H. Stith.

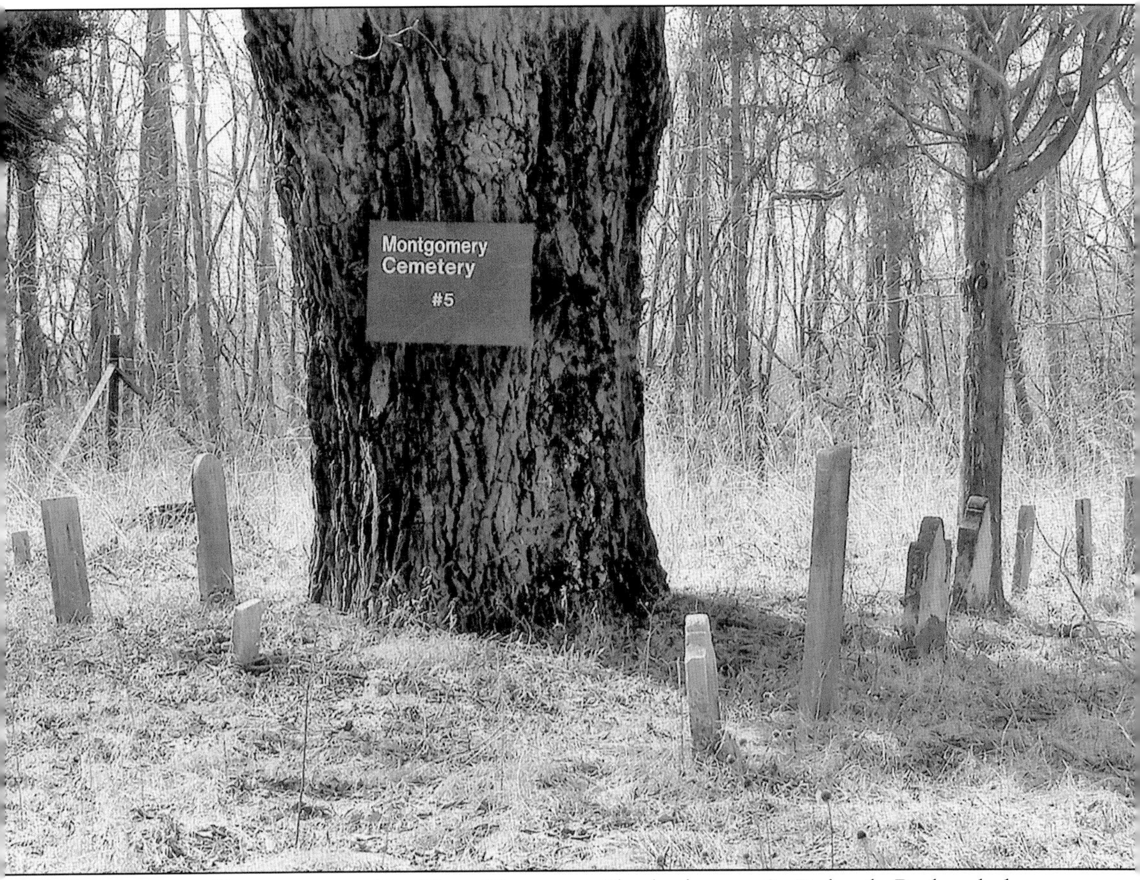

MONTGOMERY CEMETERY AT TIP TOP. The same Elizabethtown & Paducah Railroad that brought growth and prosperity to Stithton in 1873 brought about the establishment of Tip Top. With the arrival of the railroad came a depot, post office, a cluster of homes, general store, school (for a short time), and telephone service to an area just north of Stithton and a couple miles southwest of Pleasant View. The highest point on Muldraugh Hill, the area became known as Tip Top, and the name began to appear as a place name on maps in 1874. The train station in Tip Top came to be the main shipping point for the Grahampton and Garnettsville textile/grist mills, located in those respective towns (both of which were taken in the expansion of Fort Knox in 1941–1942). No evidence remains of Tip Top except for the active railroad tracks and the Montgomery Cemetery, currently located 100 yards west of the site of the bygone train depot. Some of the earliest settlers in the area lie in the cemetery. William Montgomery was the earliest burial in 1831, and the last recorded burial was Kitty A. Montgomery in 1880. The sassafras tree in the center of the cemetery was once listed as the largest in the country in *Ripley's Believe It Or Not*. A handsome stone fence, which once surrounded the cemetery, is now gone, as the stones have been taken and used in construction elsewhere.

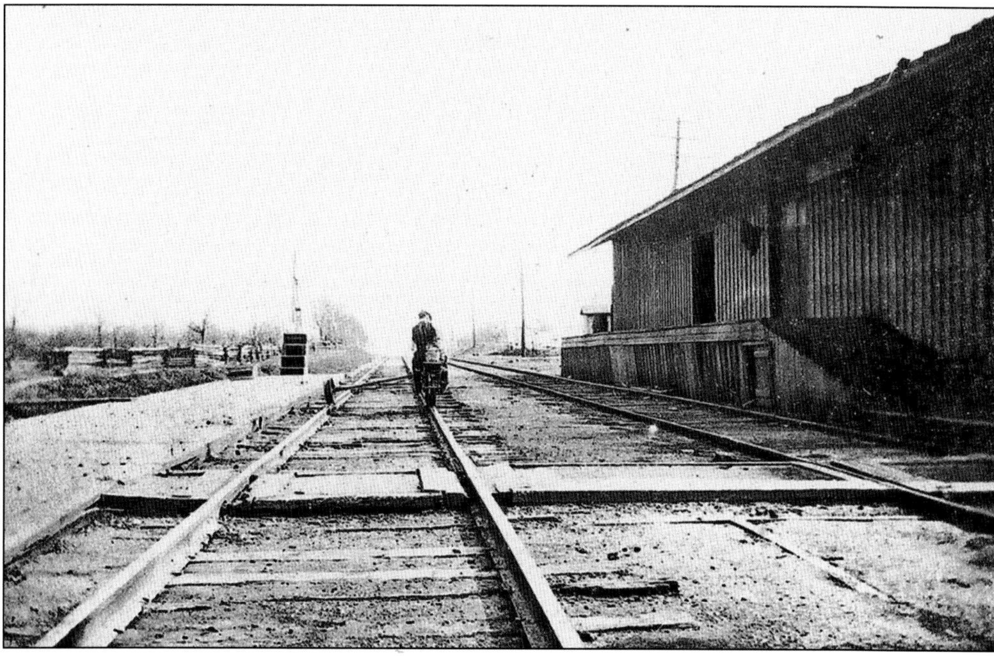

TIP TOP TRAIN DEPOT, 1918. Goods from Garnettsville and Grahampton mills, as well as produce and livestock from area farms, were shipped into and out of the Tip Top depot. Area residents who worked in Louisville took the train to work, and those wishing to shop in Louisville could also take the train. For most of its existence, S.K. Nichols was the railroad agent at the depot. Usually three or more trains per day stopped at the depot.

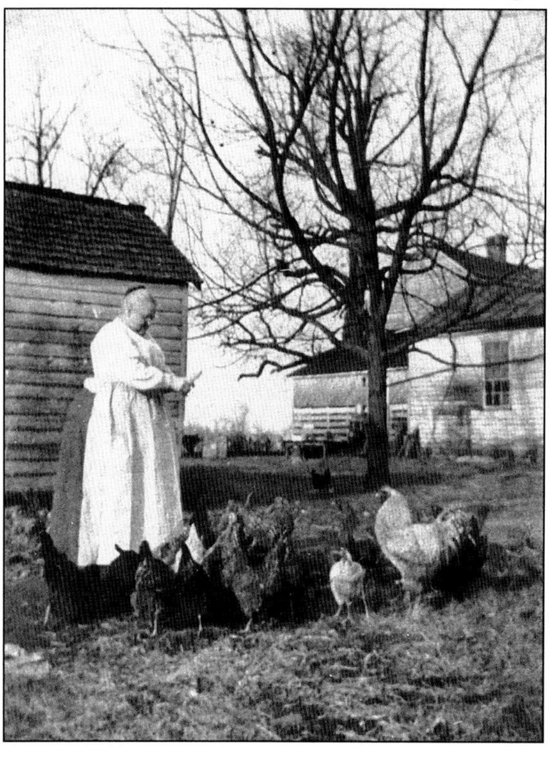

GRANNY SCHEIBLE AT HOME IN TIP TOP, 1918. Mary E. Scheible owned 446 acres of land west of the railroad tracks. The Scheible farm had 3,000 apple trees, and the Montgomery Cemetery was located on the land. A handsome stone fence, now gone, once surrounded the cemetery, and the stones have been cannibalized for other uses. Fruit trees produced a major cash crop for the area; the adjacent farm of Dr. J.C. Lewis had over 2,000 peach trees. Apples, pears, peaches, and cherries were sent to markets by train. The land that is now Fort Knox had several areas covered by extensive orchards that produced cash crops for farmers. In 1898 the Tip Top school was managed by C.H. Lampton. G.C. Schible (note the different spelling) ran the general store, and Mrs. J.M. Farris operated a boarding house.

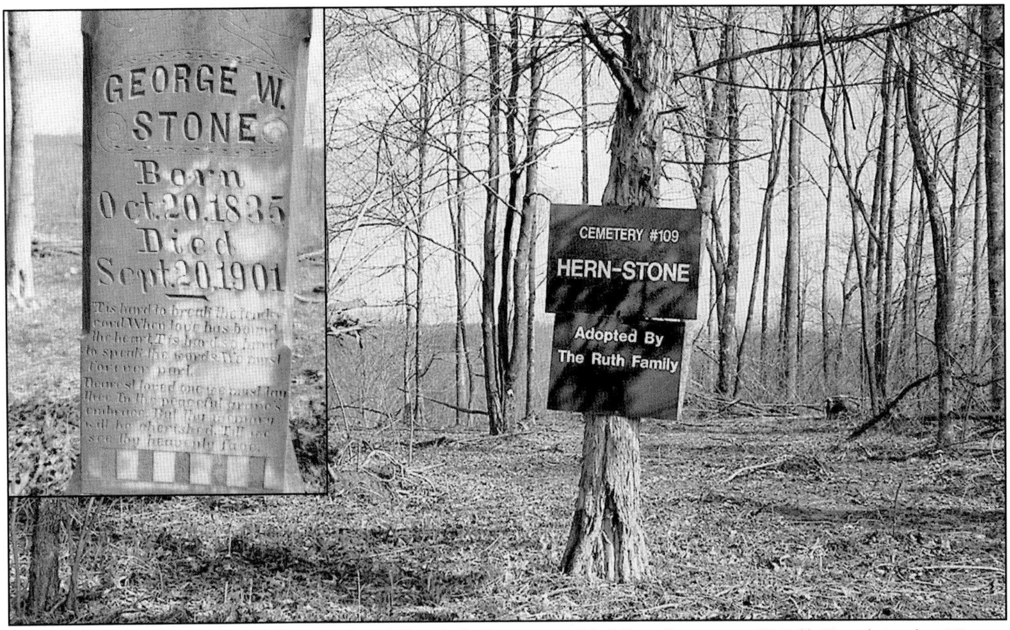

EASY GAP. About 1.25 miles south of the Salt River and 1.25 miles east of Mill Creek is the Hern-Stone Cemetery, resting atop the southeast corner of Hooker Mountain. It is not conspicuous among the 119 recorded cemeteries on Fort Knox except for it being the approximate location of the place called Easy Gap. The sign shows that the Ruth family adopted the cemetery and maintains it as part of the Fort Knox's "Adopt a Cemetery" program. Just a few days before this photograph was taken a tornado went through the area and damaged the cemetery.

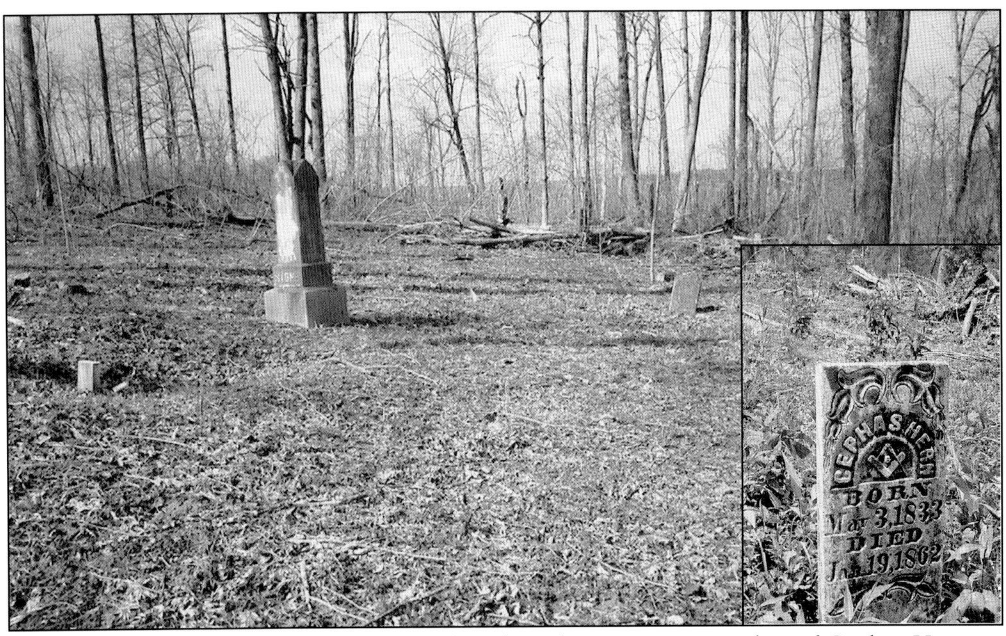

THE HERN-STONE CEMETERY. The first burial in the cemetery was that of Cephas Hern on January 19, 1862; the last burial was that of George Stone on October 20, 1901. All of the burials are from either the Hern or Stone families, who were among the early settlers in the area.

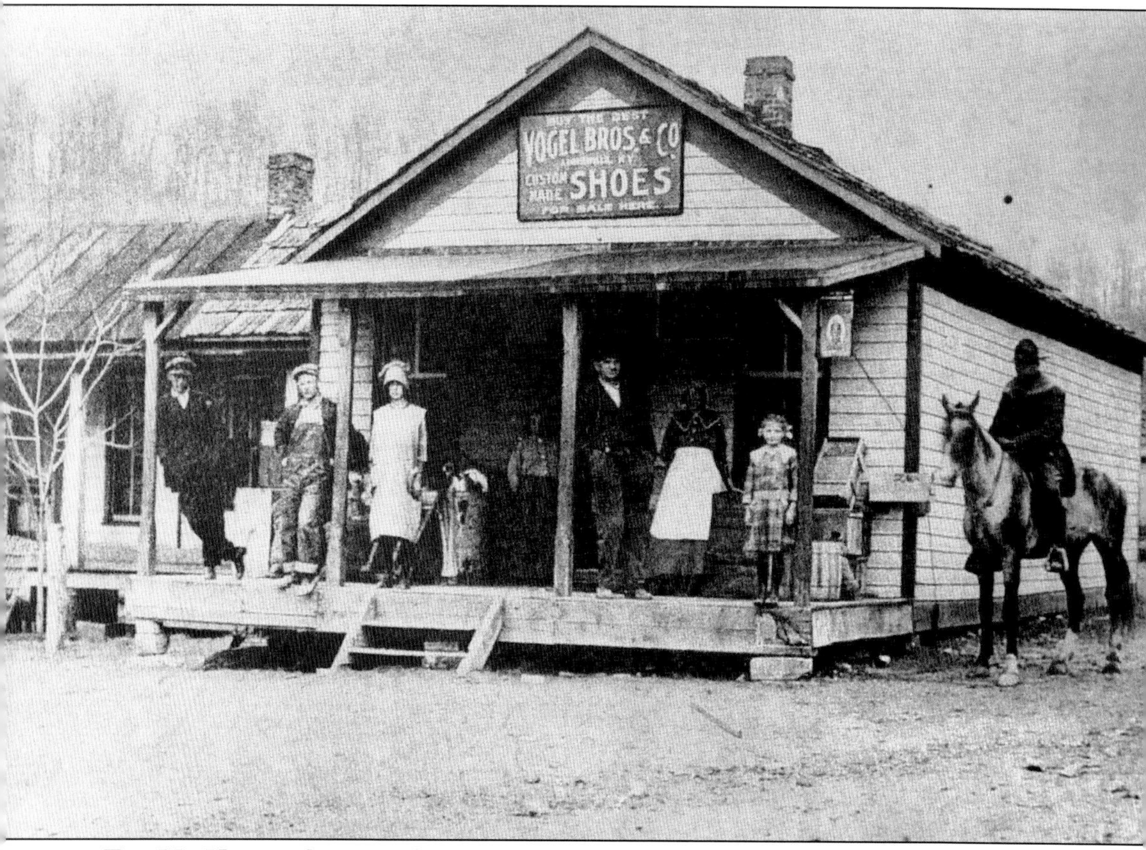

THE J.L. HARRIS GENERAL STORE AT EASY GAP, 1914. This general store at Easy Gap was typical of the many stores scattered about the area. Though West Point, Muldraugh, and Pitts Point were just a few miles away and could easily satisfy the supply needs of the scattered population of the Easy Gap area, those miles were a prohibitive distance due to the lack of roads and means of transportation. For most Easy Gap residents throughout the 19th and early 20th century, Elizabethtown and West Point were the largest and most distant towns visited. James Lewis Harris purchased this store at Easy Gap in 1912 and operated it with his wife, Sally. H.H. Carr owned the original store that opened in 1891. Easy Gap also had a post office, from 1890 to 1907. With a general store and a post office, the area earned a place name and thus appeared on maps of the time. The *Elizabethtown News* of October 18, 1905, noted in an article that "Neil Davis of Bullitt County and Miss Lola Carr, daughter of Henry Carr of Easy Gap, Hardin County were married." Shown standing below the Vogel Brothers Shoe sign are J.L. Harris, Sally (his wife), and their daughters, Georgia (left) and Ethel (right). Others in the photograph are unidentified and most likely were present for purchases or conversation. With the seizure of the land for the establishment of Camp Knox the Harris family moved to the town of Nolin and there operated a large general store.

Five

LAND ACQUISITIONS OF 1941–1942

Grahampton, Garnettsville, Pitts Point, New Stithton, Steele's Crossroads, Bartles, Dorrett's Run, and the Forgotten Town

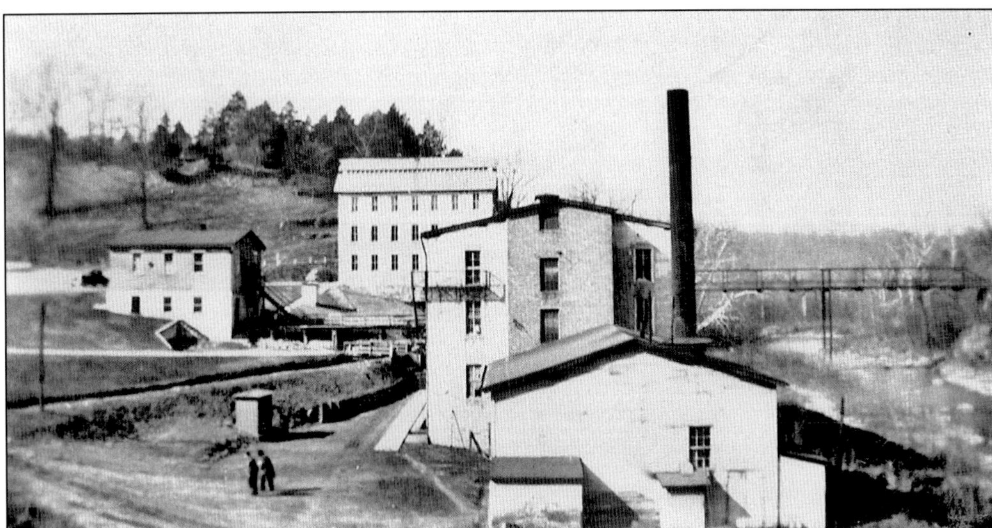

GRAHAMPTON, 1930. Among the towns that gave way to the expansion of Fort Knox was the mill town of Grahampton. This photograph depicts what once was and could have been seen in 1930 if one were to travel the route of today's Highway 60W from Highway 31W, to the bridge that crosses Otter Creek, and stand upon the bridge and look across Otter Creek to the east. The iron bridge in the background was once a wooden bridge. Both bridges carried travelers between points that present-day Highway 60 covers. The present bridge over Otter Creek is the fourth bridge in area. Atop the hill in the background to the left was the Old Grahampton Cemetery that contains the graves of some of the earliest settlers in the area and workers who once worked in the mills that operated at Grahampton.

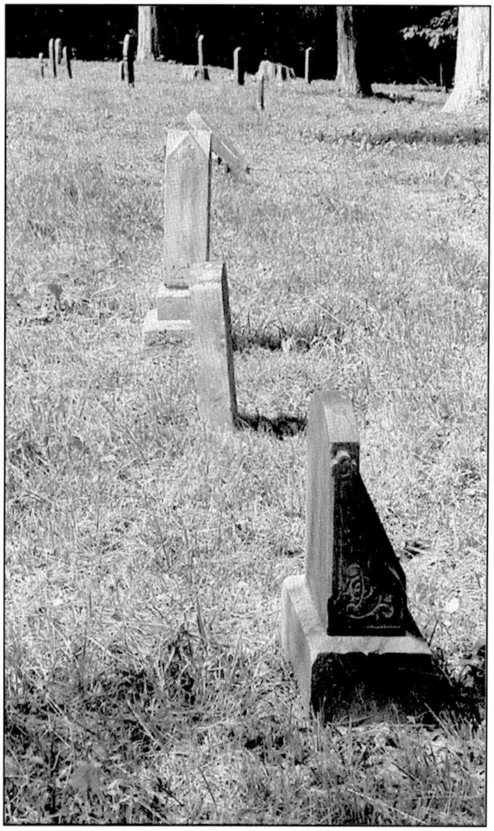

Old Grahampton Cemetery. The Grahampton Mill and associated buildings were on the west side of Otter Creek. Residents' homes and businesses at Grahampton were mostly on the east side of the creek. The Old Grahampton Cemetery was on the hill on the west side of the creek. The first burial in the cemetery was that of Martha J. McCracken in March 1846; the last known burial was that of William T. Streible on July 3, 1924.

New Grahampton Cemetery. The New Grahampton Cemetery, atop a hill south of the current Highway 60, would have been just south of the town. It contains the graves of Grahampton residents as well as others from the adjacent areas. One section is a family cemetery, another is the town cemetery, and a third is a Methodist cemetery where a Methodist church once stood. All three are active and have recent burials. In Fort Knox and other records, the three sections are regarded as one cemetery. The earliest known burials are those of Taylor M. Peak and Carl Peak, who were buried in 1911 in the Methodist portion of the cemetery.

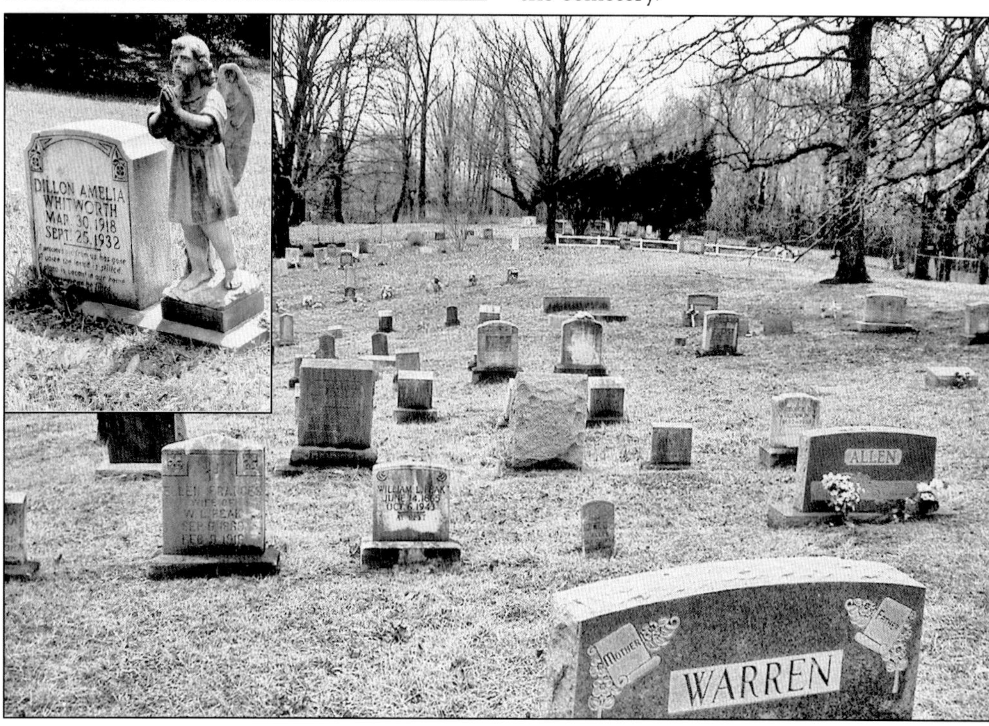

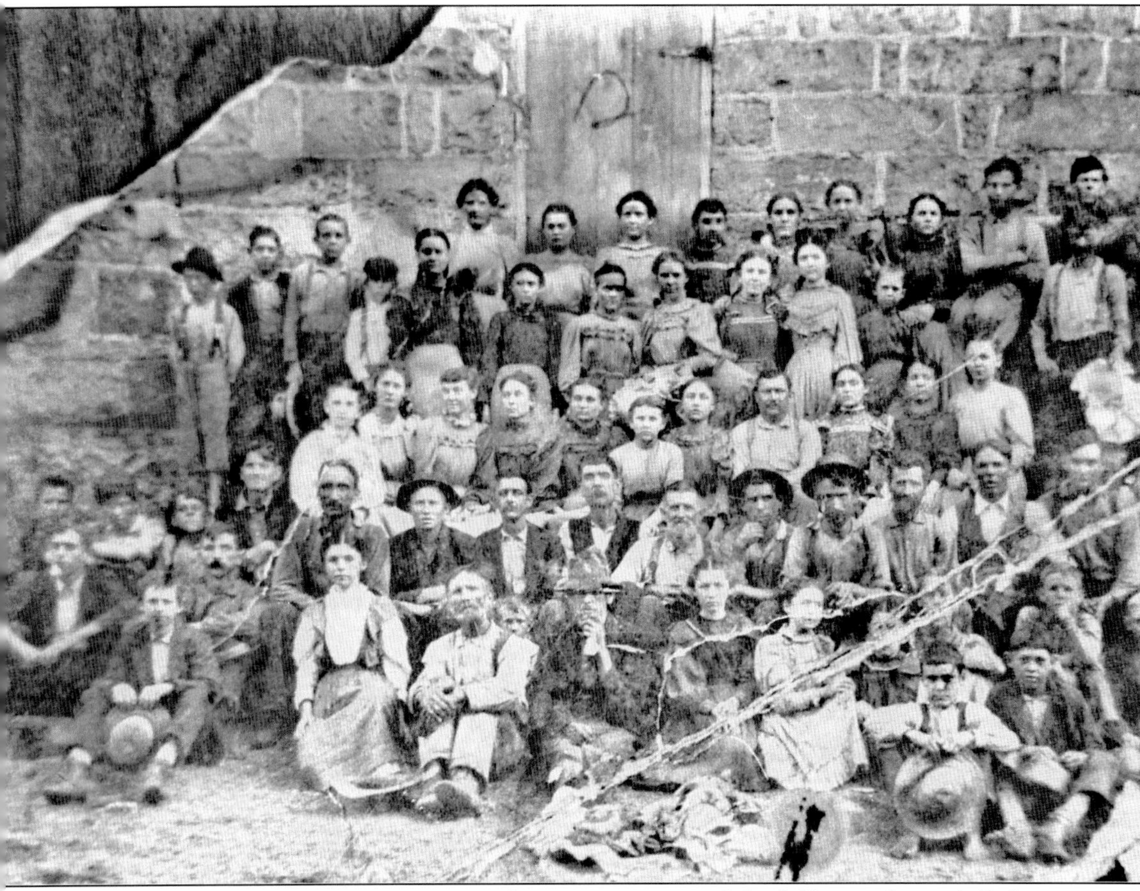

GRAHAMPTON MILL WORKERS, 1889. The town was named for Jefferson County's Robert Graham, who purchased the land from David and Susannah Brandenburg in 1835. In 1813 David Brandenburg had built a mill on Otter Creek that attracted the attention of Robert Graham. Between 1835 and 1837 Graham purchased the site and transported materials and equipment on the Ohio River from Louisville to the mouth of Otter Creek, then hauled the equipment by mule- and ox-drawn wagons to the site of Grahampton Mill. The mill operated continuously for over 100 years and became nationally important. Grahampton grew to a fair-sized town with three grocery stores, a two-room school, and three churches: Catholic, Episcopal, and Methodist. The early mill workers were mostly children who worked for 50¢ per week and women who worked for $1 to $2.50 per week. Twelve dollars a week was the salary of the mill superintendent. The mill records show one slave who worked at the mill—an African American "leased" to the mill for $35 for one year.

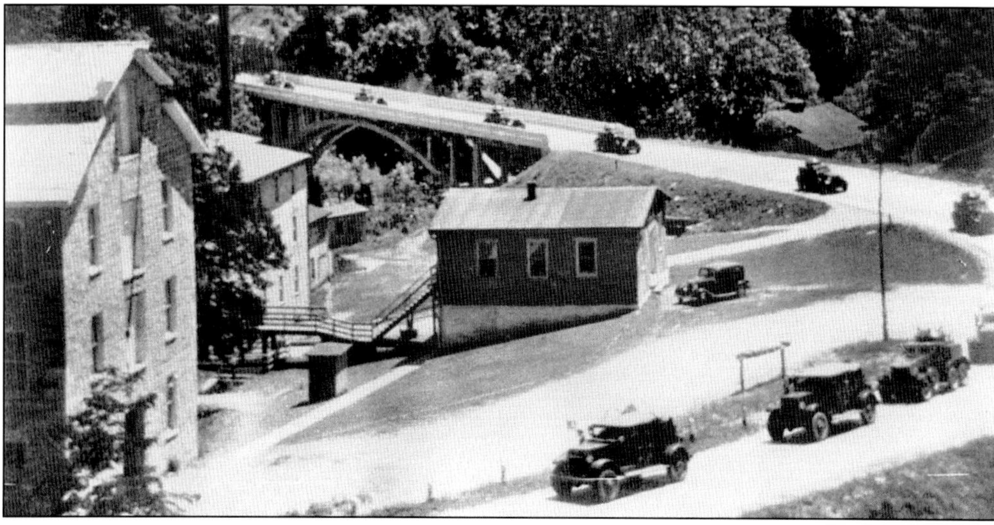

GRAHAMPTON, 1930. Before the expansion of Fort Knox in 1941, the areas that would be seized were used for military training. Here, the Seventh Cavalry Brigade, later the First Armored Division, moves into Grahampton on Highway 60. The bridge was later replaced by another to the south when Highway 60 was rerouted to eliminate the road's sharp "S" curve. The four-story building in the foreground is the Grahampton grist/flour mill. Partly obscured is the textile mill. The smaller building in the center is the mill superintendent's office.

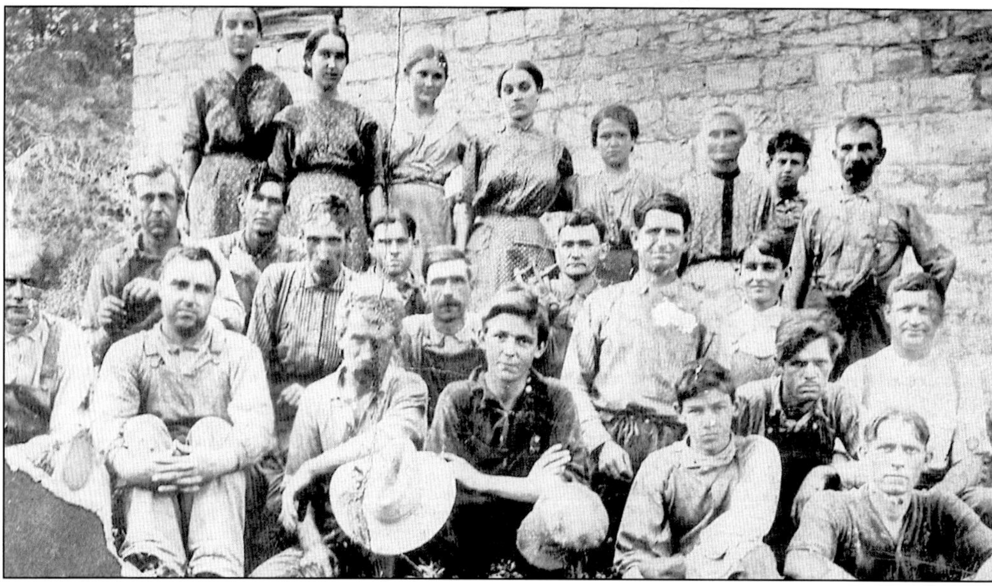

MILL WORKERS, 1930S. Before, during, and after the Civil War, in its peak production years, the Grahampton mills employed 60 to 80 workers. By the 20th century, the mills often operated just three days a week, intermittently shut down, and employed only 15 to 30 workers. The gristmill came to be used as a warehouse for the textile mill. Pictured from left to right are (front row) unidentified, John Yates, George Waldrip, two unidentified people, and Curtis Hair; (middle row) Bart Holston, Phillip Holston, Bub Mitchell, Pete Razor, Parker Schewsberry, Jesse Phillips, Rabbit Bill Peak, Walter Peak, Will (Billy Ark) Douglas, and Lewis Stocker (superintendent of Grahampton Manufacturing Company); (back row) Oma Strange, Eula Mitchell, Katie Allen, Allen Strange, unidentified, Lizzie Noe, Jim Ellan, and Dee McNulley.

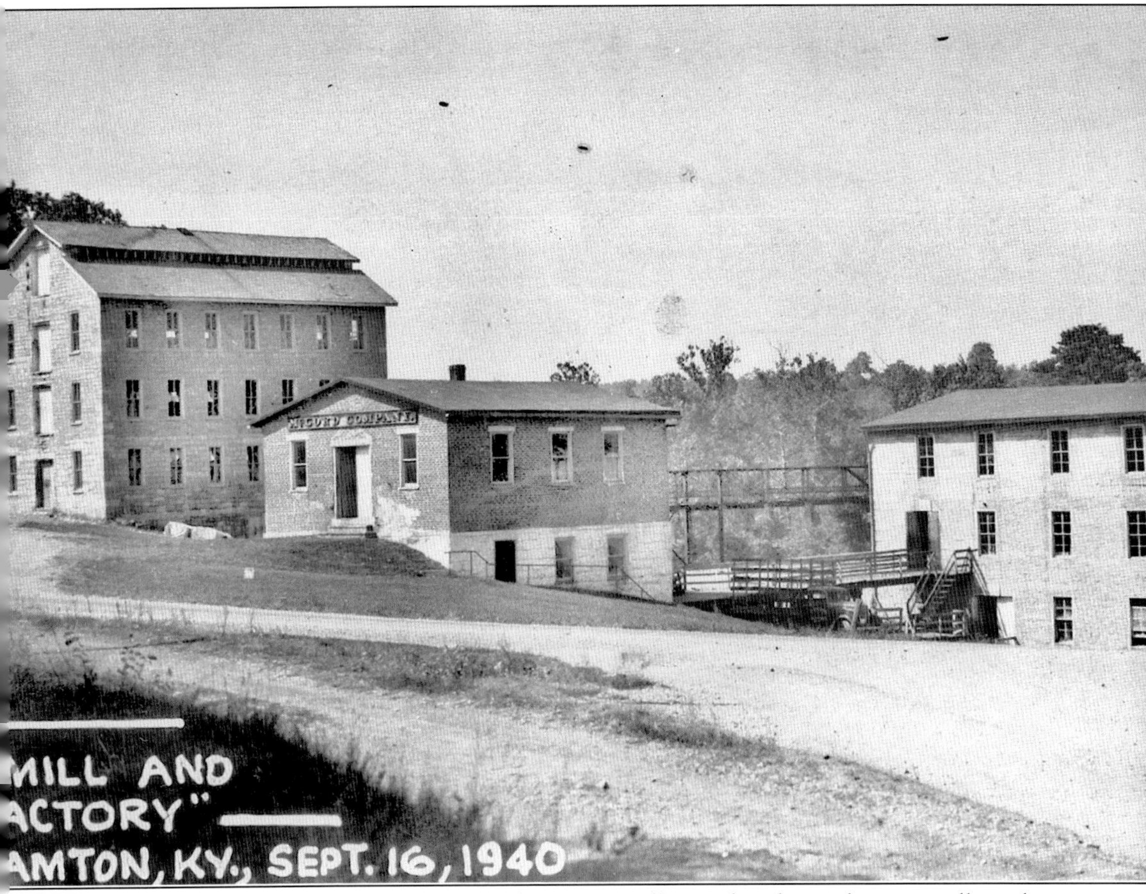

GRAHAMPTON, 1940. This view of the Grahampton Mill complex shows the grist mill on the left, office building in the center, and textile mill on the right. The textile mill was constructed and placed into operation first, around 1835. The second mill, the grist mill, was constructed in 1865; it failed to prosper and later was used as a warehouse for the textile mill. Both mills used waterpower. A millrace carried water to the textile mill, and the tailrace carried water out of the mill. The water leaving the textile mill was directed into the gristmill, where it drove the waterwheel. A tailrace then carried the water out of the mill and back into Otter Creek. The Grahampton mills were somewhat unique in that the water wheels of each were enclosed horizontally in a stone edifice under each mill. From the horizontal waterwheel a power train rose vertically from the wheel and drove a long iron mantel that ran the entire length of each mill. Belts running off the mantel then powered the machines inside the mills. The textile mill also had a steam plant for auxiliary purposes, which was apparently never necessary as it always used waterpower.

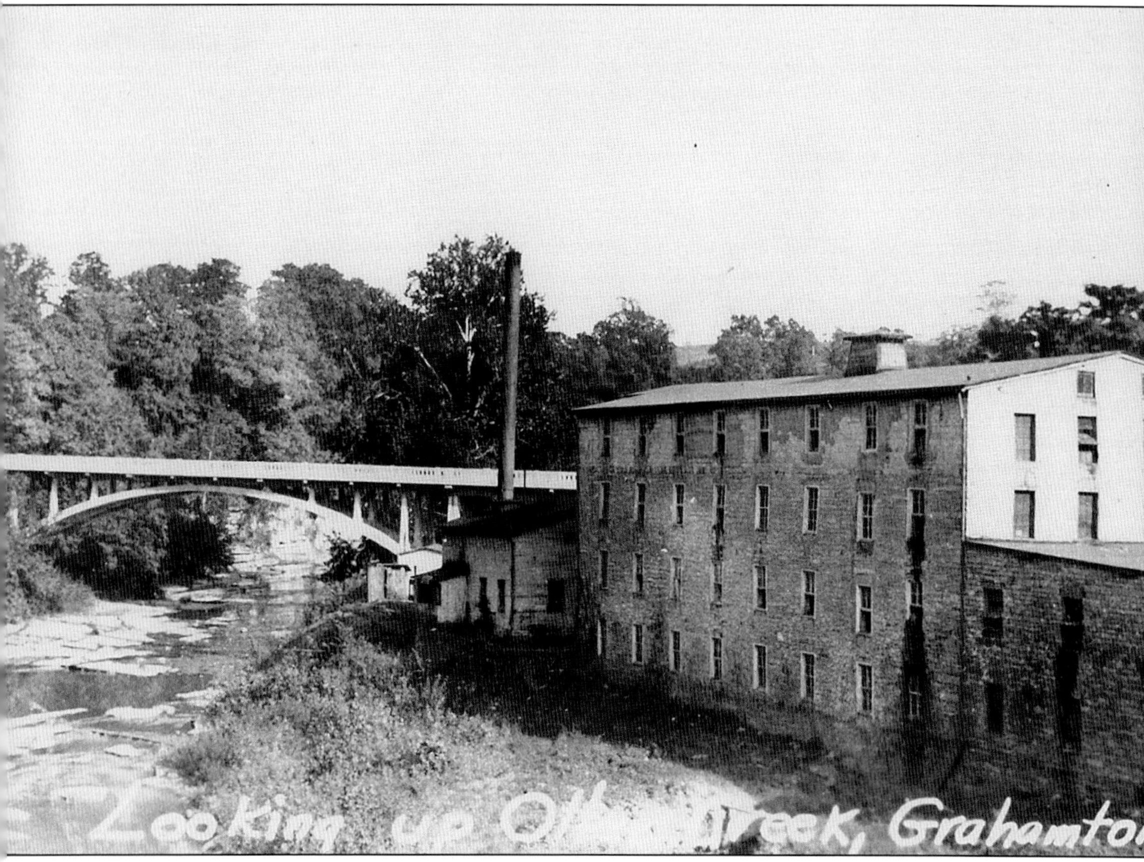

GRAHAMPTON TEXTILE MILL, 1934. This view of the Grahampton Textile Mill looks upstream toward the bridge that carried Highway 60 traffic over Otter Creek. Another bridge was later built about 200 yards further upstream. The first bridge over the creek was wooden and located about a quarter mile downstream. An iron bridge at the same location replaced the wooden bridge. The present bridge is the fourth generation bridge over Otter Creek in this area. About a quarter mile upstream (south), around a large horseshoe bend, was a dam and a gatehouse used to control the flow of water down a millrace to the mills to drive the mill water wheels. The millrace was originally wooden, but later a substantial stone and cement millrace was constructed.

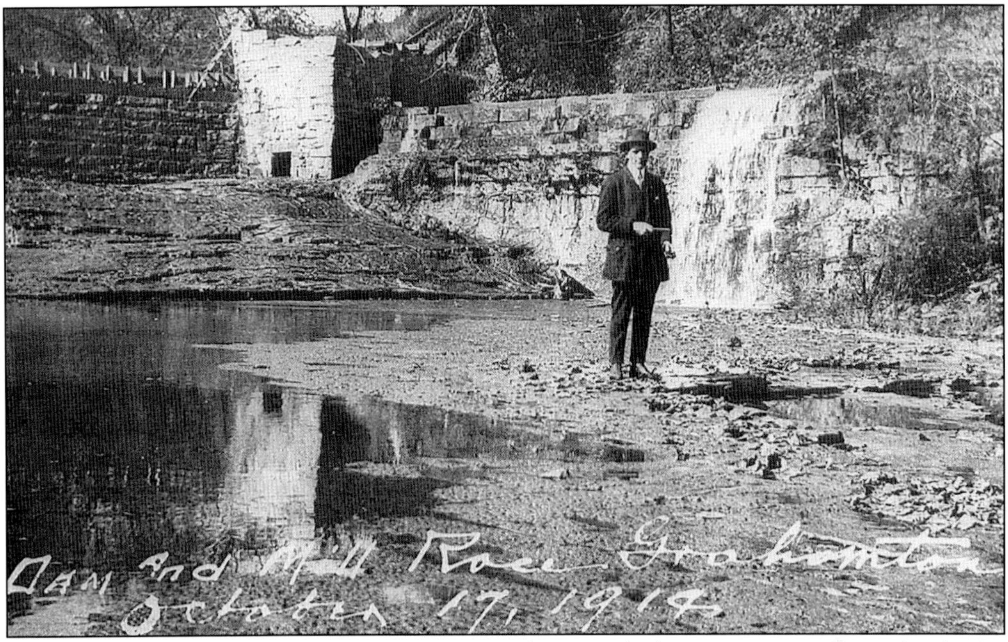

OTTER CREEK DAM AND GATEHOUSE, 1914. This view looks upstream on Otter Creek. An unidentified man stands in the nearly dry creek bed. The dam, constructed to hold water and ensure a constant supply for the mills, is in the background. The gatehouse is shown joined to the right side of the dam. Water from behind the dam was sent directly to the mills along a millrace, with the water flow controlled by the gatehouse.

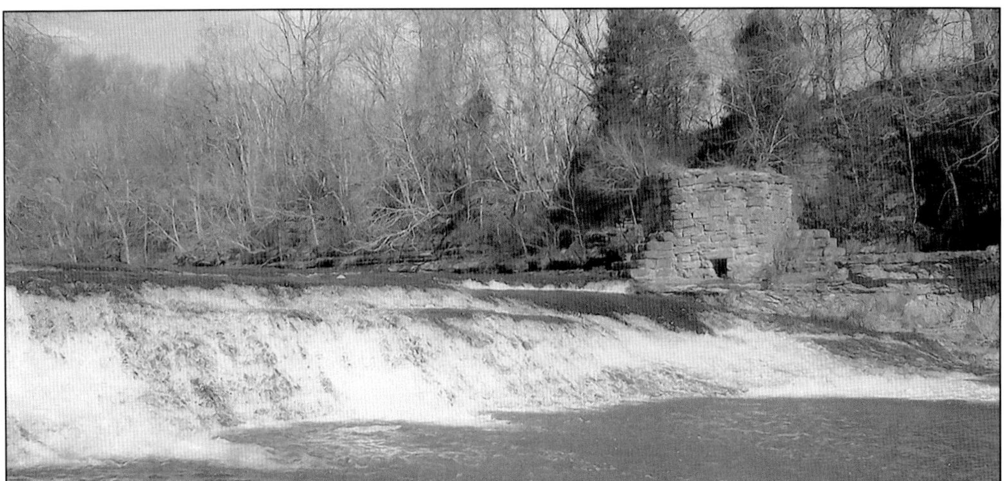

GRAHAMPTON GATEHOUSE. The only visible evidence that a water-powered mill existed in the area is this stone structure, the remnant of a gatehouse. The gatehouse, about a quarter mile from the mill, controlled the flow of water to the millrace, which carried water downstream to the Grahampton mills. A dam across Otter Creek at the site of the gatehouse ensured a constant supply of water to the mills in the dry season. In 1951 the dam was demolished during the filming of one of the three major movies filmed using Fort Knox land as a backdrop. *The Tanks Are Coming* used the area just below the dam as a main filming site for the tank company depicted in the movie. The other movies filmed in part on Fort Knox were *Goldfinger* (1964, starring Sean Connery) and *Stripes* (1981, starring Bill Murray and John Candy.).

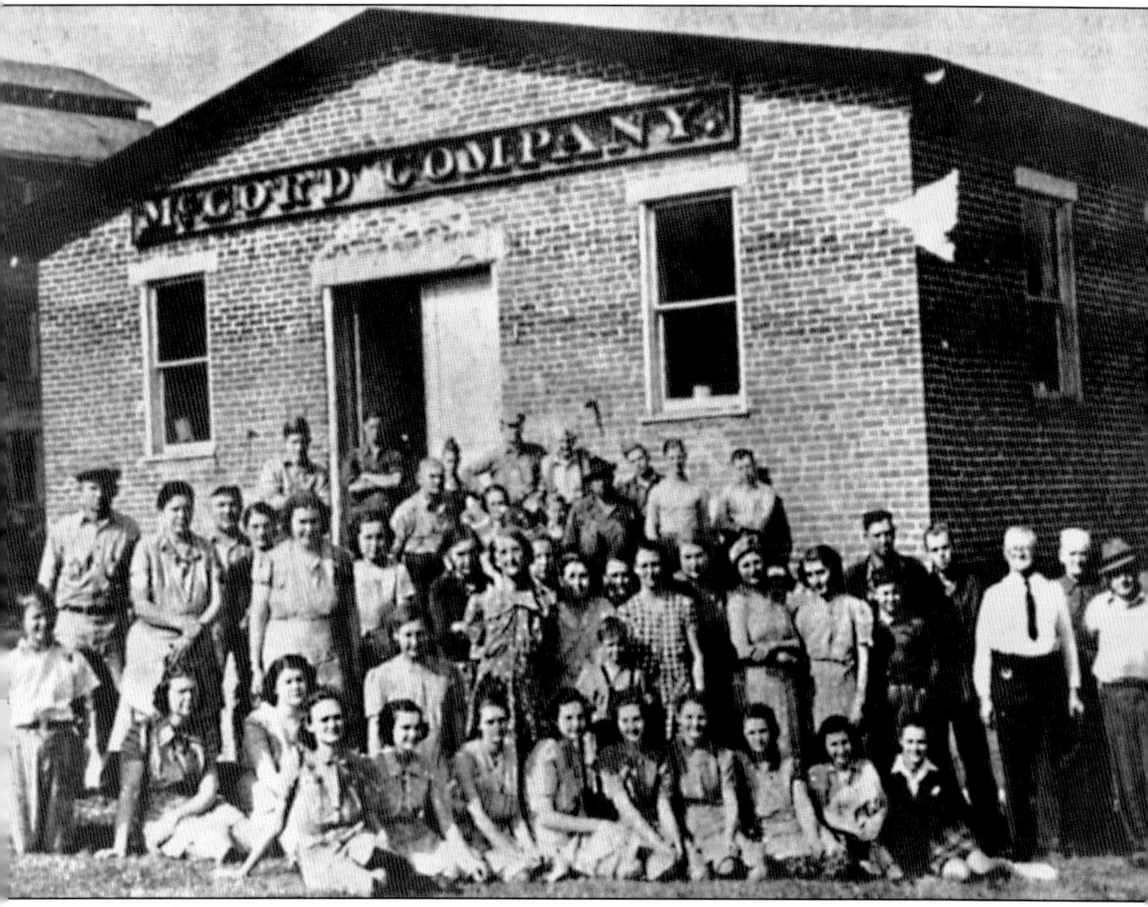

LAST GRAHAMPTON MILL WORKERS, OCTOBER 22, 1942. In its early years, the textile mill did carding, spinning, and weaving in cotton and wool. Under superintendent P.Z. Aylesworth, the mill ran almost continuously during the Civil War, except for interruptions caused by guerrillas. During the Mexican War (1846–1848), the mill produced canvas for army tents. Management and operation changed over the years, until the site was purchased in 1915 by the McCord Company at a forced sale for back taxes of $332.25. The McCord Company operated the mill exclusively as a spinning mill, confining its production to cotton yarns, especially mop yarns. By the time the government took Grahampton for the Fort Knox expansion, the mill was barely profitable, unable to compete with the more modern mills. Grahampton mill workers, from left to right, are (front row, kneeling) Irene McNally; (front row, sitting) Grace Holston, Georgia Holston, Shirley Phillips, Lula Miller, Teresa Miller, Alma Phillips, Margie Peak, Laurea Reesor, Margaret Stocker, Margie Pike, and Margaret Tate; (second row, standing) Viola Holston (under window, hands clasped; mother of Louis Holston), Mildred E. Holston, Emily Pike, Mary Strieble Thomas, Nell Padgett, Nell Pike, Bobby Pike, Violet Epperson, Allie Peak Seeley, Louise Reesor, Della Peak, Bobby Stocker, Edwin Yates, James Wilkins, Louis Stocker Sr. (white shirt and tie; mill superintendent), Ernest Meadows, Robert Stocker, Julia Thompson, Evan Thompson, William Padgett, Leonard McNally, Ervin Nelson, Jim McNally, and E.K. Hand; (third row) Leslie Tanner (between left corner of building and window, with hat and black belt), George Hackett Strieble, Clay Padgett, Everly Padgett, Maggie Strieble, and Faye Tanner; (fourth row) Jess Phillips, Minnie Phillips, Jackie Dague, and Fred Wilkins; (fifth row) Earl Douglas, Paul Wilkins, Donald Phillips, Paul Reesor, Eliza Strieble, James Tanner, Joe Reesor, and Louis Holston (under window, arms folded, wearing white shirt.)

GRAHAMPTON METHODIST CHURCH, 1940. The first Methodist church in Grahampton burned and was rebuilt in the early 1900s. Each week there was a prayer meeting and Sunday school, but the preacher only came once a month, as he was a circuit preacher. Some of the preachers included Rev. Clemmie Streebles, Loyd Logston, John R. Marten, ? Day, Comore Lyons, Earl Ashley, Clarence Nichols, and Arthur Cooper, who was serving the church when it was closed. A cemetery was started behind the church. Taylor and Carl Peak (killed in an accident) were the first to be buried there in 1911. The cemetery is still active.

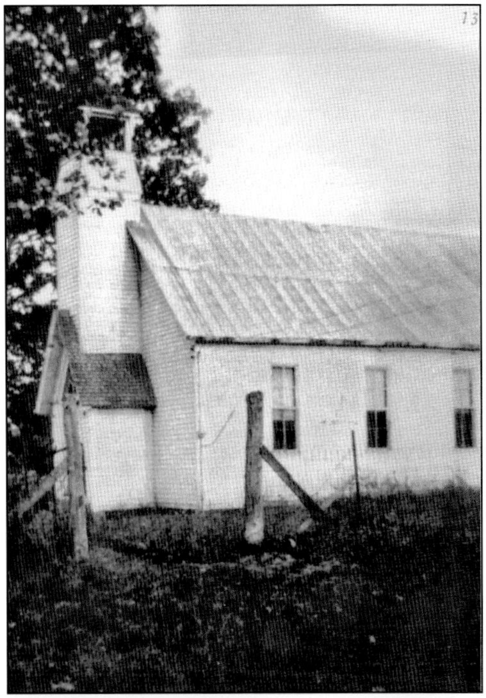

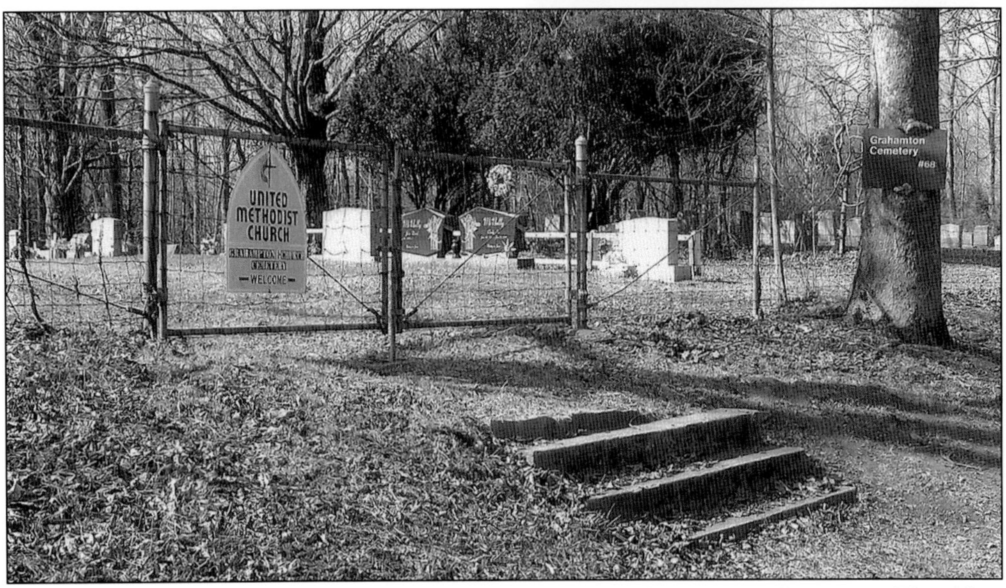

NEW GRAHAMPTON CEMETERY AND SITE OF THE METHODIST CHURCH. The New Grahampton Cemetery (so called because of an older cemetery atop a hill north of this one called the Old Grahampton Cemetery) is a large cemetery with three distinct sections. The large middle section is a Methodist cemetery and is still active. The steps in this view would have been the front steps to the Methodist church that once rested on the site. At this church a serious incident occurred—Nick Holston shot and killed Ben Case in 1904. Ben Case is buried in the Old Grahampton Cemetery and Nick Holston is buried in the Methodist church portion of the New Grahampton Cemetery. Nick served time in prison and then returned to Grahampton and raised a family.

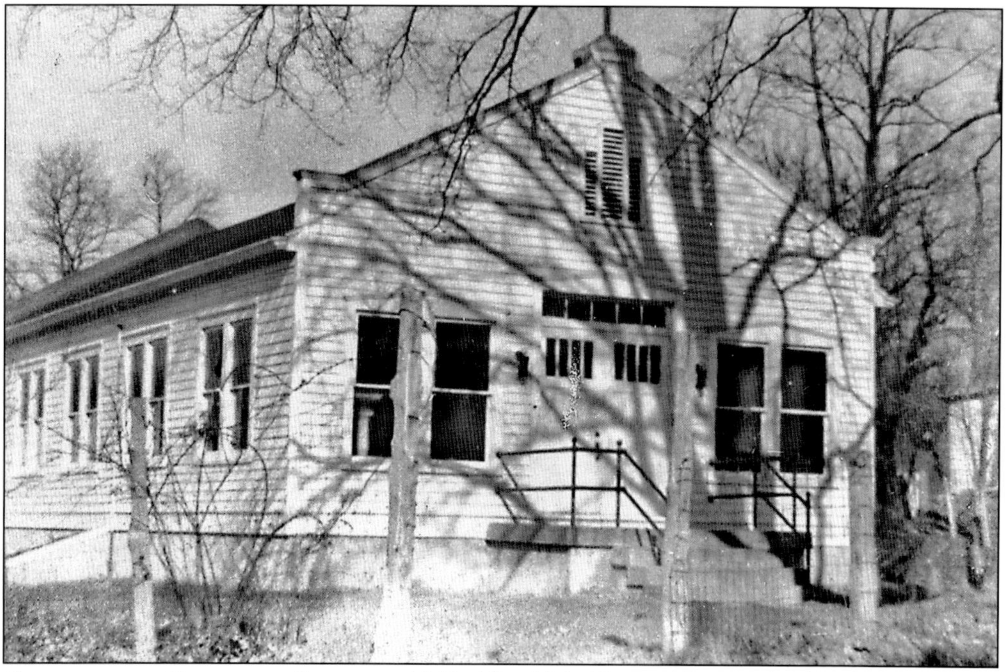

GRAHAMPTON EPISCOPAL CHURCH, 1940. The Holy Trinity Episcopal Church was located on the north side of Front Street on the other side of Otter Creek from the Textile Mill. Front Street was the main road into and out of Grahampton. Front Street (first generation Highway 60) crossed Otter Creek via a bridge about 300 yards north of the present bridge. The old bridge is long-gone, but the abutments can still be seen from the present bridge that carries Highway 60 over the creek.

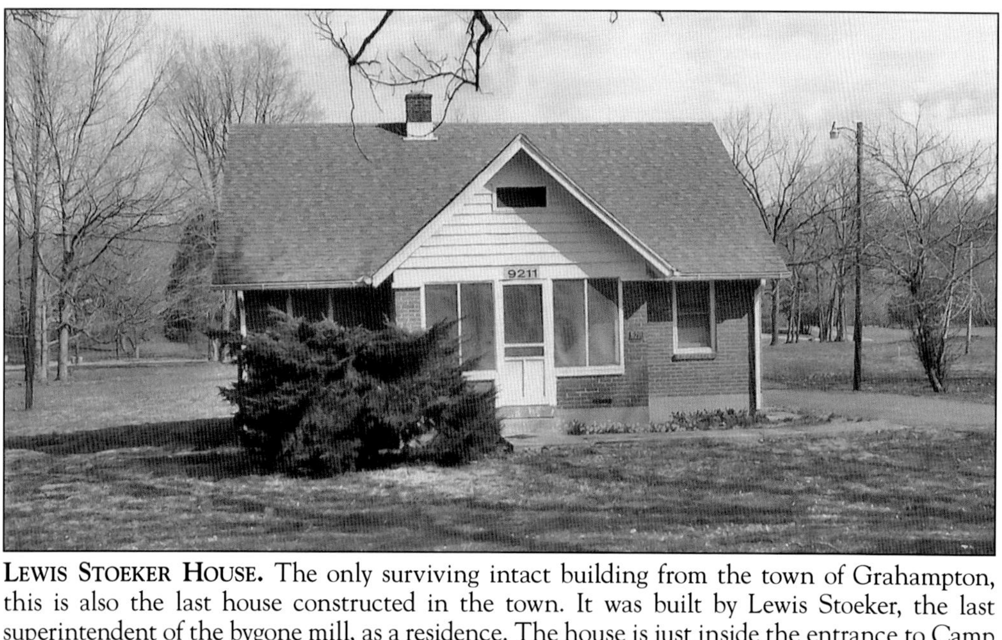

LEWIS STOEKER HOUSE. The only surviving intact building from the town of Grahampton, this is also the last house constructed in the town. It was built by Lewis Stoeker, the last superintendent of the bygone mill, as a residence. The house is just inside the entrance to Camp Carlson Army Travel Camp, which is operated by Fort Knox. The Grahampton Episcopal Church was just south (toward Highway 60) of the house.

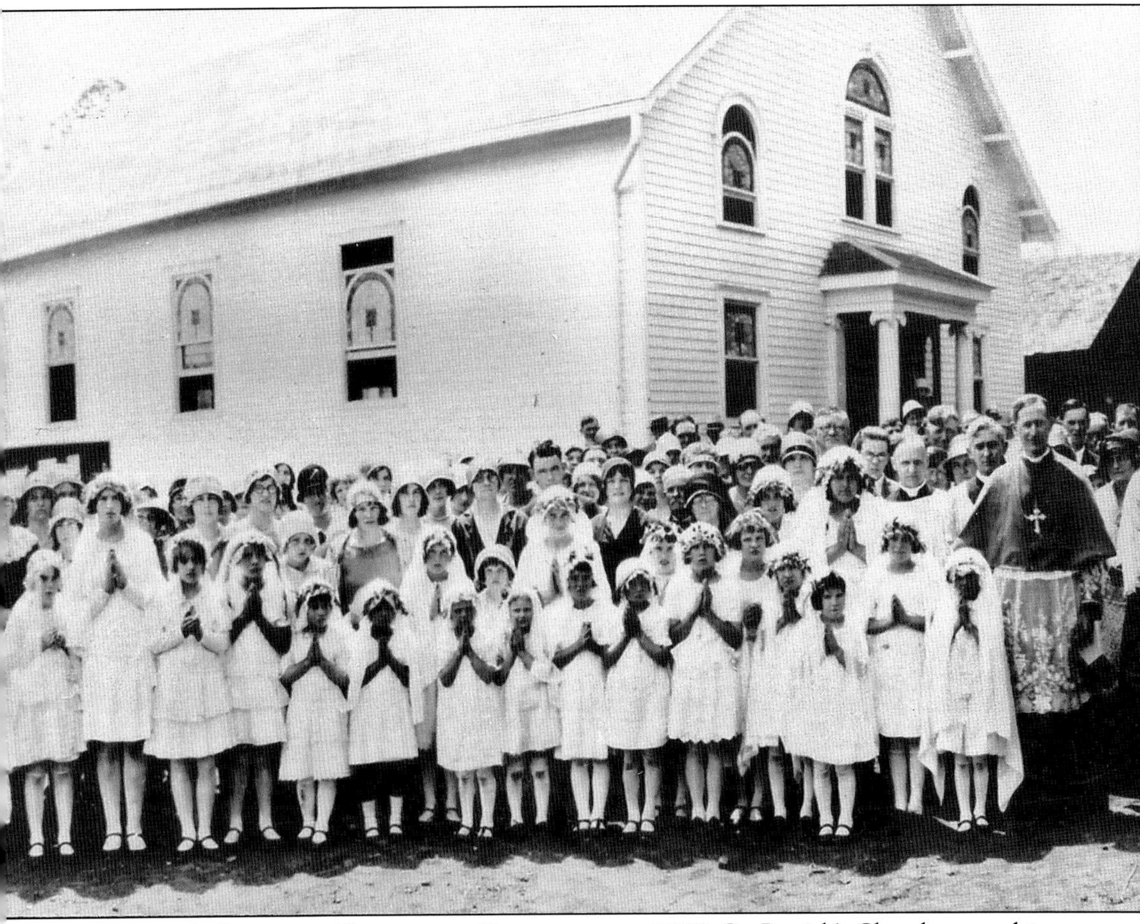

ST. PATRICK'S CATHOLIC CHURCH OF GRAHAMPTON, 1929. St. Patrick's Church opened its doors in 1929. Rev. Guido Liagi Mensa is shown here with the first confirmation class standing in front of the church at the dedication of the new church building. This photograph is one part of a 10 inch by 40 inch photograph showing the entire congregation of the church. With the appropriation of land for expansion of Fort Knox, the church building was used as the Fort Knox Rod and Gun Club. Later, the building was disassembled and transported several miles to the north side of the Fort Knox cantonment area, reassembled, and is presently used as the French Range Shooting Club and office.

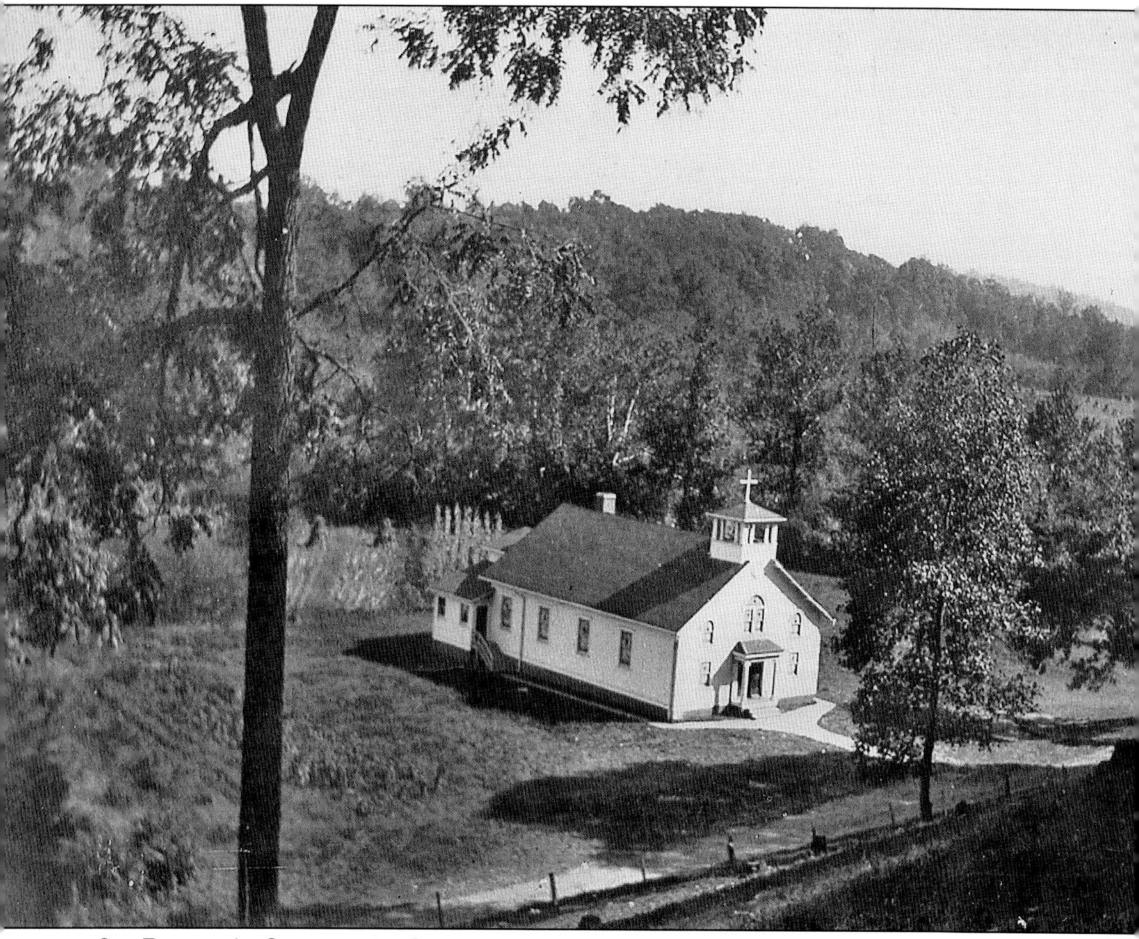

ST. PATRICK'S CHURCH OF GRAHAMPTON, C. 1935. The St. Patrick's Catholic Church of Grahampton building served the Catholic community in Grahampton and the surrounding area for less than 13 years before being acquired for the expansion of Fort Knox. It stood for a few more years as the Fort Knox Rod and Gun Club. It was later disassembled and carried to French Range, north of the Fort Knox cantonment area, where the walls were erected and later covered with sheet metal. The building now serves as the French Range office and clubhouse. The location of bygone Grahampton can be reached by traveling west on Highway 60 and approaching the bridge across Otter Creek. Across the bridge, on the bank of Otter Creek just before the bridge's west end, is the site of the long gone Catholic church. In the time of the acquisition of Grahampton for the expansion of Fort Knox, the town was not what it once was. The once active and profitable textile mill operated only intermittently, and the town itself was in decline. Nevertheless, the town was said to be one of the most scenic and beautiful in Kentucky.

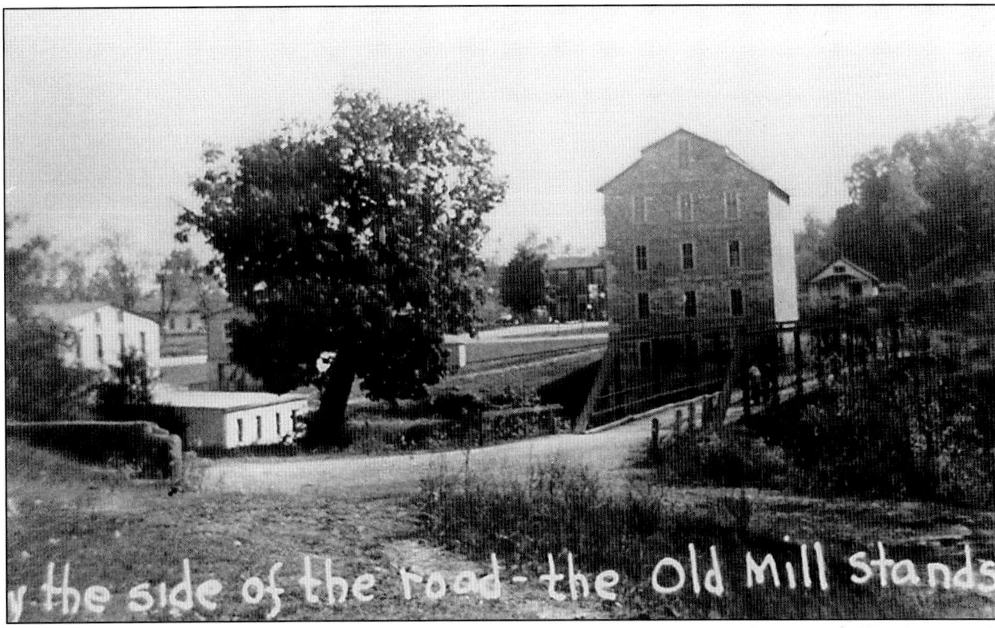

GRAHAMPTON, 1940. This view looks south across Otter Creek to the gristmill. The textile mill is to the west; a portion of the textile mill can be seen in the far left of the photograph. The iron bridge, previously a wooden bridge, carried all the traffic in the area across the creek. It carried Highway 60 traffic through Grahampton for many years.

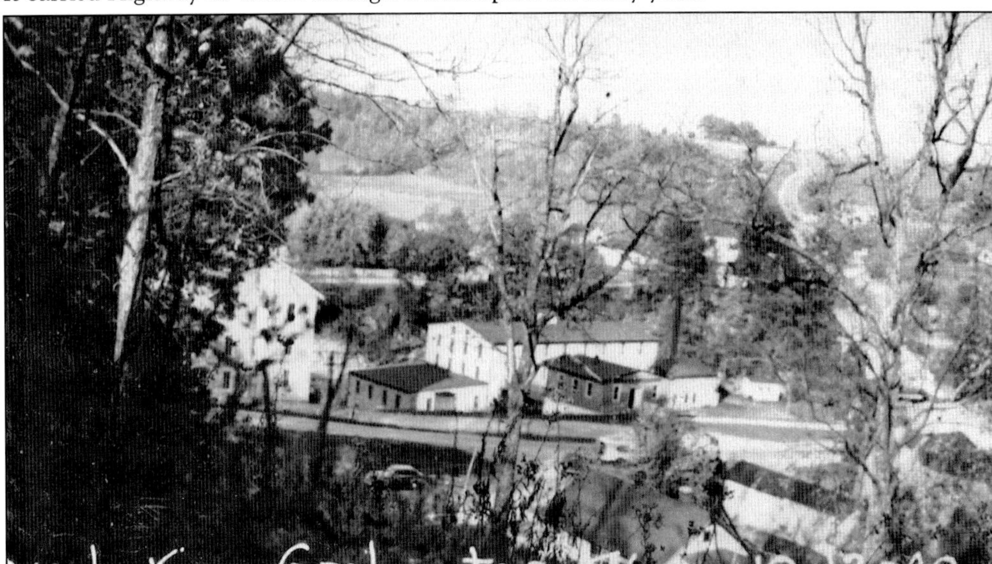

GRAHAMPTON, 1940. This view looks north into Grahampton from the Old Grahampton Cemetery atop the hill just south of Otter Creek. The building in the foreground is the Stoeker store. In the middle of photograph are the textile mill to the right and the gristmill to the left. Between the Stoeker general store and the mills was Highway 60 and Otter Creek. When a final concrete bridge was constructed, Highway 60 was redirected to the east in order to bypass the congestion of Grahampton. Each new generation of the bridge over Otter Creek moved Highway 60 more to the east.

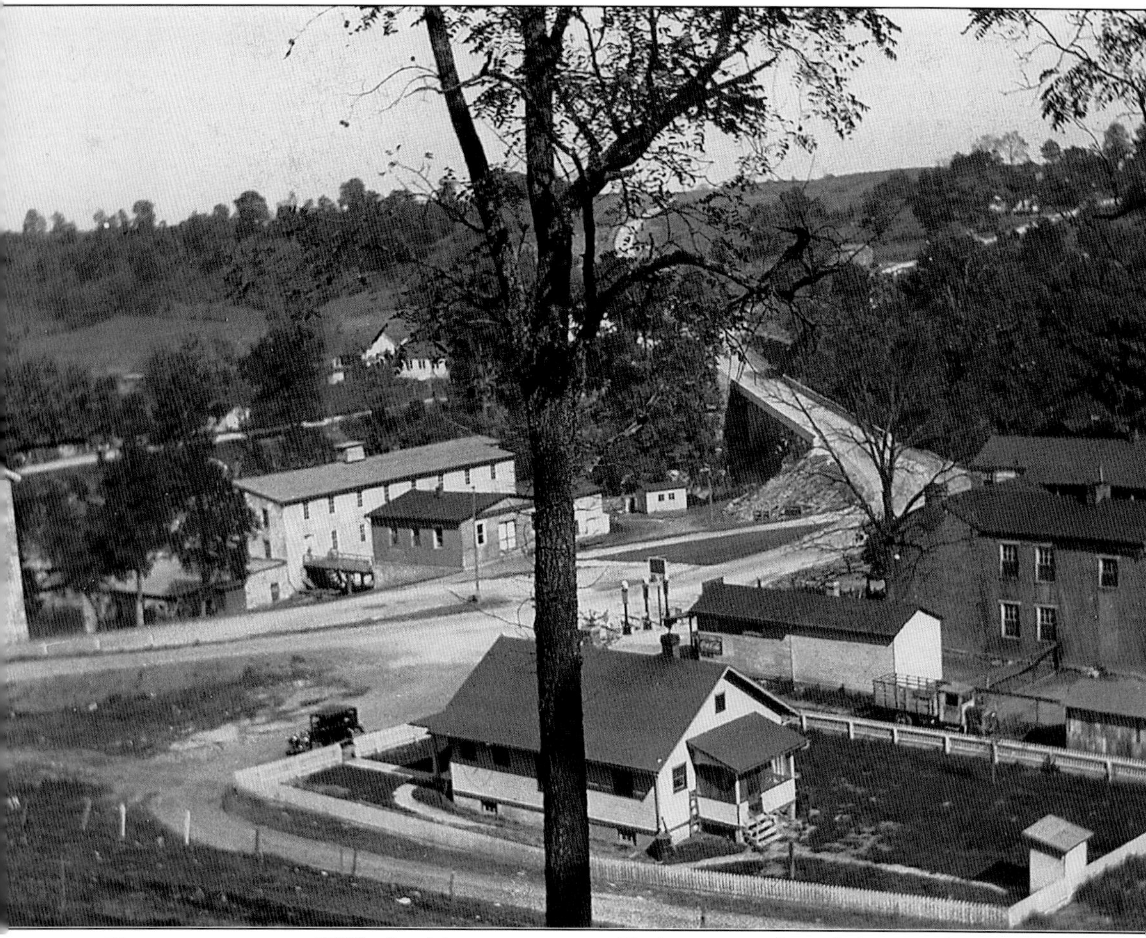

GRAHAMPTON, C. 1935. Looking east across Grahampton, from left to right are (in the foreground) the home of Lewis Stocker; the Stocker and Yates Store with three gas pumps out front; the two-story brick home of Elijah Streible, who was the watchman for the mill complex; and a partially obstructed view of the two-story Laura Reesor home. St. Patrick's Catholic Church was beyond and somewhat behind the Reesor house. In front of these buildings is old Highway 60 with its third generation bridge across Otter Creek. The highway was eventually rerouted to the south to bypass the town, and a fourth bridge, the current bridge, across Otter Creek was built. Across the highway and down the hill, the four-story Grahampton Textile Mill can be seen. Beyond the mill is Otter Creek, and beyond the creek is the rest of the town of Grahampton. The remnants of old Highway 60, which once ran through Grahampton, can still be seen from atop the present bridge that crosses Otter Creek. Beyond the limits of this photograph, to the left, the old road continues up and around a hill where the Old Grahampton Cemetery is located. The road pavement is still intact on that portion. Grahampton Road, which ran between Tip Top and Grahampton, is in the background, running diagonally across the photograph and crossing Highway 60.

CHARLIE PEAK STORE, 1939. Charlie Peak stands in the front door of his store, which was on the second floor of a two-story building. It sold everything from ladies hats to coffee, sugar, harnesses, kerosene lamps, and other such items necessary for the times, and many items not seen today. The first floor was a meeting hall and office for the Woodmen of the World Life Insurance Society.

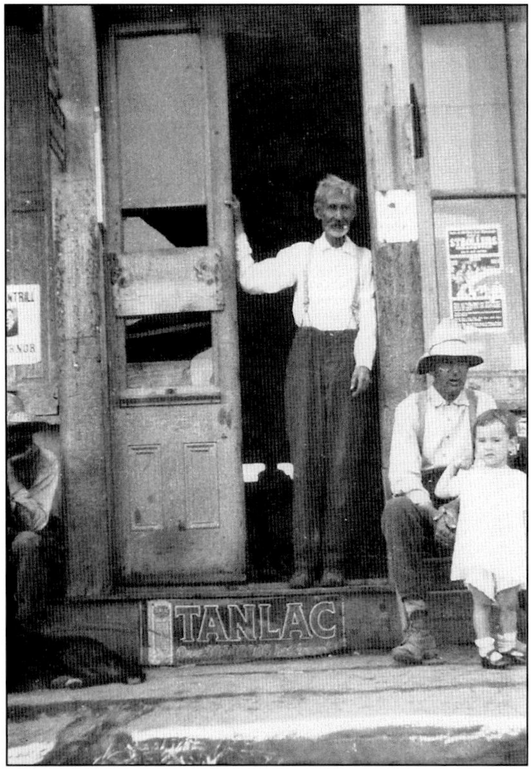

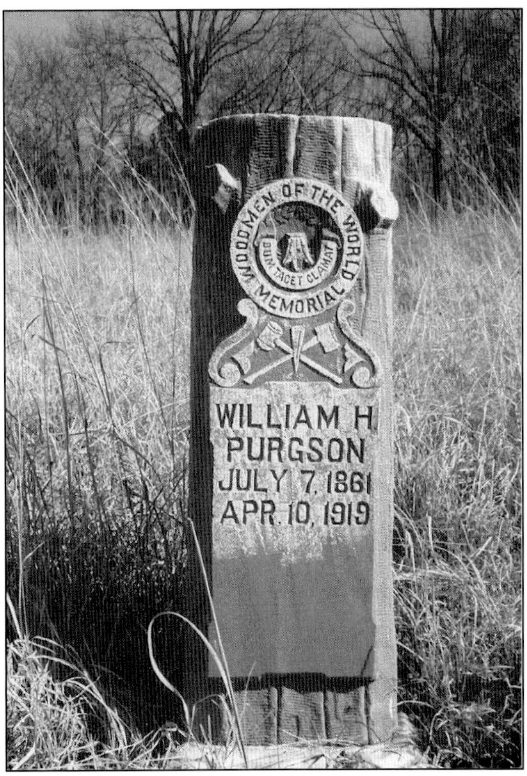

WOODMAN OF THE WORLD MONUMENT. The Woodmen of the World is a nonprofit, fraternal benefit society, committed to members, their families, and their communities. The society is active today and offers life and health insurance. When the society was formed in 1893, the only policy offered was simple term insurance. To give honorable burial to members, a gravestone bearing the society's symbol was furnished free of charge. This practice was discontinued in the 1920s. Woodman of the World gravestones can be found within Fort Knox cemeteries and in cemeteries throughout the country. This gravestone is in Pleasant View Cemetery, which was part of the town of Pleasant View that was taken in 1918 for the establishment of Camp Knox.

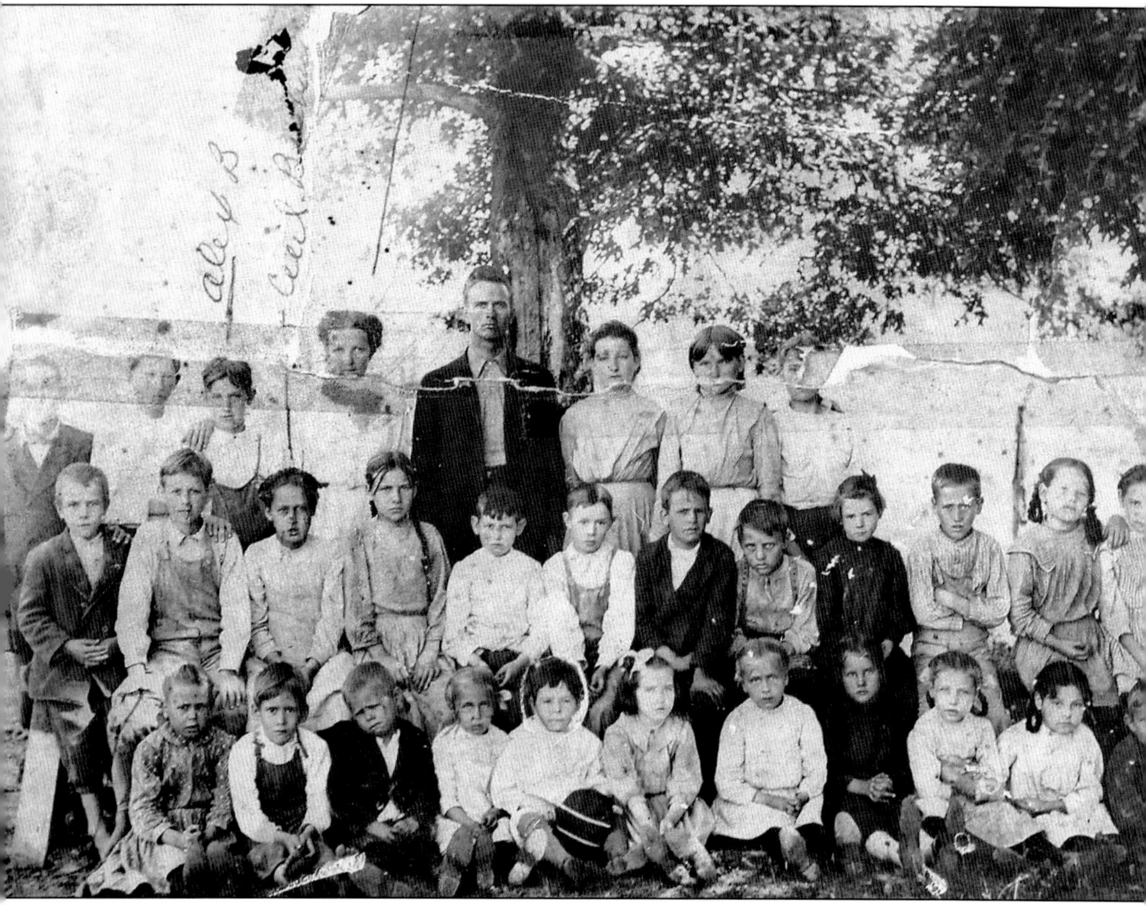

Grahampton School, 1910. This photograph was provided by Iva Mae Cannon (nee Meadors-Clark) during an interview on December 4, 1998, at her home in Henryville, Indiana, regarding her recollections of Grahampton. Iva was born in 1902. Another former resident of Grahampton, Edith Buckler Byerly (born in 1903), was interviewed in her Vine Grove home on August 29, 1997. They were close friends at school in Grahampton, and Iva had dated Edith's brother Dewey. The ladies had fond memories of each other even though they had not corresponded in over 70 years. The following students are listed from left to right: (front row) two unidentified students, ? Seeley, ? Seeley, Wilbur Cannon, ? Miller, ? Seeley, ? Seeley, unidentified, Iva Mae Cannon, and ? Seeley; (middle row) ? Seeley, Edgar Cannon, ? Basham, ? Seeley, unidentified, Dewey Buckler, ? Seeley, ? Seeley, Edith Buckler, ? Seeley, Hollie Peak, Ada Ola Cannon; (back row) two unidentified students, Alex Basham, Mollie Peak, Mr. Onsbey (teacher), ? George, ? Allen, and unidentified.

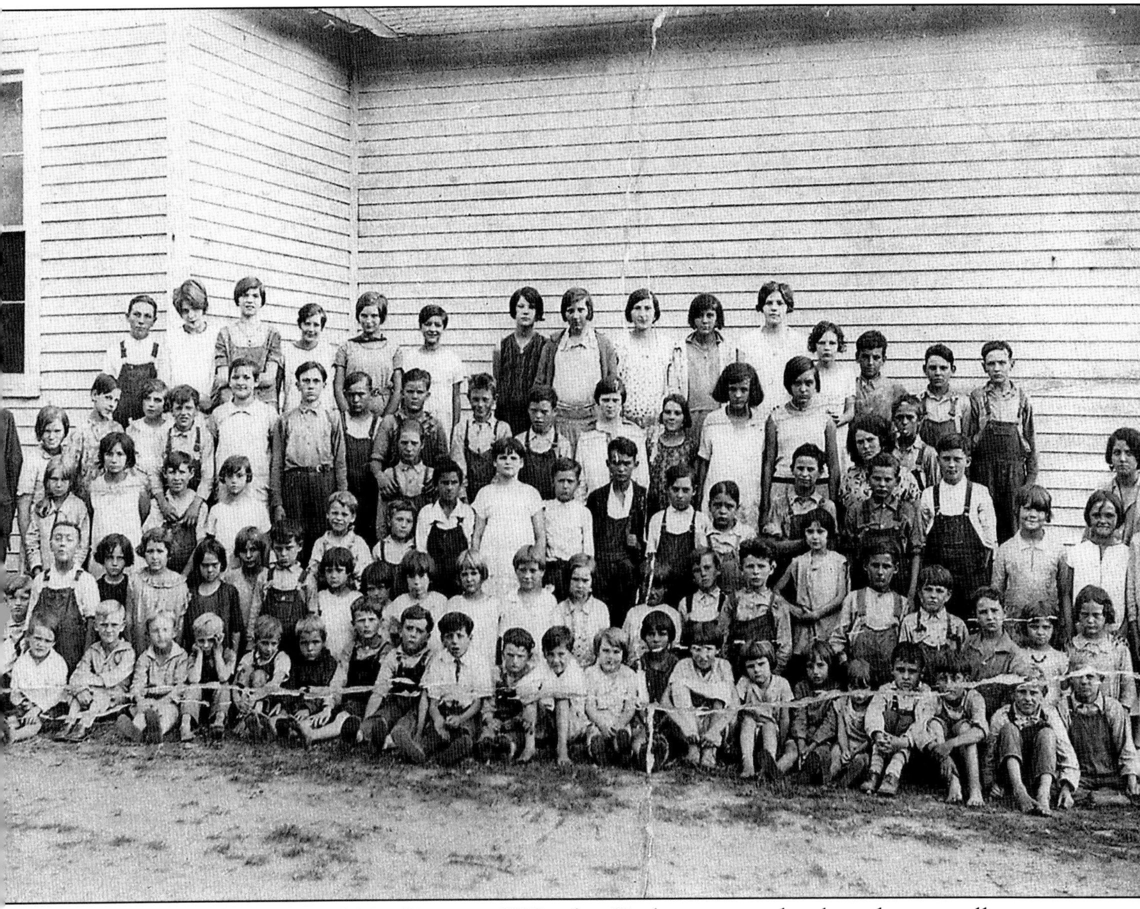

Grahampton School, 1930. Prior to 1930, the Grahampton school student enrollment necessitated the building of a two-room school. The old one-room school was then used by a Catholic congregation until they could build their own church in 1929. Pictured on the first row, though not identified, are Alvin Phillips, Joe Reesor, Dan Thompson, Wean Thomas, Harold Allen, Freddy Allen, Ronald Thomas, Lillian Peak, Virginia Seelye, Boo Peak, Margie Peak, Haynes Hunt, Raymond Clark, and Minnie Bell Thomas. Pictured from left to right, are (second row) Pete Holston (bibbed overalls), unidentified, Mildred Miller, nine unidentified people, Raymond Clark, unidentified, Wilber Thomas, Lula Miller, Joe Clark (wide suspenders), Everett Peak, Bobby Stocker, Josephene Miller, and Pauline Sally Holston; (third row) Dillon Whitworth, unidentified, Donnie Pike (the boy behind him has arms over his shoulders), three unidentified people, Jessie Seelye (dark hair, dark bibbed overalls), Virginia Peak, unidentified, Arthur Phillips (tall boy, dark jacket), John Raymond Yates, Chester Peak, Chester Seelye, unidentified, Raymond Hune, Grace Holston, Shirley Phillips, and Virginia Thomas (standing far right of row); (fourth row) Elizabell Douglas, Elsie Pike, Aillene McNally, Arther Peak, Louise Reesor, Charles Whitworth, Robert Phillips, Dick Thomas, Chester Strieble, Robert Toby Whitworth, Louis Holston, Cathrine Hunt, Alice Clark, Evlyne Thompson, Eulanay Thomas, and Stanley Seelye; (fifth row) Martin McNally, Sylvia Lusk, Alberta Lusk, Estelle Allen, Antoinette Peak, Elizabeth Allen, Georgia Holston, Beatrice McNally, Leona Bryant, Bernice Thomas, Estelle Lusk, Alma Peak, Jack Peak, Martin Peak, and Wayne Boss Peak. The spellings of names are presented as they appeared on the back of the photograph.

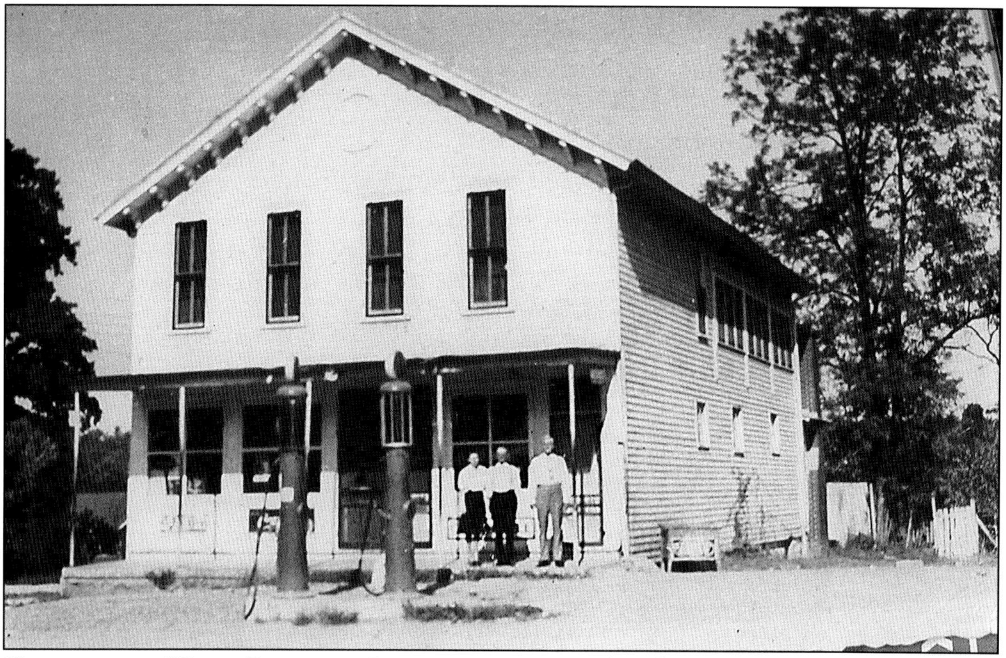

CHARLES AND NORA CAMPBELL STORE, 1938. Pictured is the Campbell store before it was moved to accommodate the rerouting of Highway 60 and construction of the third bridge over Otter Creek. The Campbell's store had many owners: W.G. Anderson, A.M. and Mary Robinson, P.Z. and Ann Aylesworth, Samuel Randall, Matt and Emma Carr, Will and Hattie Byerly, and Charles and Nora Campbell. First located at the end of Front Street on the east side of Otter Creek, near the iron bridge, the store was moved to the south, beside the Episcopal church. Charles believed relocating his store would enhance his business. Standing in front of the store are, from left to right, Nora Campbell, Will Byerly, and Charlie Campbell.

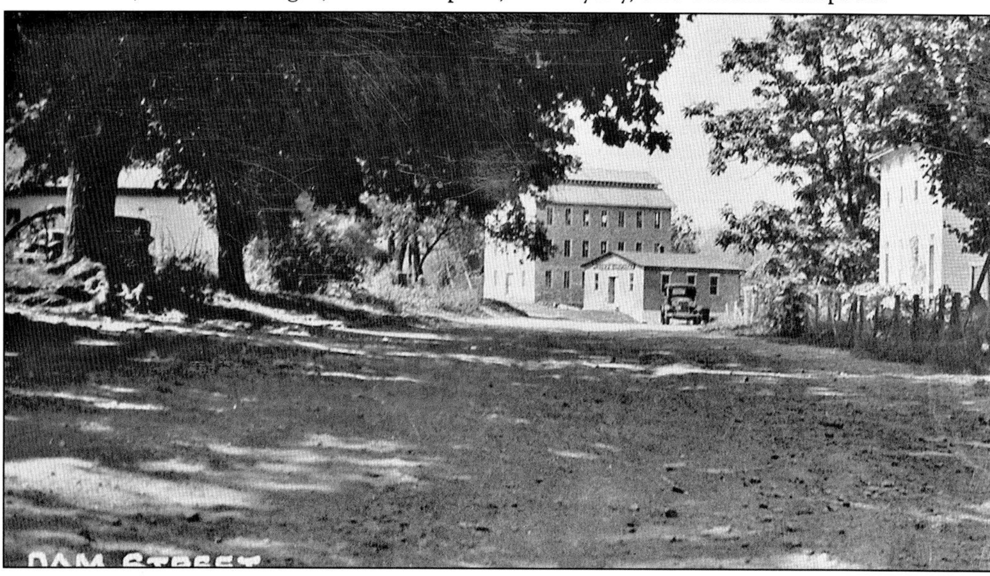

MILL DAM STREET, GRAHAMPTON, C. 1930. In this partial view of the Grahampton Mill complex, looking north on Mill Dam Street, the gristmill is in the background. The mill office building is just behind the automobile in the photograph.

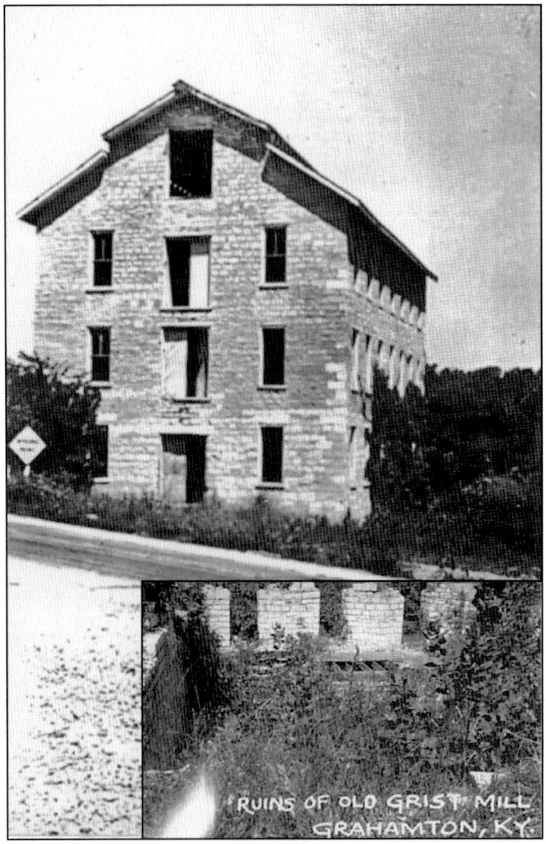

RUINS OF GRAHAMPTON GRIST MILL. Both the Grahampton grist mill and the textile mill were large, well-built structures constructed of local limestone blocks. Following the demise of Grahampton for the expansion of Fort Knox in 1941–1942, the buildings were systematically demolished. The mills were left standing for a time, but stone blocks were carried off for use in construction elsewhere. The base of the tank monument at the foot of Muldraugh Hill, just south of West Point on Highway 31 West, was constructed of stone from the Grahampton grist mill. By the 1950s no trace of the mills remained on the bank of Otter Creek at Grahampton.

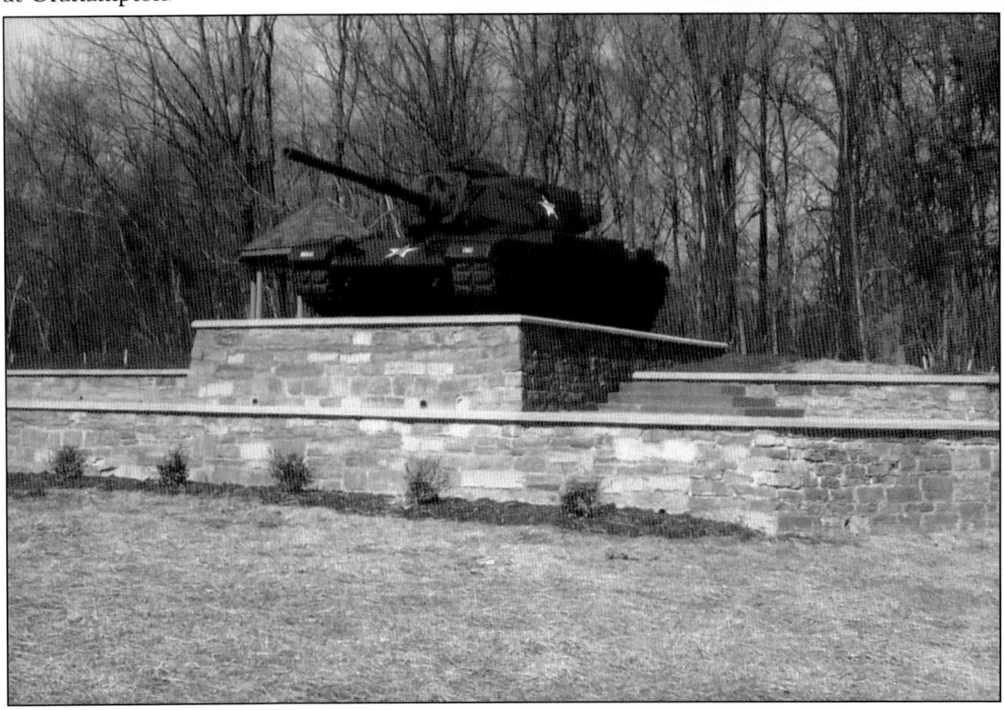

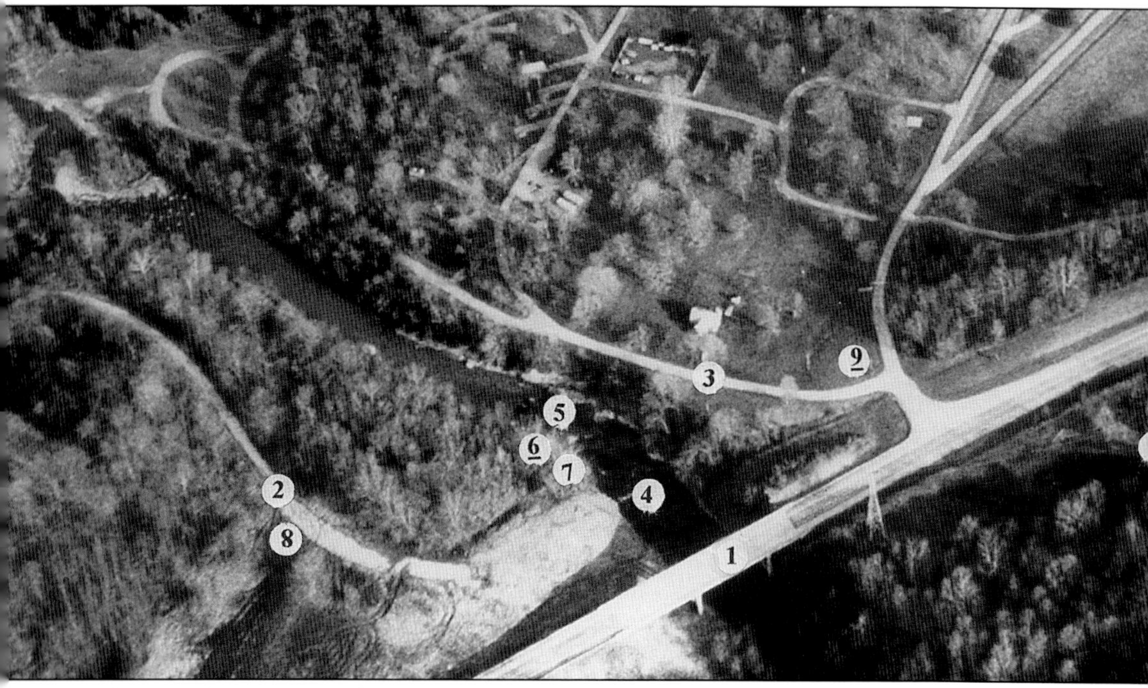

AERIAL VIEW OF THE GRAHAMPTON SITE. All of Grahampton is now gone, except for one intact building. The site, on the north side of Highway 60, now serves as Camp Carlson, the Fort Knox Army Travel Camp. This aerial view shows Highway 60 running east and west, and Otter Creek running south to north. The following numbers on the map correspond to the locations of various features once in and around Grahampton: (1) Highway 60 and fourth generation bridge over Otter Creek; (2) Old Highway 60, the second highway through Grahampton; (3) first generation of Highway 60 through Grahampton, which was called Front Street as it traveled through the town; (4) site of the third generation bridge, a cement-arched bridge, over Otter Creek; (5) site of the first (wood) and second (iron)generation bridges over Otter Creek; (6) site of the grist mill; (7) site of the textile mill; (8) site of the Stoeker store; and (9) site of the Episcopal church and current entrance to Camp Carlson. Approximately five miles north of this site, Otter Creek empties into the Ohio River at Hughes Landing, which was adjacent to the town of Bartles, another town seized in the expansion of Fort Knox in 1942.

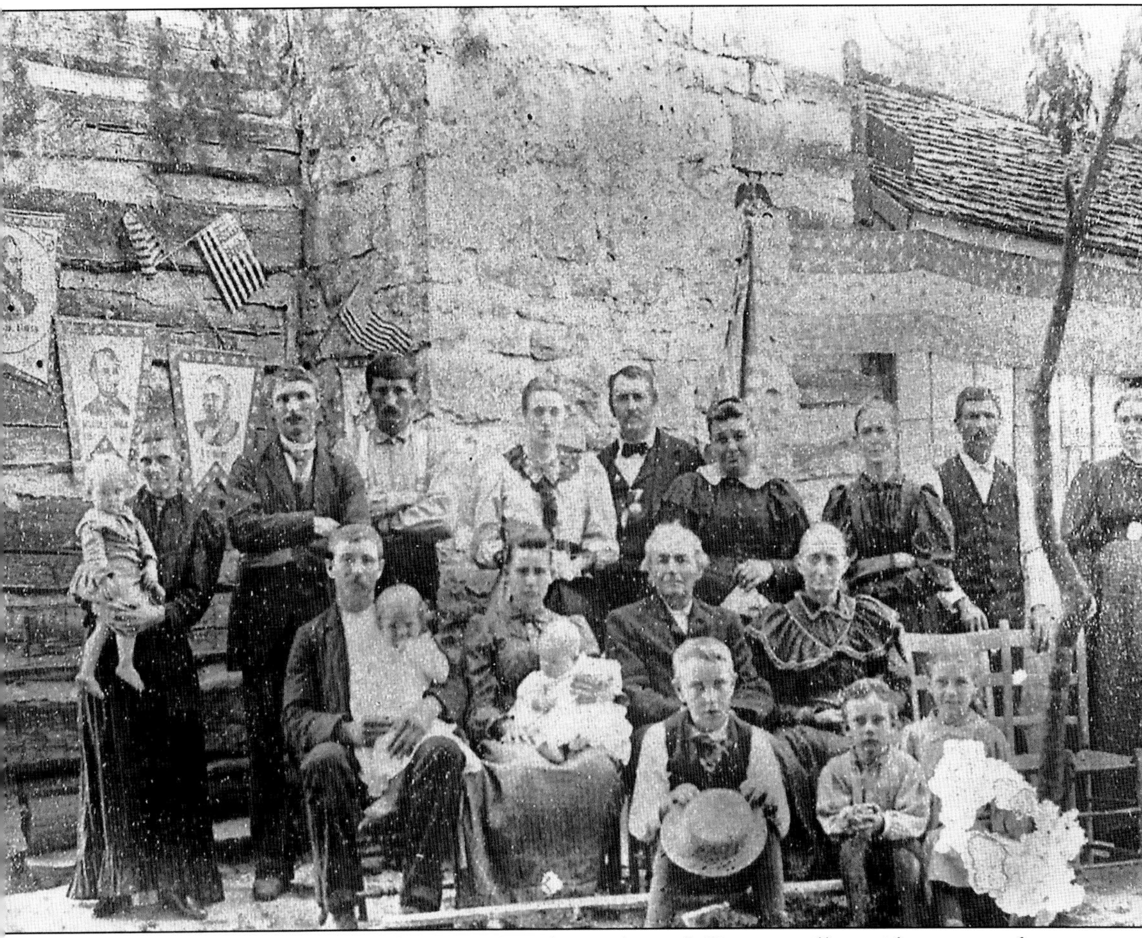

GARNETTSVILLE STAGECOACH STOP, 1890. A number of Garnettsville residents pose for a photograph by the Garnettsville stagecoach stop, which was on a road that connected Louisville and Hardinsburg. The posters and banners in the background suggest it is an election year. Garnettsville was named for William Garnett, born about 1777 in Virginia. By 1812 he was in Kentucky and shortly thereafter took over a mill on Otter Creek that was built in 1808. His mill produced meal and lumber for many years. The town that grew to the northeast of the mill became Garnettsville. It was in Hardin County until 1824, when Meade County was formed from Hardin and Breckinridge Counties. When the new county was formed, Garnett became one of its first justices of the peace and sheriffs. A few businesses existed in the coalescing town in the 1830s, but the 1840s and 1850s witnessed the town's real growth and established it as an important area crossroads. Although Garnett's mill was only a couple of miles northeast of the Grahampton mills, the two did not compete as their products were different. Taverns, mercantile stores, blacksmith shops, schools, churches, and other trades and professions were established in and around Garnettsville. A tailor, millwright, and doctor plied their trades in Garnettsville. In 1866 Salem College was established (incorporated by the Kentucky State Legislature) in the town and operated for many years. The expansion of Fort Knox consumed Garnettsville; nothing remains except the large Garnettsville cemetery that is not on Fort Knox and is still active. The bridge that carries Highway 1638 traffic over Otter Creek rests nearly atop the extinct town of Garnettsville.

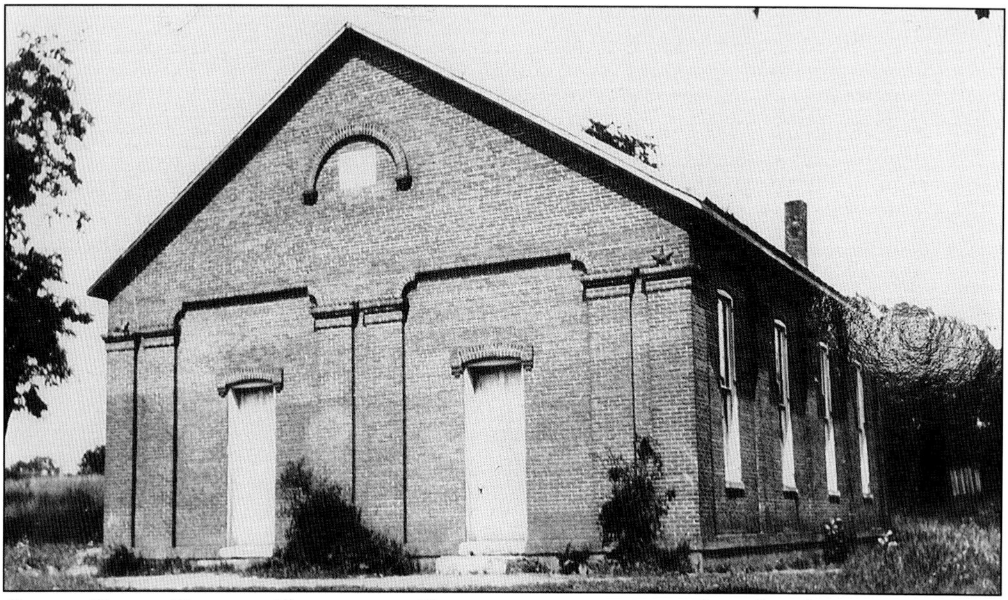

OTTER CREEK BAPTIST CHURCH IN GARNETTSVILLE, 1930. This church was originally a log building; this brick building later replaced it. Marguerite Lewis attended this church and recalled several ministers who served here in the first half of the 20th century. From the latest to the earliest, Marguerite recalled pastors C.J. Bottom, Rainey, Whitlow, Shreder, Williams, Hiebert, and D.E. Jones. About 500 feet west of the Baptist church was the Episcopal church, and further west was Otter Creek.

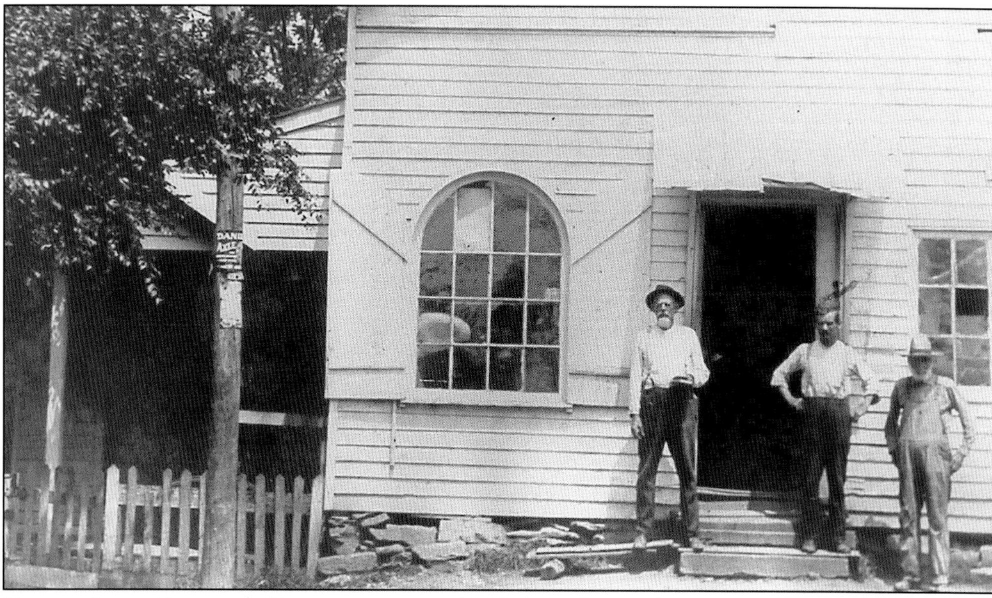

CASPER LANE STORE IN GARNETTSVILLE, 1905. The Casper Lane store was on the south side of Main Street, the main east-west road through Garnettsville. In the center of town, Main Street intersected with Walnut Street running north and Garnettsville Road running south. Main Street crossed Otter Creek north of the town, where the north flowing Otter Creek bends east in the shape of a horseshoe, and then again continues north. The Casper Lane store was on the southwest corner of Main Street and Garnettsville Road.

ORVILLE AND EMMA MARKUM IN FRONT OF THEIR STORE, 1941. Orville was born in Garnettsville, and his wife, Emma Stone was born in Grahampton. This is one of the last photographs taken of the Markum store, as it was demolished for the expansion of Fort Knox. The store was located at the west end of town, on the north side of Main Street. The store was "a stone's throw" northeast of the Garnettsville Mill on Otter Creek.

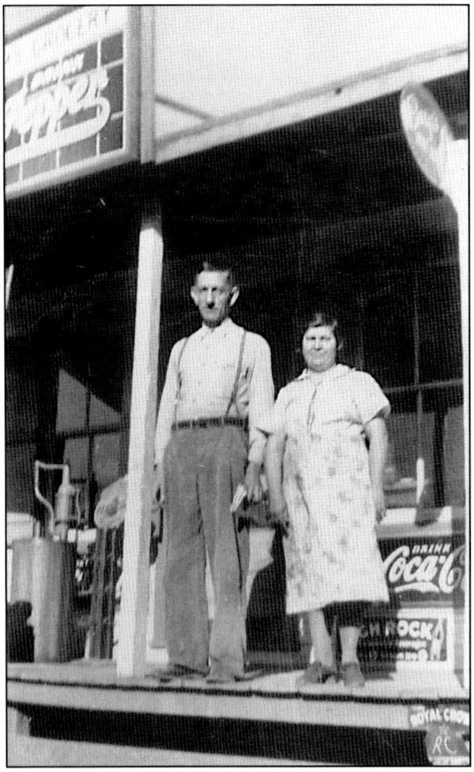

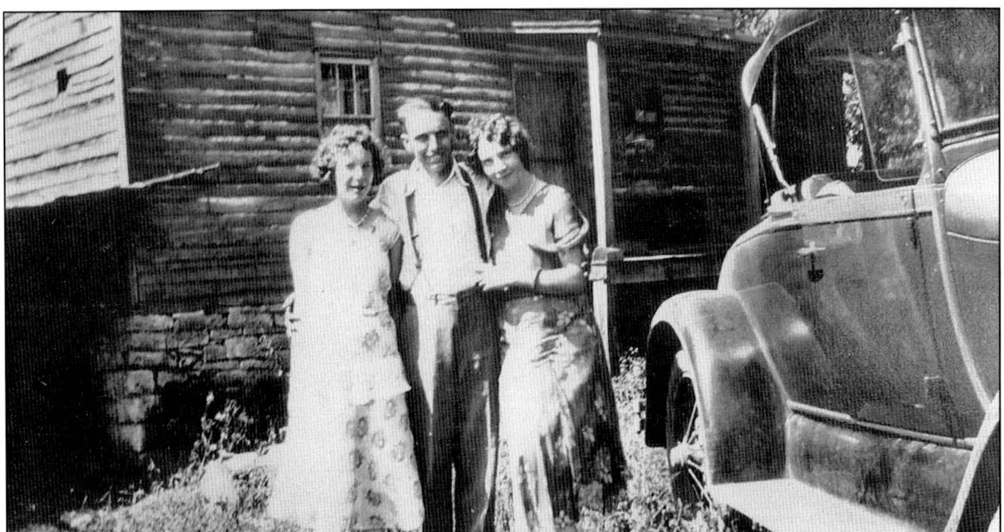

GARNETTSVILLE MILL, 1929. Marguerite, William, and Elizabeth Lewis stand in front of the mill, beside their 1929 Ford Roadster. Their home and farm was just north of the Garnettsville Baptist Church. Marguerite was born in 1915 in a house built by her great grandfather, Dr. H.K. Pusey. Five generations lived in the house before it was seized for the expansion of Fort Knox. At one time, four generations lived together there. The only evidence that Garnettsville existed is the cemetery, which is still active. Cemetery trustees have held a meeting and "homecoming" on the first Sunday in July each year since the demise of Garnettsville.

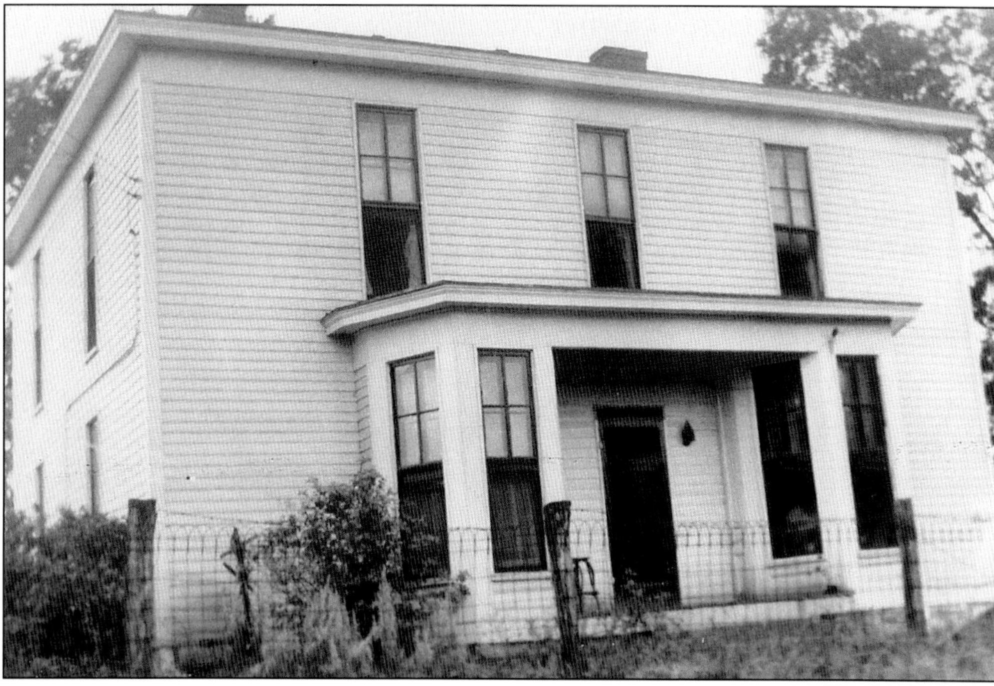

PUSEY HOUSE IN GARNETTSVILLE, 1940. Built by Dr. Henry K. Pusey, this house replaced the boarding house, destroyed by fire c. 1870, where he and his wife had lived and operated. After Dr. Pusey's death, his wife moved to Elizabethtown with their second daughter, Mollie Gardiner. The eldest daughter, Betty Lewis, continued living here with her husband, William.

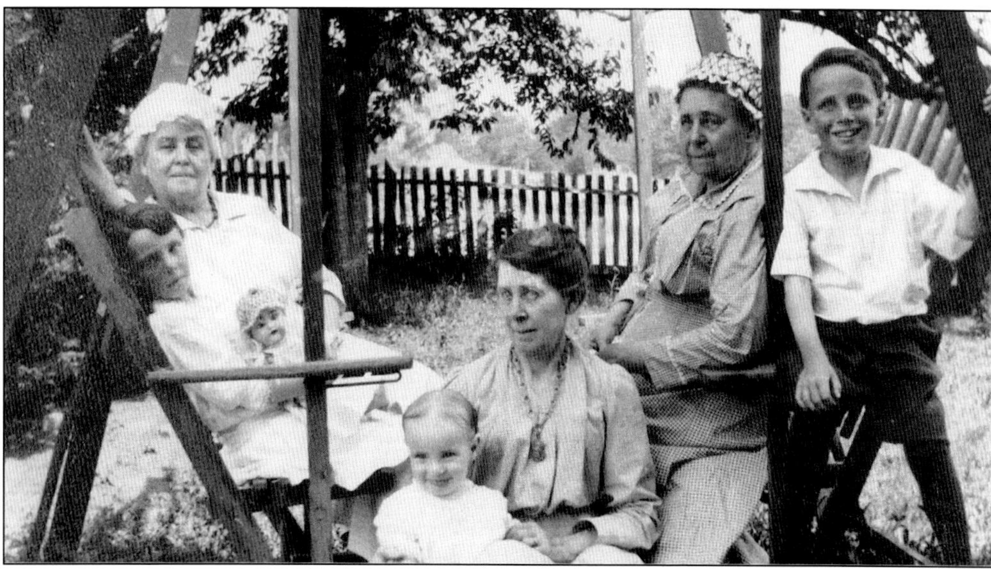

THE LEWIS HOME IN GARNETTSVILLE, 1917. The Lewis home and farm was a prosperous farm, north of the Baptist church. Salem College was at one time just east of the home. In the months prior to the government's purchase of the land, residents became aware of the pending event and began to look for and secure new homes and farms. Pictured from left to right are Elizabeth Lewis, Orrie German (young girl with doll in her lap), Marguerite Lewis (child), Mollie Taylor, Lizzie Lindsay (grandmother of Marguerite Lewis), and Lindsay Lewis.

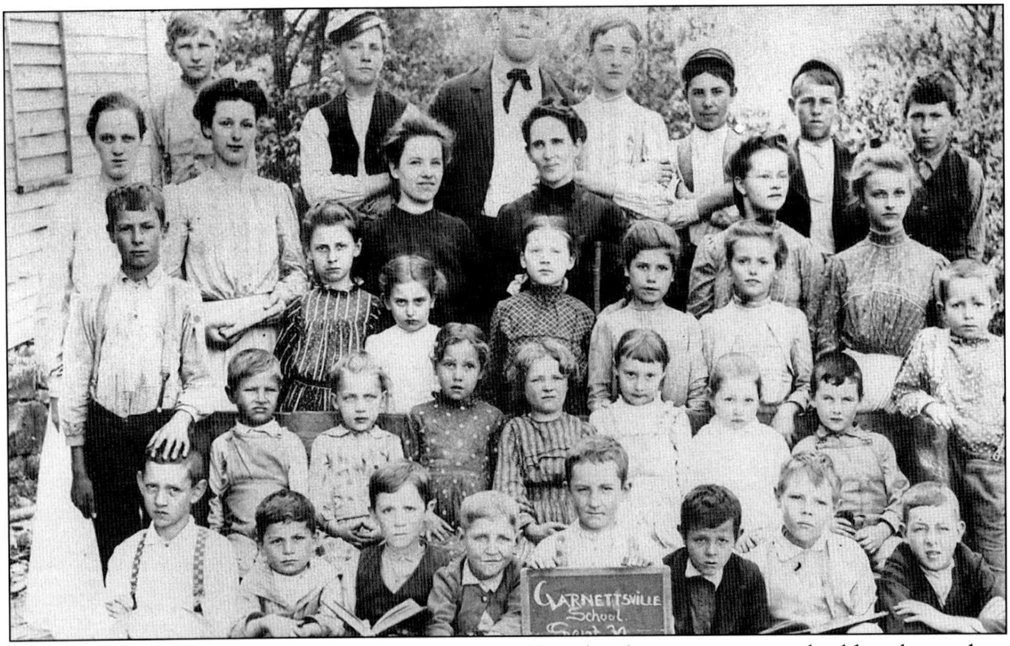

GARNETTSVILLE SCHOOL, 1903. The Garnettsville School was a one-room building located on the south side of Main Street at the east end of town. The dress worn by the students suggests prosperity. Holding the chalkboard is Olen Chapman. Others known to be in the picture are Orvil Markum, Hazel Chapman, Wilbur Chapman, Amanda Owens, Pearl Chapman, and Betty Kincaid.

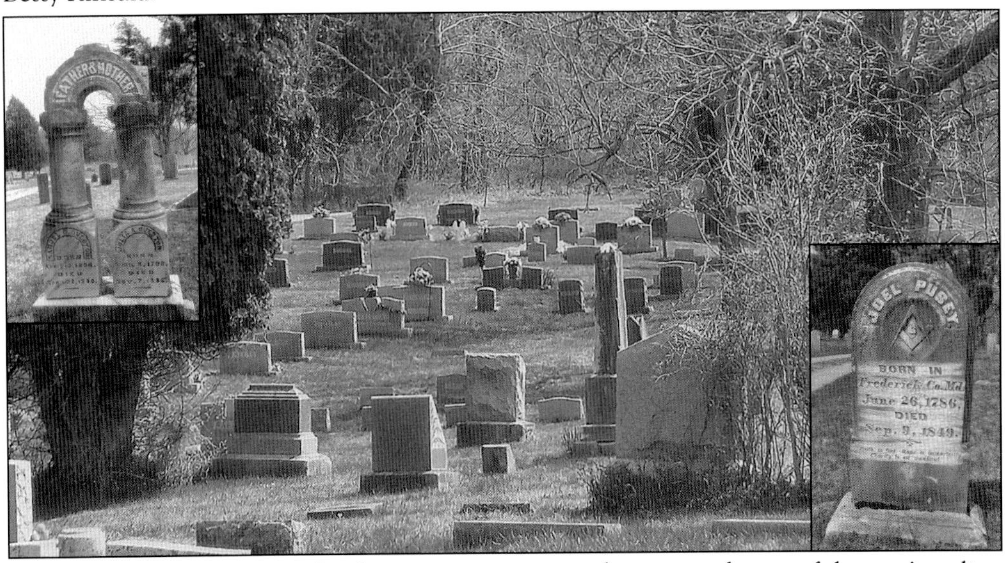

GARNETTSVILLE CEMETERY. In the town cemetery are the graves of some of the area's earliest settlers. The town stretched just south of the cemetery along Main Street. The Baptist church was at the east end of town, and an Episcopal church was halfway between the cemetery and the Baptist church on Main Street. The Garnettsville School was at the east end of town, across Main Street from the Guy Chapman farm. The Garnettsville Mill was south of the cemetery, across Main Street and Otter Creek. Present-day Highway 1638 was constructed south of the town, and the mill would have been on the west side of the highway, just east of the creek.

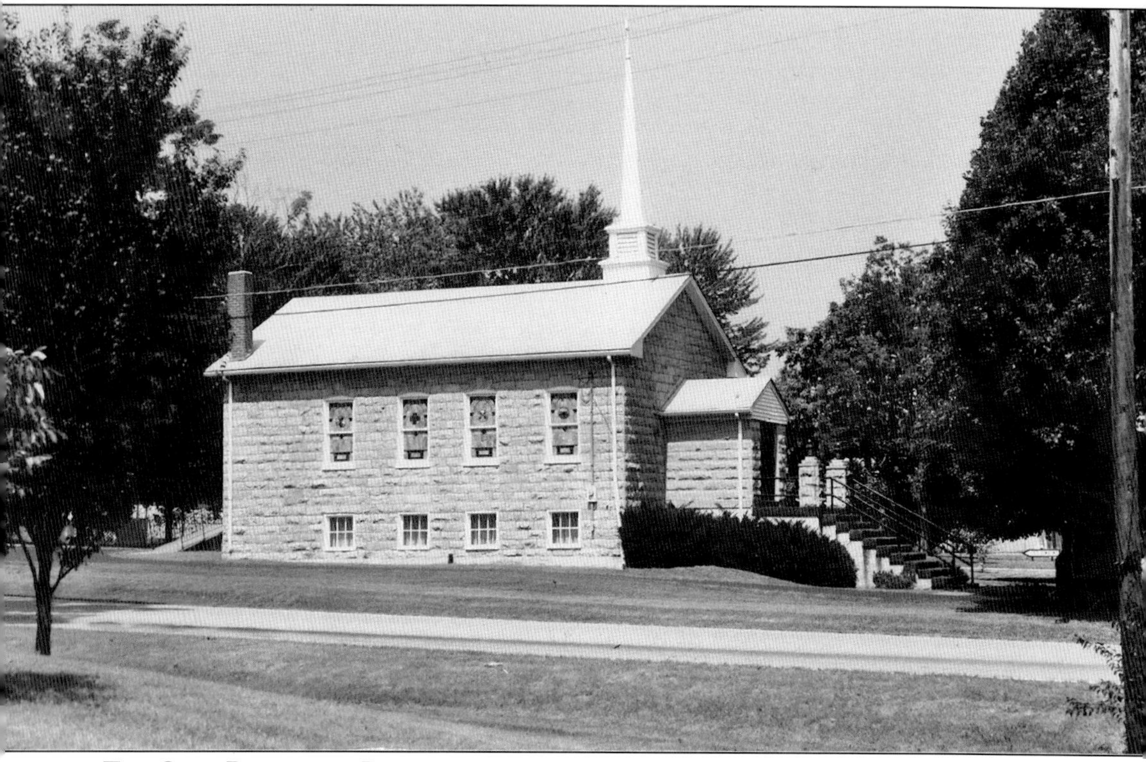

The Only Remaining Building from the Bygone Town of Garnettsville, 1995. In 1870 a Methodist church was erected in Garnettsville with stone taken from a nearby hillside. The individual stones were hand-dressed and laid by several men who were supervised by William C. Hutcheons. Some of the stones bear the names of A.L. Upton, John Maurrer, and R. Wheatley. The Methodist church stood in the flat area downhill from the Garnettsville Cemetery on land donated by Dr. Henry Pusey. With the decline of the town of Garnettsville in the early 20th century, services at the Methodist church were discontinued. In Muldraugh, a growing Methodist congregation desired a building; Curt Watts and William Kunnecke spearheaded the effort to move the church in Garnettsville to Muldraugh. Beginning in 1928 and completed in 1930, the church was relocated to a lot bought from Thomas L. Crutcher. As the church was dismantled, each stone was numbered, loaded onto horse-drawn wagons, and moved three miles to Muldraugh. Jack and Richard Kunnecke, high school students at the time, worked after school under the supervision of Mr. Nutter. The church is the only building that remains from the extinct town of Garnettsville; it has an active congregation to this day.

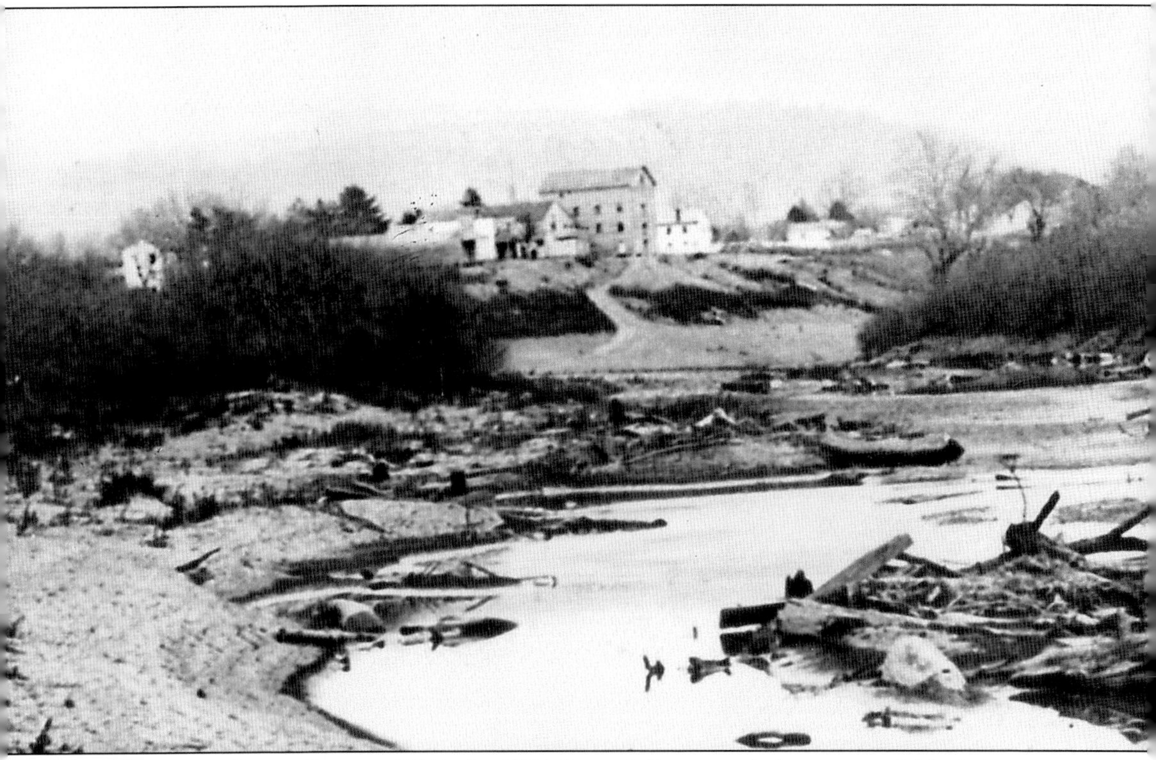

THE TOWN OF PITTS POINT, 1873. In 1776 Samuel Pearman led a group of Virginians to the confluence of the Salt and Rolling Fork Rivers. Their hopes of establishing a permanent settlement were not realized then because Native Americans drove them back to Virginia. Pearman returned years later with James Young and established the town of West Point at the mouth of the Salt River. Records show that brothers John and James Pitt bought 600 acres on the southwest side of the junction of the two rivers from Abraham and Hannah Froman in 1831 for $1,500. At the time Abraham Froman operated a ferry across the rivers. By 1831 Native Americans had been driven from the area, and numerous settlers occupied the land. The salt works at nearby Bullitt's Lick (near Shepherdsville) were at high production, and traffic on the Salt River carried salt, farm produce, and lumber downstream to the Ohio River and West Point. A town, first called Pittstown, was incorporated in 1861 as Pitts Point with a population of 300. Pitts Point became a big player in the development of the area, first as a shipping point for salt produced at Bullitt's Lick and later as a customs inspection point for tobacco, hemp, and salt. Farmers came from miles around to ship their goods to West Point and on to markets in Louisville, New Albany, and other ports on the Ohio River. Only two cemeteries remain from the town, which was seized for the expansion of Fort Knox. Each year on Memorial Day descendants of former residents are allowed onto the military base to decorate graves and walk the paths of their forefathers.

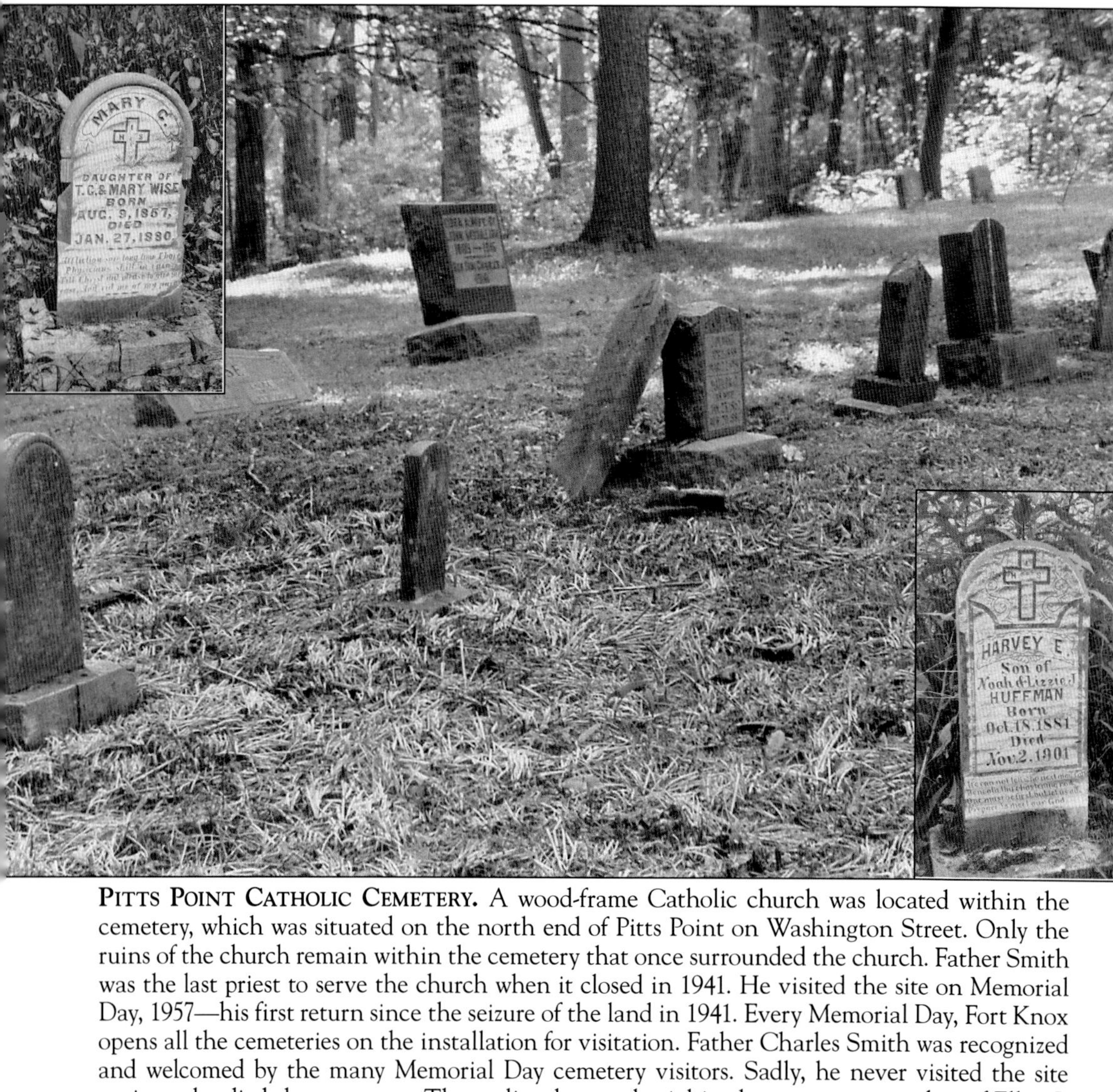

Pitts Point Catholic Cemetery. A wood-frame Catholic church was located within the cemetery, which was situated on the north end of Pitts Point on Washington Street. Only the ruins of the church remain within the cemetery that once surrounded the church. Father Smith was the last priest to serve the church when it closed in 1941. He visited the site on Memorial Day, 1957—his first return since the seizure of the land in 1941. Every Memorial Day, Fort Knox opens all the cemeteries on the installation for visitation. Father Charles Smith was recognized and welcomed by the many Memorial Day cemetery visitors. Sadly, he never visited the site again, as he died the next year. The earliest known burial in the cemetery was that of Ellen J. Ryan in October 1872. Eddie Ryan was buried in November of the same year. The last recorded burial was E.B. Reesor in March 1938.

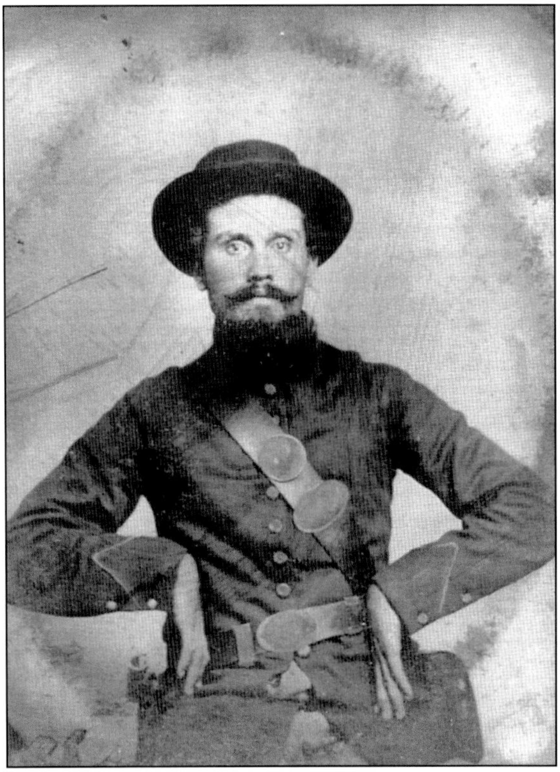

JOHN WALTER HOWLETT, 1866. John Walter Howlett lived in the Pitts Point area and attended the Pitts Point Catholic Church. He and his wife, Mary Huffman, are buried together in the Catholic cemetery. John enlisted in the Union Army on September 26, 1864, and was discharged June 23, 1865. He served in the Kentucky 23rd Infantry, Company F. The Kentucky 23rd lost four officers and 81 enlisted men in battle, and 107 died of disease. Pitts Point was unique in the area because it sent a regiment of men to fight for the Union cause; the area had predominately Southern sympathies. During Howlett's absence a battle took place in the streets of Pitts Point against a band of guerrillas led by the Southern sympathizers, the Wigginton brothers. The "Home Guard" drove off the guerrillas and killed one of the brothers.

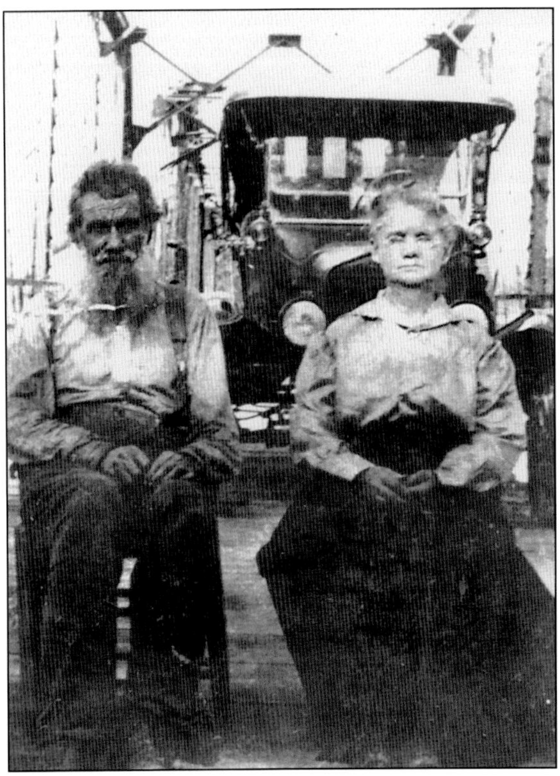

JOHN AND MARY HOWLETT, 1917. John Walter Howlett and his wife, Mary, sit on the Wooldridge Ferry Bridge in 1917. John and Mary had six children—Clarence, Eugene, Lawrence, Emma, Isabel, and Lona. They lived their entire married lives in a farmhouse in Hardin County, just 50 feet from the Wooldridge Ferry Bridge. The bridge crossed the Rolling Fork River and connected Hardin and Bullitt Counties. It also gave access to the town of Pitts Point for Hardin County families who wished to avail themselves of the town services. The bridge is long gone.

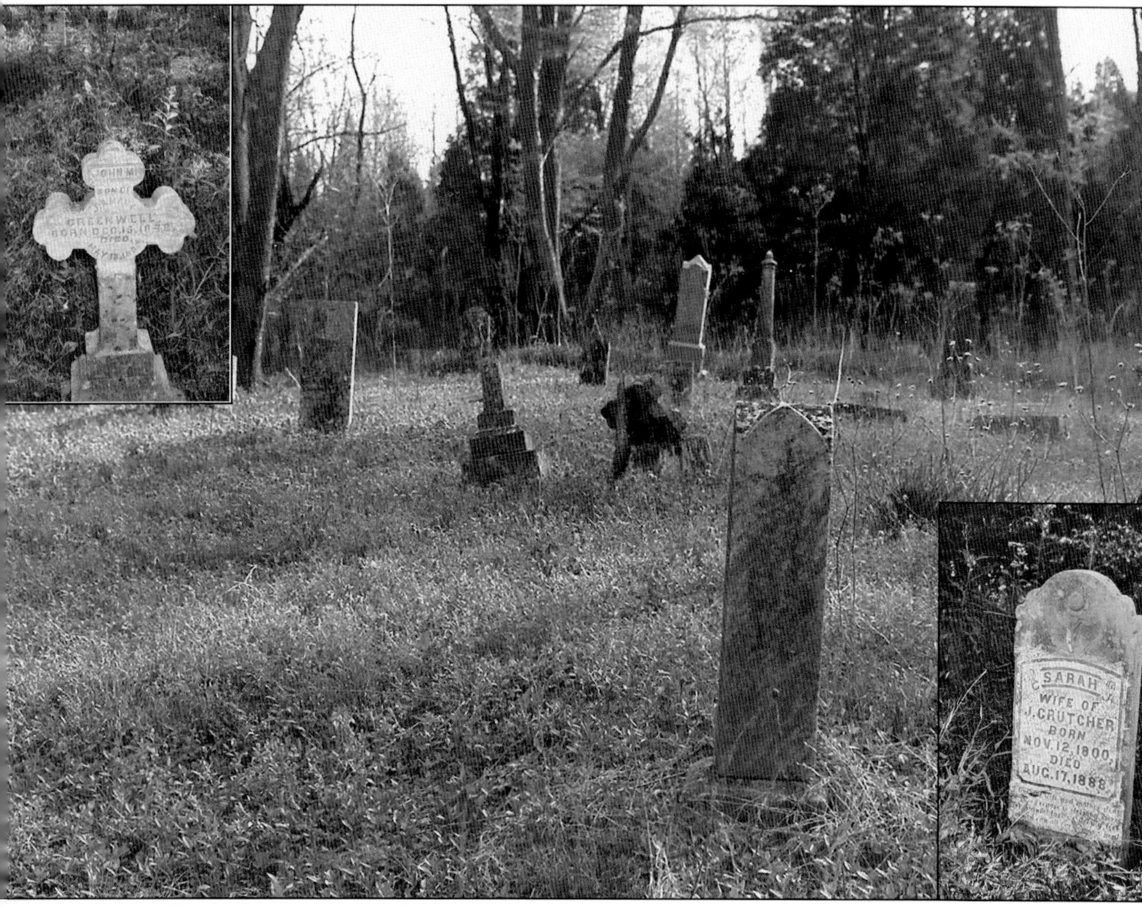

Pitts Point Protestant Cemetery. Pitts Point Road, a county road that when approached from the south was the entrance to Pitts Point, became Main Street in the town. One could also enter Pitts Point by boat on the Salt or Rolling Fork Rivers or by ferry across the rivers. If entering town by the road, the Protestant church and cemetery were on the left side just south of town. The earliest known burial in the cemetery was Robert Henry Lee in November 1868. The last burial was Laura Mae Rountree in August 1939, two years before the last town residents were removed for the Fort Knox expansion. By the late 19th century, the railroads had taken most of the river traffic that had caused the growth and prosperity of Pitts Point, and the salt works to the east had ceased production. These factors caused a decline in the fortunes of this once prosperous river town. By 1942, when the government took the town, less than a dozen families resided here. Among those were the Atcher, Druin, Gentry, Hill, and Dawson families.

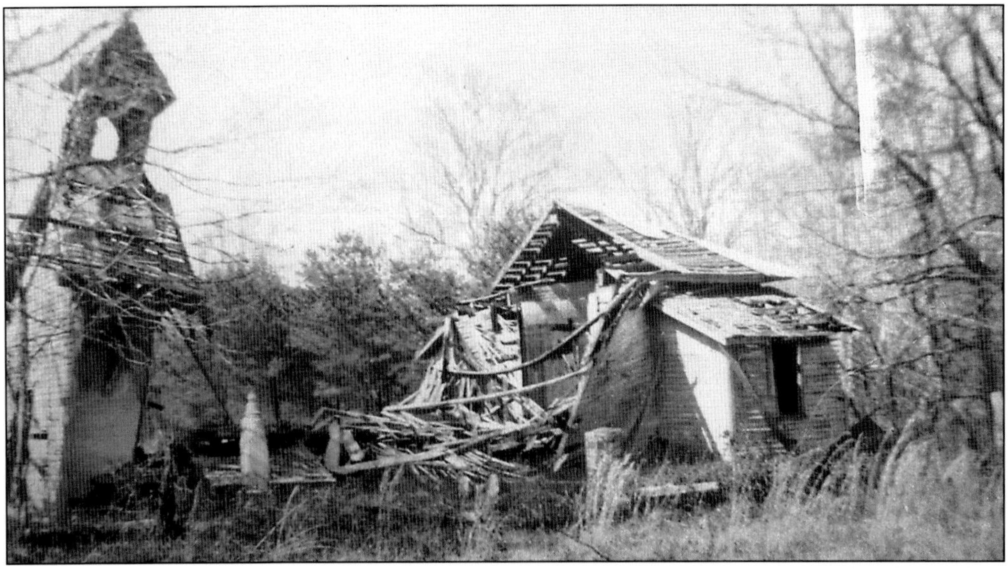

Pitts Point Catholic Church, 1957. In the later years of Pitts Point, the church had only monthly services. The town was declining from the reduction in river traffic brought by the expanding railroad networks and the closing of the salt works. For a few years after the government's seizure, a few dilapidated buildings remained. This photograph is what Father Smith, the last priest to serve the church, saw in 1957 on his final visit. By 1980 little was left of the town. A year later, a range fire removed any buildings left standing.

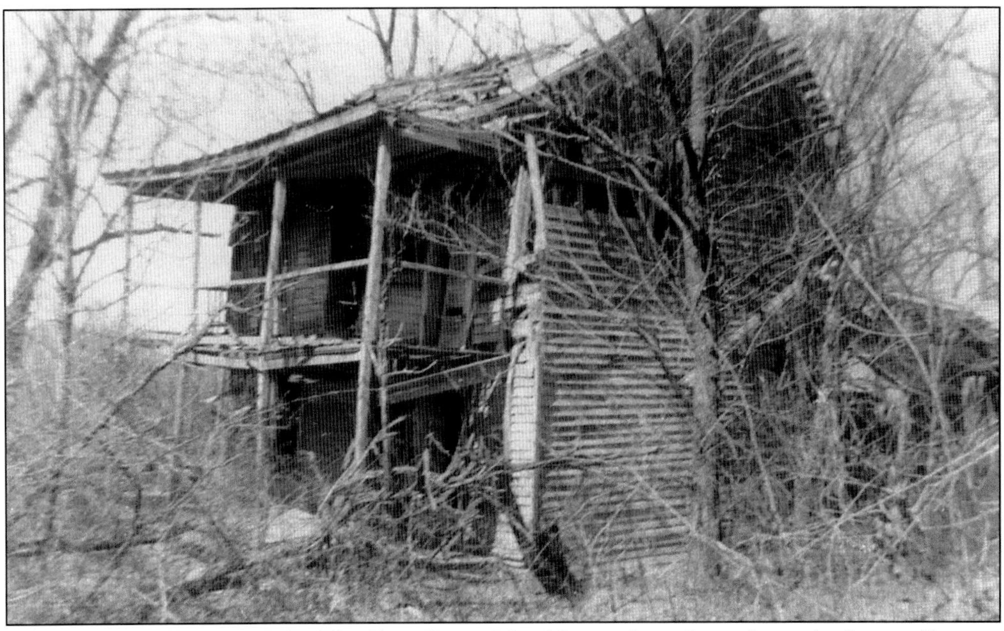

Pitts Point Hotel, 1957. The Pitts Point Hotel housed residents from the Louisville area on hunting and fishing excursions. Early on, travelers and workers on the riverboats also stayed here. In 1913 John Chris Atcher moved from Stithton to Pitts Point with his family. He purchased the hotel, the Pitts Point general store (previously the Hardy Store), and the Pitts Point Academy building. He turned the academy, founded in the 1860s, into a commercial hunting lodge. His wife operated the store. The Atchers used the hotel as their residence.

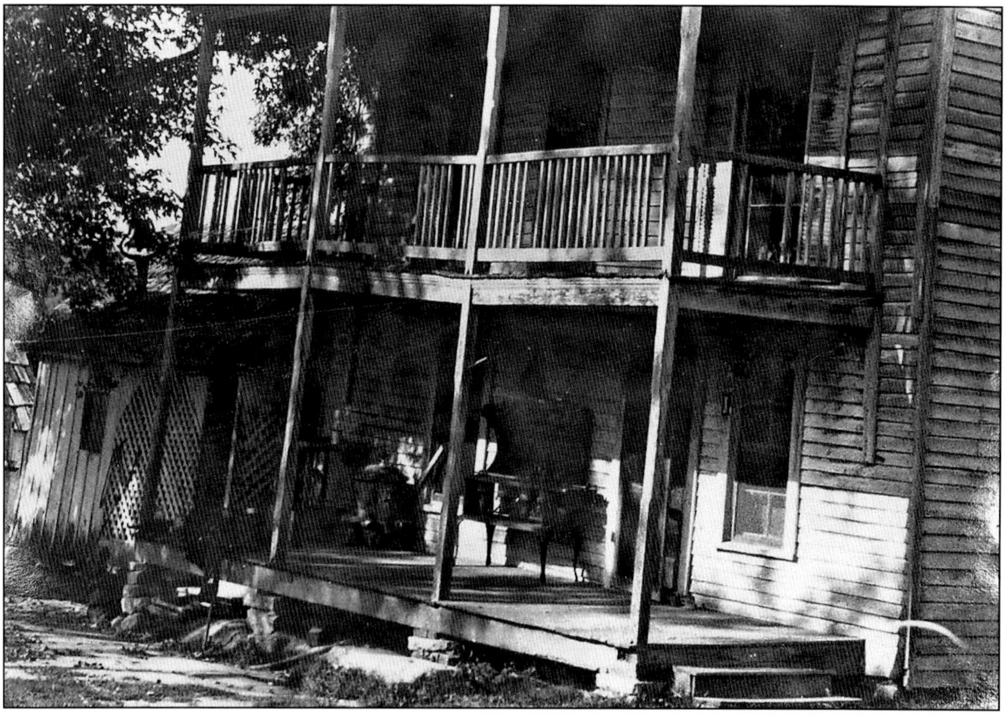

Atcher Home (once the Pitts Point Hotel) in Pitts Point, 1930. Ruby Atcher Zepperlein moved with her family to Pitts Point from Stithton in 1913. Her father, John Chris Atcher, and mother, Mary Elizabeth, owned a farm just outside Stithton. Ruby recalled that the house, previously the Pitts Point Hotel, was heated with wood stoves and lighted by gas lamps. In 1930 the building was in a state of disrepair, as were most of the buildings in the town. Less than a dozen families occupied the town by the late 1930s.

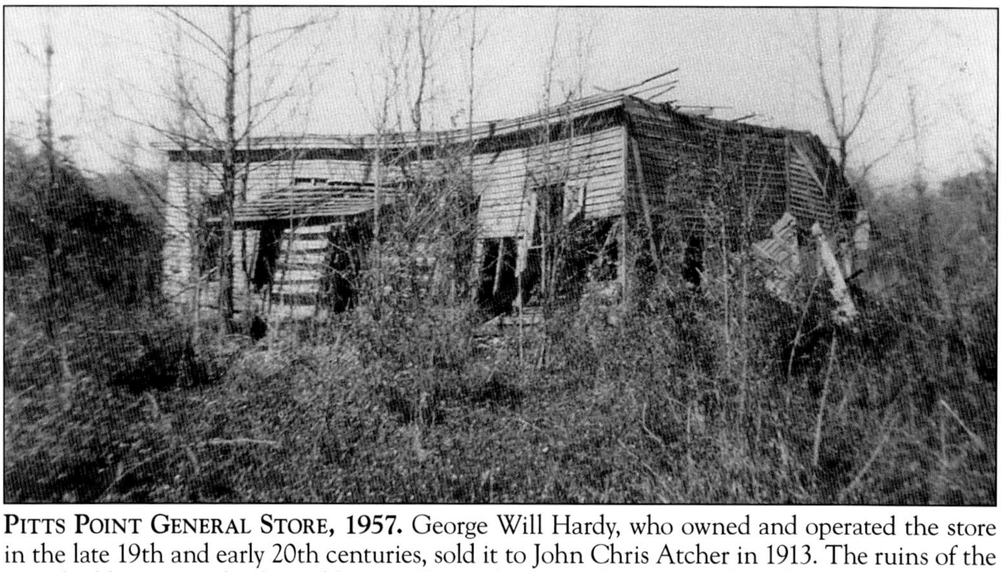

Pitts Point General Store, 1957. George Will Hardy, who owned and operated the store in the late 19th and early 20th centuries, sold it to John Chris Atcher in 1913. The ruins of the store building were clearly visible in 1957. In the 1980s fires swept through the area that was once Pitts Point and completely destroyed the last vestiges of any remaining buildings. Nothing remains of the town except for the two cemeteries that were part of the town's churches.

TOM AND MOLLY HILL, 1930. Tom and Molly Spencer Hill, among the last residents to live in Pitts Point, worked as tenant farmers on the Daugherty farm in the Flats, south of Pitts Point. Prosperous tenant farmers, the Hills were both were born into slavery; their parents had also worked on farms in the Flats. They retired to Pitts Point, where they purchased two houses. One was a one-story log cabin overlaid with clapboards, used as their winter home because it was easier to heat in the winter. The other was a two-story building they used in the summer. Molly was a midwife and delivered many babies born in the area. Both were respected members of the community.

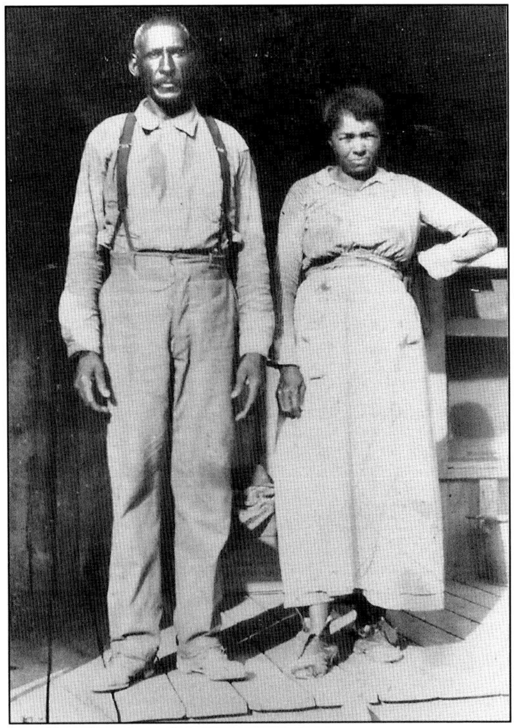

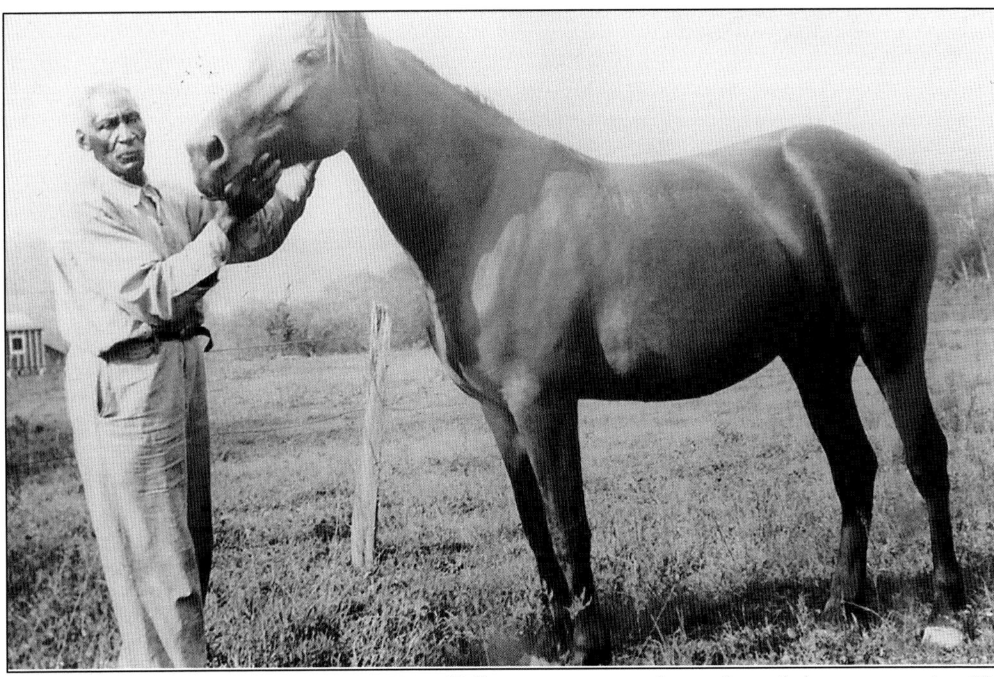

TOM HILL IN PITTS POINT, 1937. Tom Hill was a respected member of the community. He retired to Pitts Point and did odd jobs and cared for horses. Known as "the Pitts Point banker," he lent money at interest. Reportedly, his wife, Molly, was a child of mixed race. It has also been claimed that Molly's white father was a prosperous farmer and provided monetary support for Molly until his death.

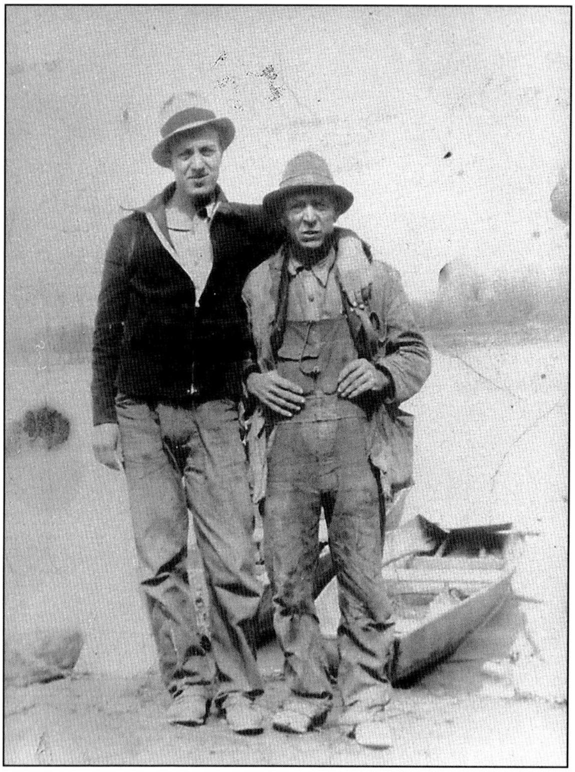

WILLIAM DRUIN AND HIS SON, LEE, IN PITTS POINT, 1936. William Druin built cabins on the Salt River in Pitts Point; he rented them, as well as boats, to hunters and fishermen from Louisville and other cities on sporting vacations. Lee Druin, a fisherman and trapper who lived in Pitts Point with his wife Angie Bell Clark, trapped beaver, mink, raccoon, and fox. The Druins were among the last to depart Pitts Point with its seizure for the expansion of Fort Knox.

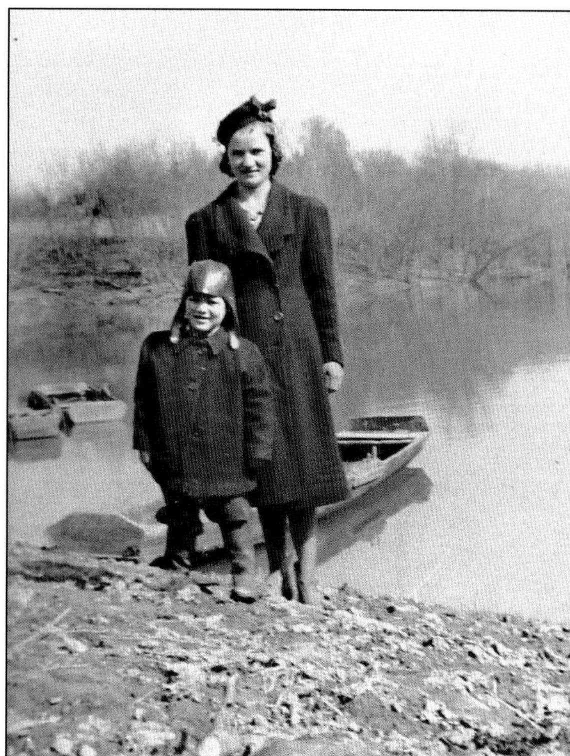

ANGIE BELL DRUIN WITH SON, CHARLES WILLIAM DRUIN, IN PITTS POINT, 1941. Angie was the wife of Lee Druin and the great granddaughter of William and Cynthia Brumfield, who in 1812, were among the earliest farmers to settle in the area. The Brumfields lived just west of Pitts Point in Hardin County, and they also lived for a time within Pitts Point. Angie and her son, Charles, soon left Pitts Point for the very last time.

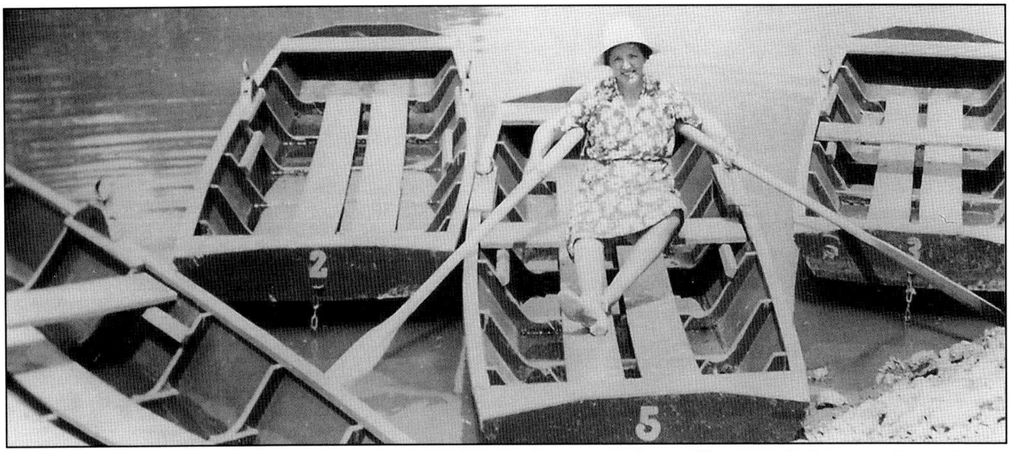

SADIE ATCHER AT PITTS POINT, 1940. Sadie Atcher is on the Rolling Fork River at Pitts Point. Giles Kelly owned and rented the boats and ferried people across the river. Hardin County children, on the west side of the river, paid 5¢ per day to be ferried across the river to attend the Browns Run School in Bullitt County. Rua Larrimore was a student who attended Browns Run School in this manner. Mary Dawson was the last teacher at the Browns Run School. The Atchers, the Druins, and Tom and Molly Hill were among the last residents of Pitts Point. Sadie would soon leave Pitts Point and return only on Memorial Day cemetery visitation.

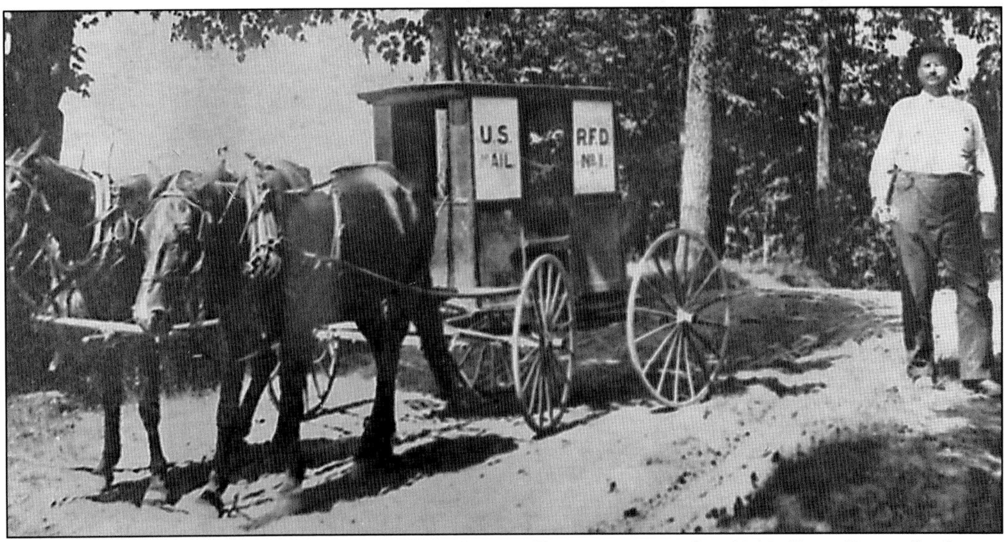

GEORGE BRADBURY CARRIES MAIL TO PITTS POINT, 1917. In 1860 Pitts Point had one Baptist church, one seminary, one Masonic lodge, one steam flouring and saw mill, two hotels, two general stores, four physicians, two attorneys, two carpenters, one baker and confectioner, one blacksmith, two beef and pork packers, one cabinet maker, one chair manufacturer, one cooper, one dentist, one gunsmith, one saddle and harness maker, one nurser and seedsman, one plow maker, one rope manufacturer, one shingle maker, two stone and brick masons, one tin and sheet ironware manufacturer, one surveyor, one tailor, and one tobacconist, as well as a population of 300. A post office was established in 1842 with J.V. Froman serving as postmaster. By the time of its seizure for the expansion of Fort Knox, Pitts Point was nearly a ghost town. Gone were all the businesses and almost the entire population. By 1917 the post office was gone, and mail was delivered from Belmont to the east. George Bradbury was the mail carrier for deliveries between Belmont and Pitts Point for many years.

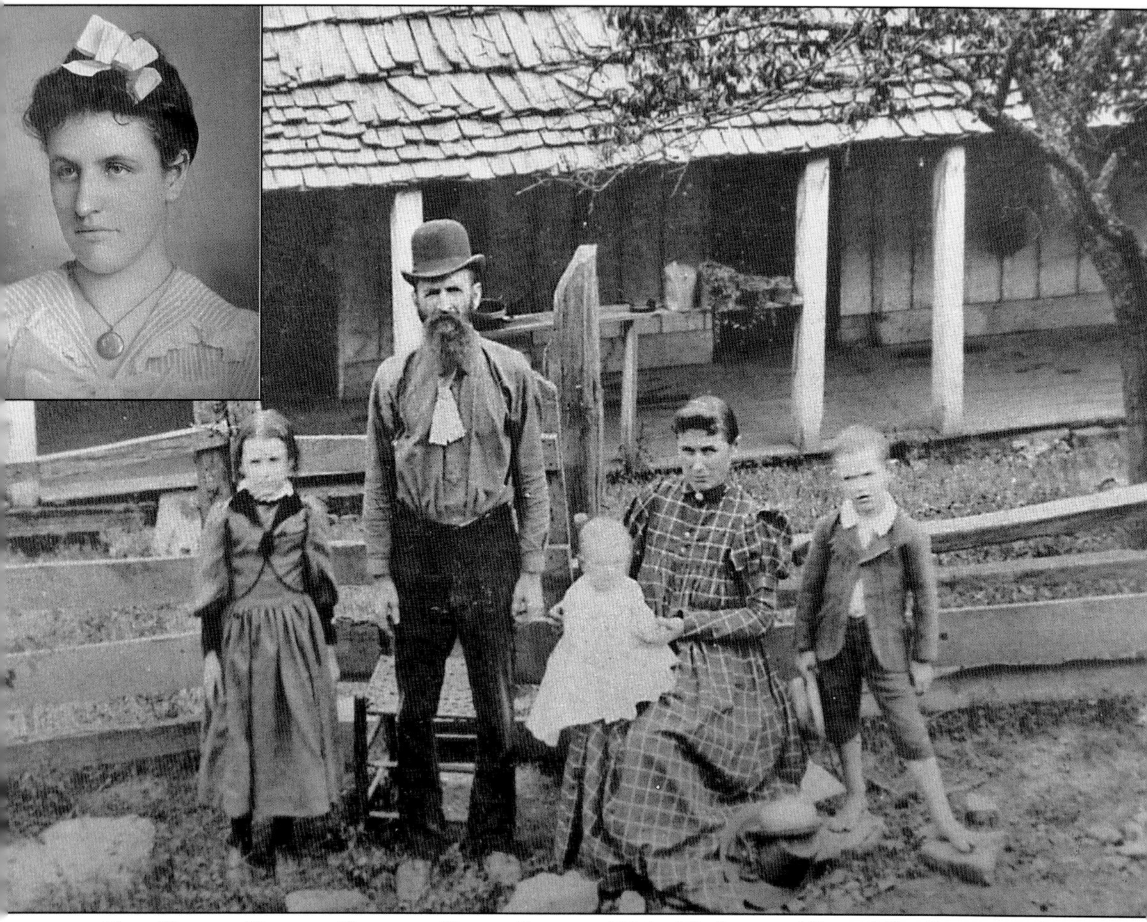

THE KELLEY FAMILY OUTSIDE PITTS POINT, 1891. Claiborne Allen Kelly (born 1843) was among the farmers around the Pitts Point area who depended on the town for services such as mail, merchandise purchases, equipment repair and purchase, church, school, and social activities. Claiborne saw the town in its prime, before the railroads and highways diminished the river traffic that was so vital to the town. The Kelly family outside their farmhouse, from left to right, are Virginia Lee Kelly, Claiborne Allen Kelley, Barnett Pearl Kelley, and Theodore Matthew Kelley. Such farmers raised fine families, and their children went on to raise fine families of their own. Virginia Lee Kelly married Vernon Whitehouse and had five children. Virginia is shown as a 29-year-old woman in the inset of the photograph above. At the time of the expansion of Fort Knox, just a few large farms were adjacent to Pitts Point. To the north and east were the farms of Lee Dawson (116 acres), James and Howard Dawson (165 acres), and William Dawson (276 acres); to the south were the farms of Hillary Dawson (165 acres) and Charles Dawson (108 acres); to the west was the Rolling Fork River and Hardin County.

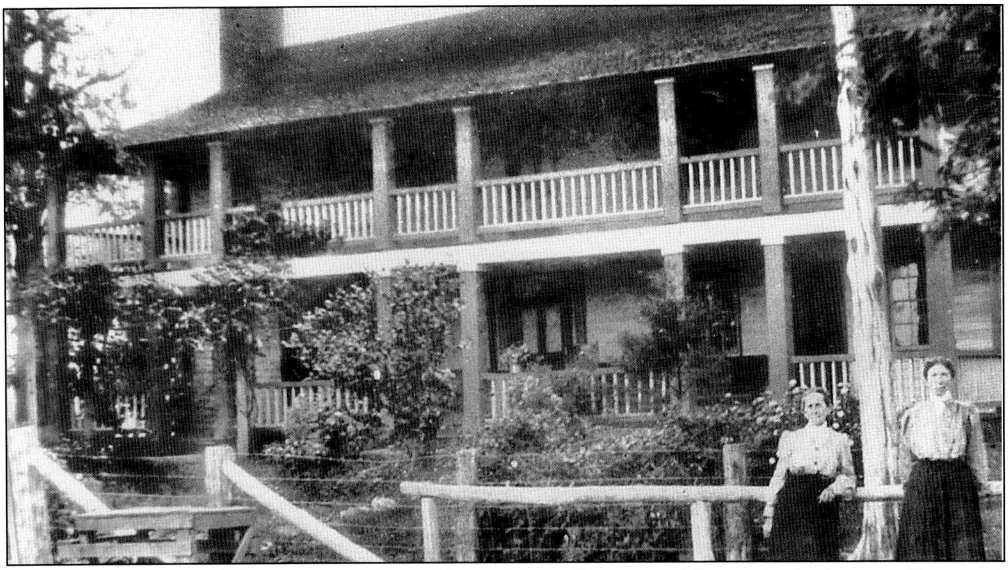

BLOOMINGTON INN/STAGECOACH STOP, LATE 19TH CENTURY. Shown is the home of Jesse and Susan Hays Wooldridge, whose family—except for one son who stayed to finish law school in Louisville—moved to Missouri in 1858. The home, on the Louisville-Nashville Turnpike (now Wilson Road), served as an inn and stagecoach stop. Bloomington was located in the vicinity of today's Anderson Golf Course. The September 30, 1862 issue of the *Cincinnati Commercial* chronicled the passage of 50,000 troops under the command of Union General Buell through Bloomington to West Point along the turnpike. New Stithton came to be superimposed on Bloomington. The schoolhouse in Bloomington retained the name Bloomington School until about 1923 when the New Stithton schoolhouse was built.

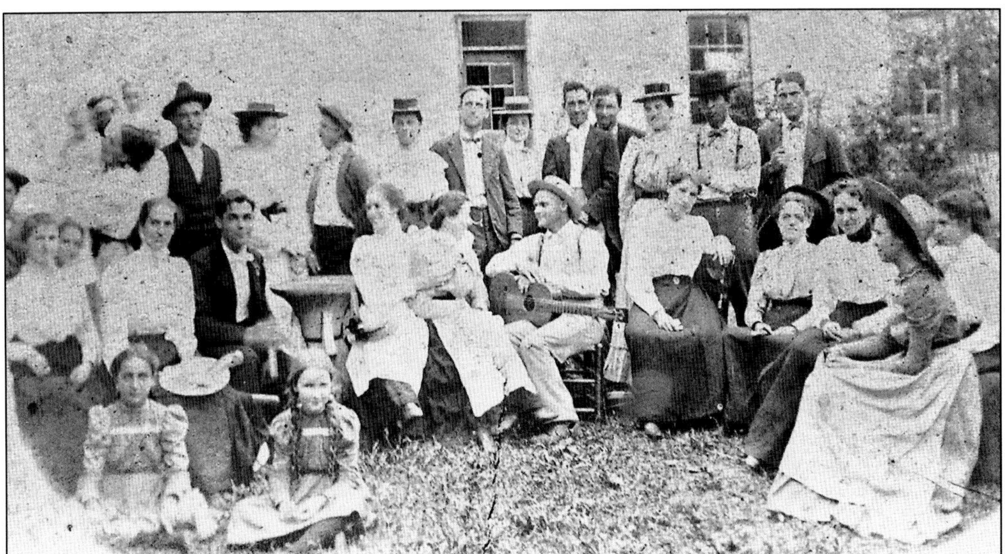

BLOOMINGTON SCHOOL, 1891. At this time, Bloomington School was a private school and the teacher was William Green Cowley, in the center of the photograph with the hat and guitar. Located about a half a mile west of the Tarpley Cemetery, the school became a public school with Whitcum Stovall as the teacher in 1899. In 1923 the schoolhouse was shared by the New Stithton Methodist Episcopal Church until they built a church in New Stithton in 1934.

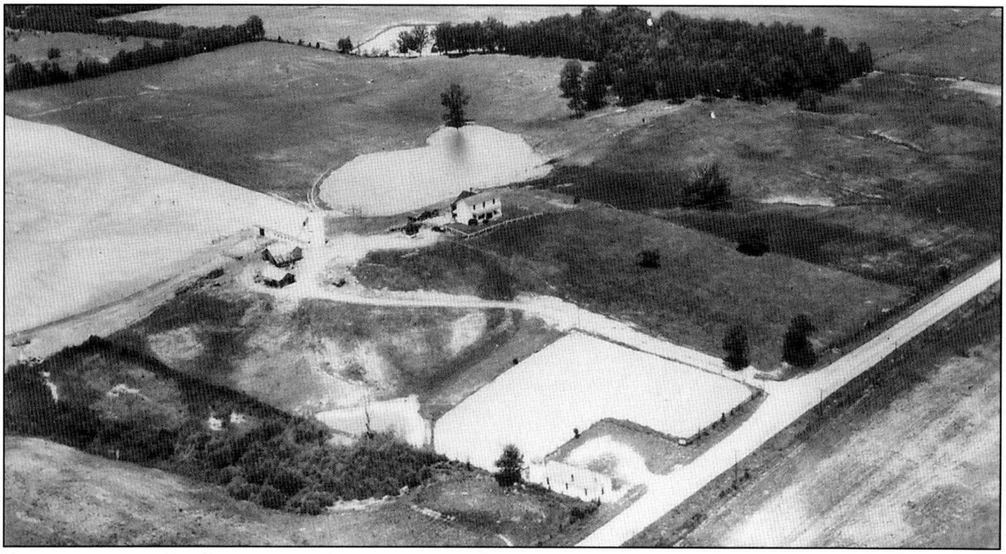

Burton and Cy Bennett House and Farm in New Stithton, 1930. This home and farm was seized when Fort Knox expanded in 1941. The businesses and residences of New Stithton, which was established following the acquisition of Stithton in 1919, were taken for the expansion of Fort Knox in 1942. Redmar Plaza was established about three-fourths of a mile south of this farm. The road in the foreground of the photograph is Wilson Road, once Dixie Highway, and before that the Louisville-Nashville Turnpike. The pond just behind the farmhouse is gone, but the smaller pond in the background remains and was a source of water for the Anderson Golf Course that later occupied the one-time Bennett farmland.

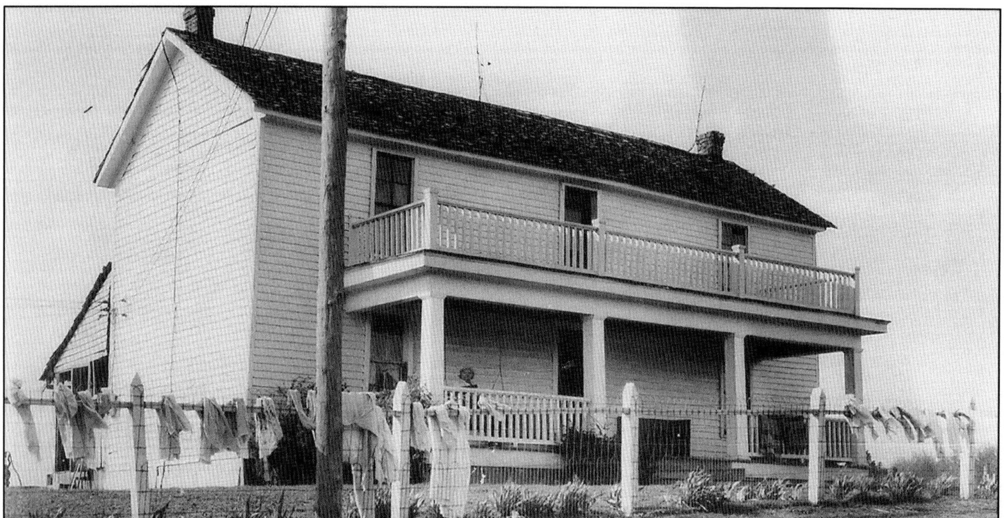

The Bennett House in New Stithton, 1936. In 1942 every home, business, church, and school near New Stithton was taken for the expansion of Fort Knox. Burton and Cy Bennett were the last owners of this house, located north of the Fort Knox boundary on Wilson Road atop a hill that would become part of Anderson Golf Course. Sitting on the porch is Matilda Bennett, grandmother of Al Burton Bennett. The house was believed to have been built in the 1890s as a log cabin and served as the office of Doctor Bennett. It was clapboarded and greatly enlarged.

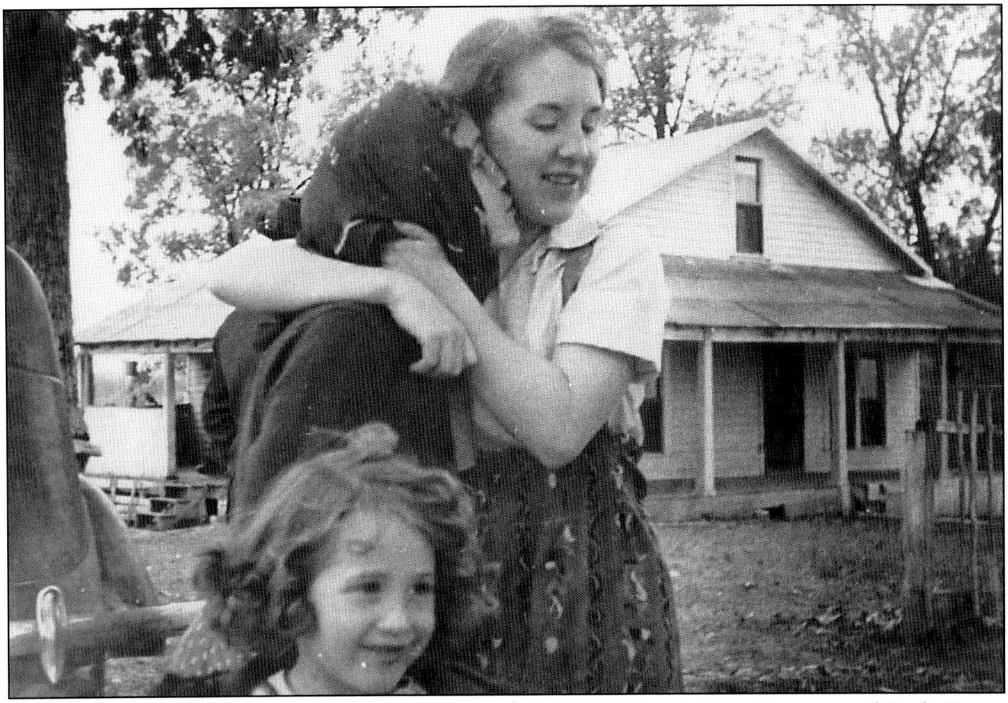

DAVIS HOME IN NEW STITHTON, 1926. From left to right are Lilian, Vivian, and Earla Davis in front of their home that was soon taken for Fort Knox. It was a wood-frame structure and had a front porch, typical for homes in the New Stithton area. The house was about a half mile east of the Davis store on Goldsmith Street, now known as Poor Man Range Road on Fort Knox.

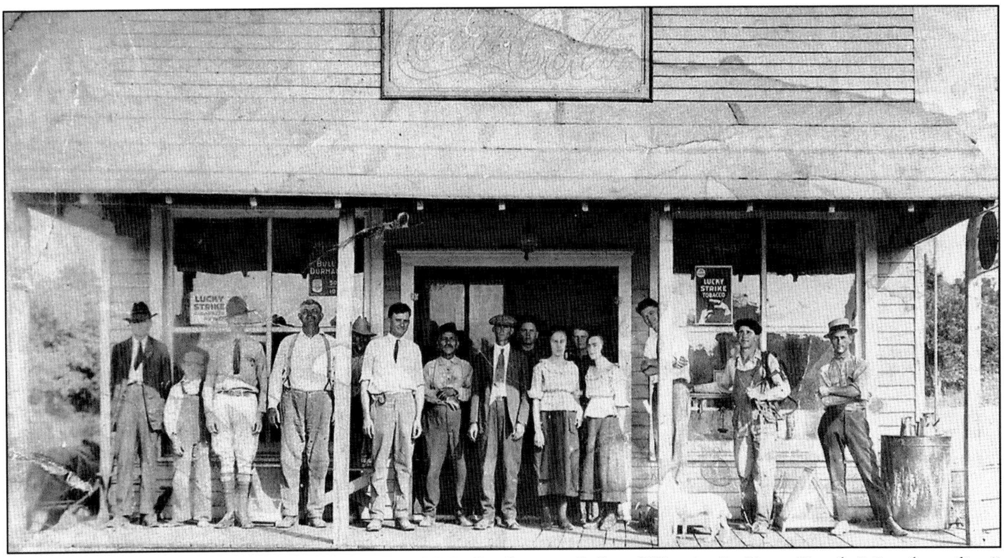

DAVIS STORE IN NEW STITHTON, C. 1920. In front of this "Davis & Son Genl. Merchandise" store are a group of customers, passersby, and some people probably there to converse. Truman Cowley is known to be at the far right of the photograph (with the brim hat). Next to him is Herman Clay Davis (bibbed overalls), and Emmett Davis is behind the porch post (third from the right). John Davis, wearing suspenders, is the fourth man from the left, and Joe Northcut is beside him with the white shirt and tie.

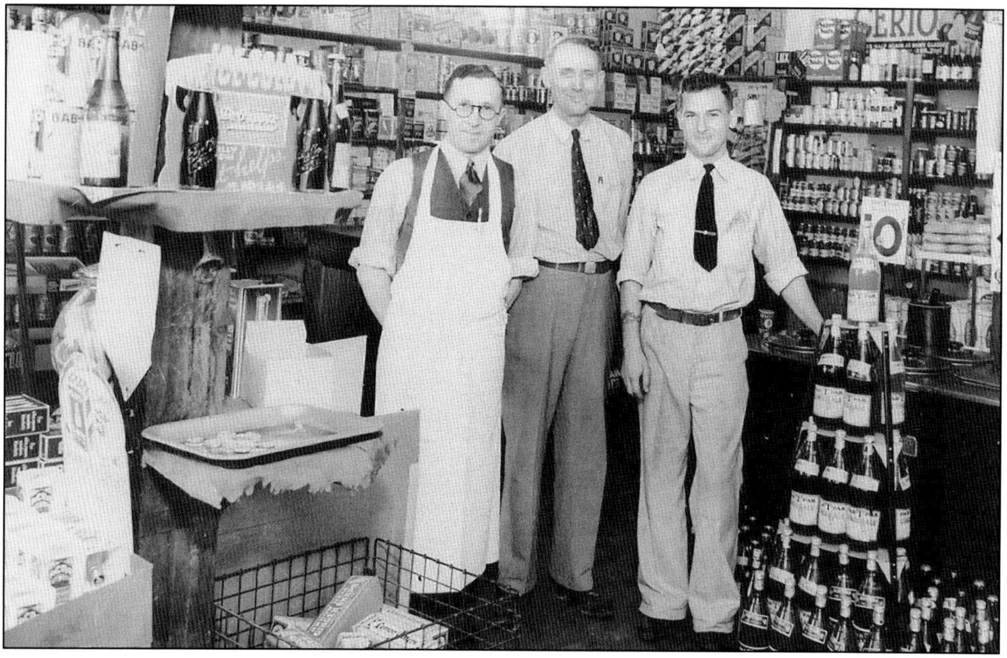

THE BROWN STORE IN NEW STITHTON, 1939. The Brown Store was located outside the boundary of Fort Knox on the east side of Wilson Road (the Louisville-Nashville Turnpike) at the north end of New Stithton before its establishment. Seen inside the store, from left to right, are Earl Brown, William Martin Brown, and Burley Graham.

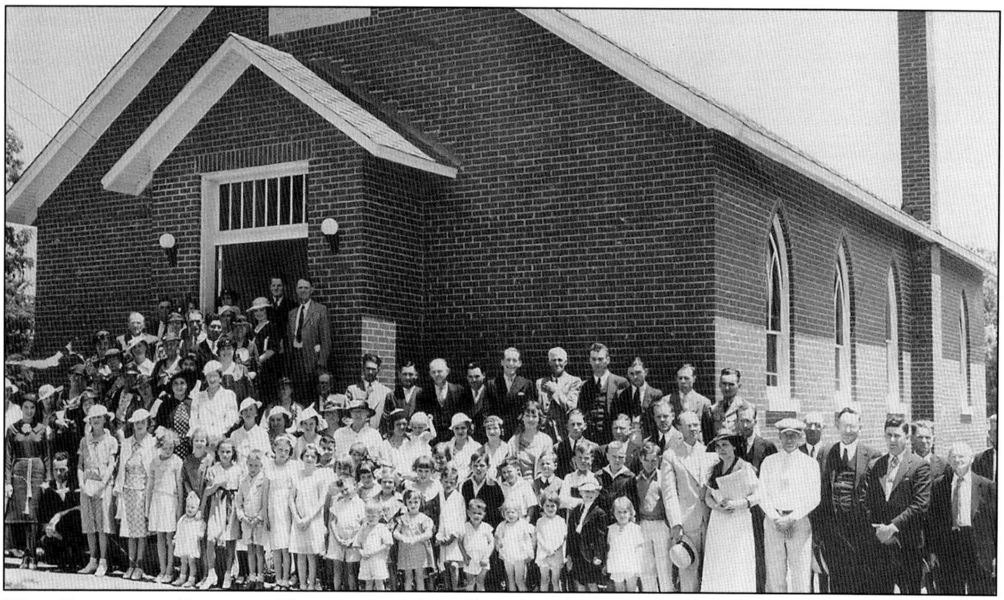

NEW STITHTON BAPTIST CHURCH, 1940. This church, one of only two brick buildings in New Stithton, was located on the east side of Wilson Road, inside today's Wilson Road entrance to Fort Knox and across from Tarpley Cemetery (also called Stithton Cemetery). Some of the church's parishioners attended Stithton's Baptist church, which was seized in 1918 for Camp Knox. The last pastor was Rev. Carlyle Marney. Parishioners saw their church constructed a few years prior to this picture, and within one year, the church was demolished.

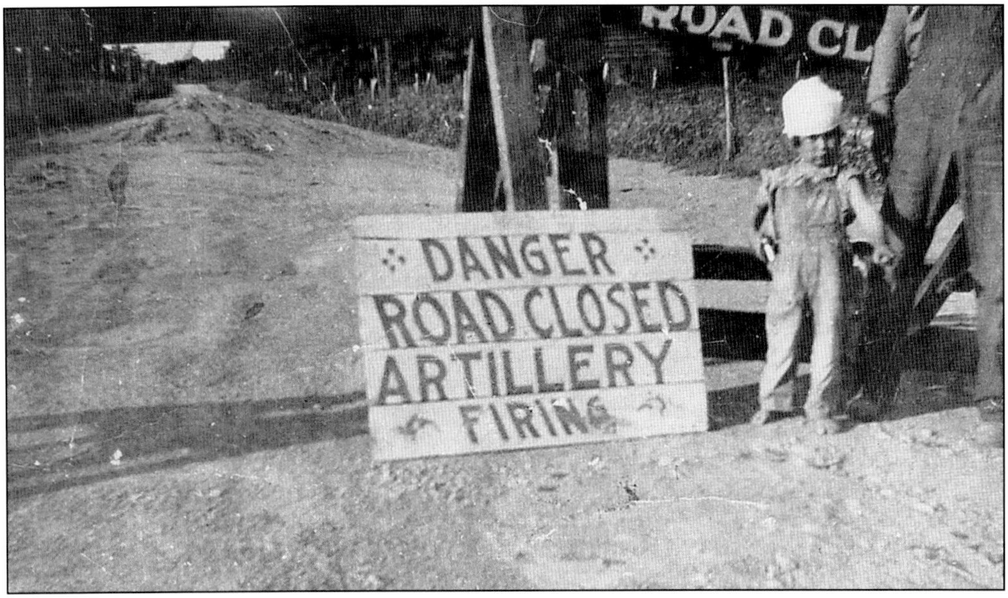

NEW STITHTON, 1922. Fort Knox, which was on the west and north borders of New Stithton, was still known as Camp Knox when this picture was taken. The child standing in the road is (Dr.) John Davis. His head is bandaged because of a fall the previous day that resulted in stitches. He is standing in front of the Davis Store, which was on the east side of Wilson Road at the northern border of New Stithton. Much farther north on this road was the active military base. Roads leading into the base were closed when military firing was occurring.

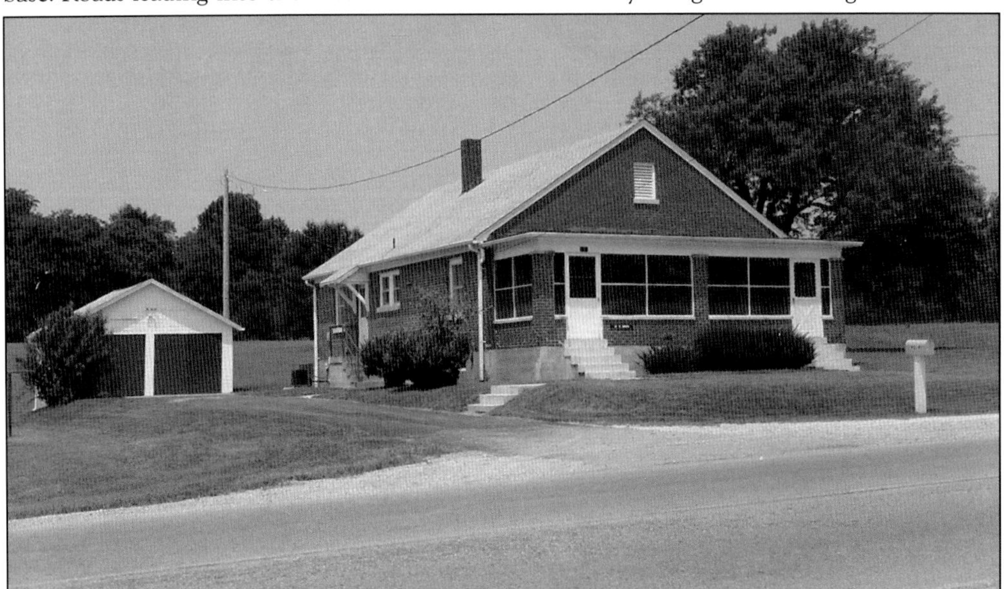

THE ONLY SURVIVING BUILDING FROM NEW STITHTON, 2002. Just inside the Wilson Road entrance to Fort Knox, on the west side of the road, is the only remaining building from New Stithton. One of two brick buildings in New Stithton, it was built by Dan E. New in the mid-1930s as a duplex that he rented to soldiers. It is currently used a single-family residence for soldiers. Just north of this house was the home of Dan New, from which he operated a small grocery store. Farther north was the New Stithton Methodist Church.

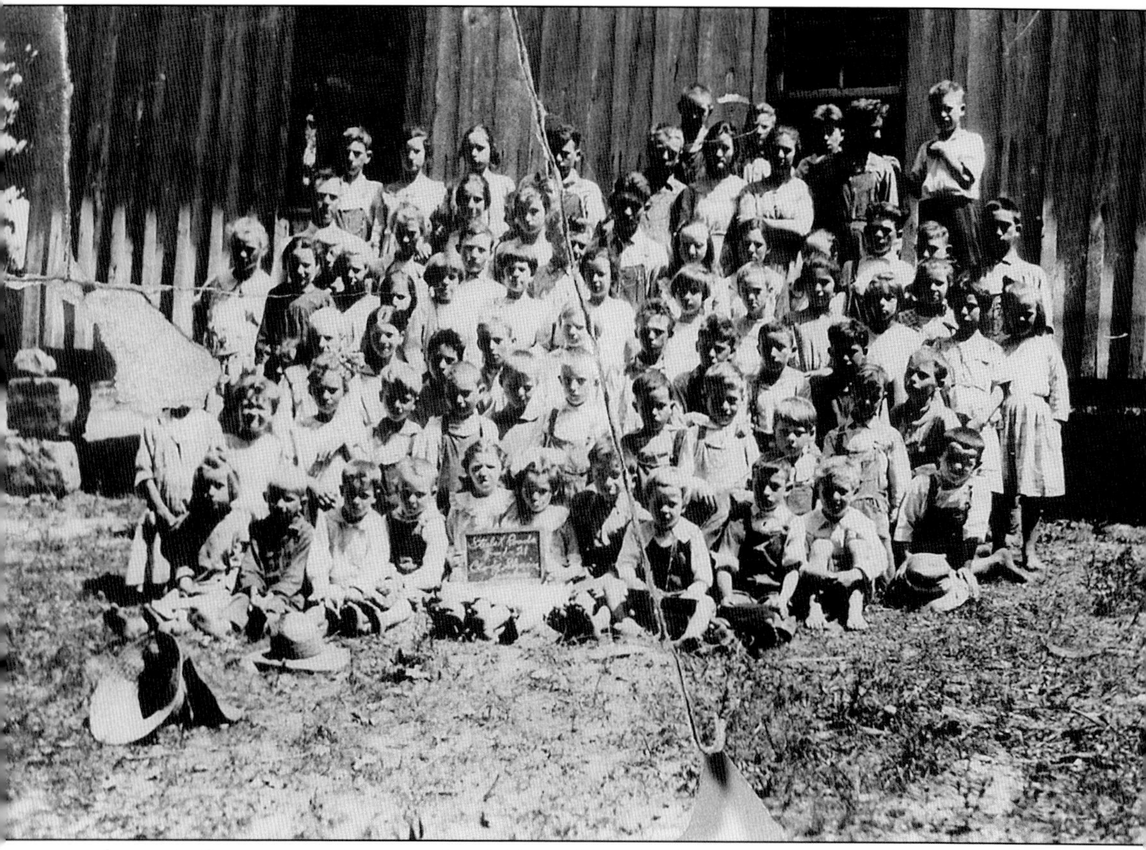

STEELE'S CROSSROADS SCHOOL, 1921. East of New Stithton, in the area of the current Seventh Armored Division Road and "Old" Highway 251, was a school, church, and merchandise store in close proximity. The area acquired a place name and appeared on maps as Steele's Crossroads. Along with New Stithton, it was taken for the expansion of Fort Knox. Regarded as a community early in the 19th century, Steele's Crossroads was settled by members of the Steele family. Alphonzo Steele, reportedly the last survivor of the Battle of San Jacinto and who died in Texas in 1912, was a descendent of these early settlers. Steele's Crossroads School was located close to the Phillips Cemetery. This photograph indicates a large enrollment. Only four people have been identified in the photograph: teacher Claude Shane, in the second to last row on the far left; Mildred Crutcher, fifth from the left, four rows down from the back; Hazel Phillips, sixth from the left in the second to last row (near the window); and Ruth Lassiter, second from the left in the second row from the front. Other teachers at the school were Goldie Dunaway and Mrs. Fowler. The *Elizabethtown News* of 1891 listed Steele's Crossroads (Steel X Roads), "school as District 75, with R.P. Daugherty as the teacher." The newspaper reported, "57 students in the district, with 23 enrolled." It is further stated, "The house is a bad one. Parents not interested. This is the teacher's second school. Trustees are: C. Wise, Floyd Davis, C.A. Morrison."

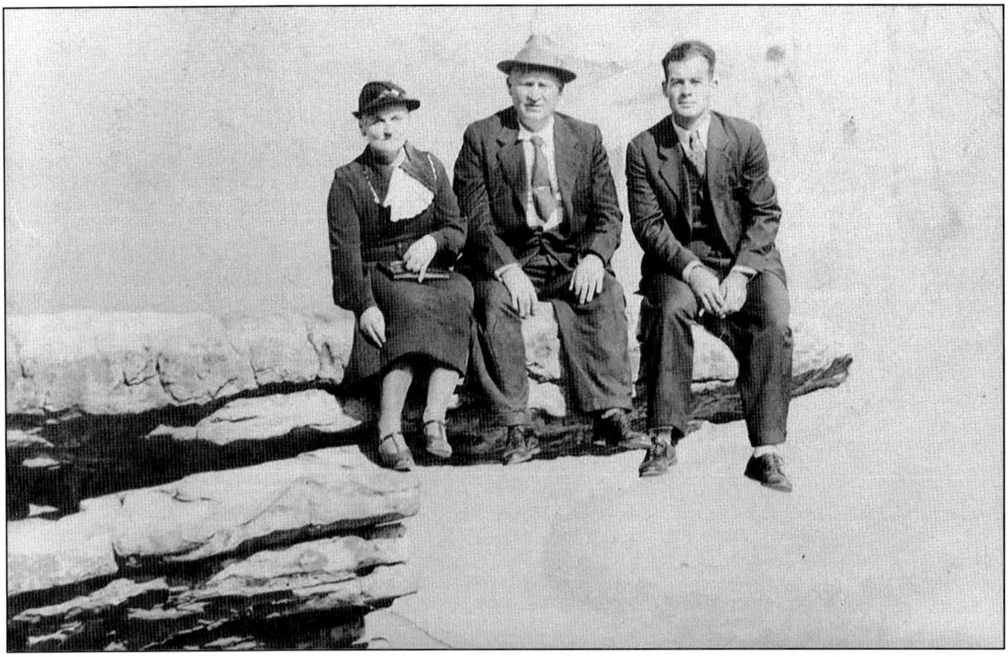

THE LASSWELLS ON VACATION, C. 1940. Pete and Delia Lasswell owned the store at Steele's Crossroads, and Anis Lee Keith worked at the store. The three are shown on vacation at Lookout Mountain in Tennessee. Anis was born near Steele's Crossroads. His parents were Pearl and George Keith, and he married Beulah Elizabeth Stone, daughter of Roderick and Rosa Mae Stone. All was not always peaceful among the residents of Steele's Crossroads. The *Elizabethtown News* of August 8, 1890, reported, "Last week at Steele's Cross Roads, Peter Yates and his son, Turkee Yates had an argument. The father shot the son in the thigh. The son broke three of his father's ribs with stones."

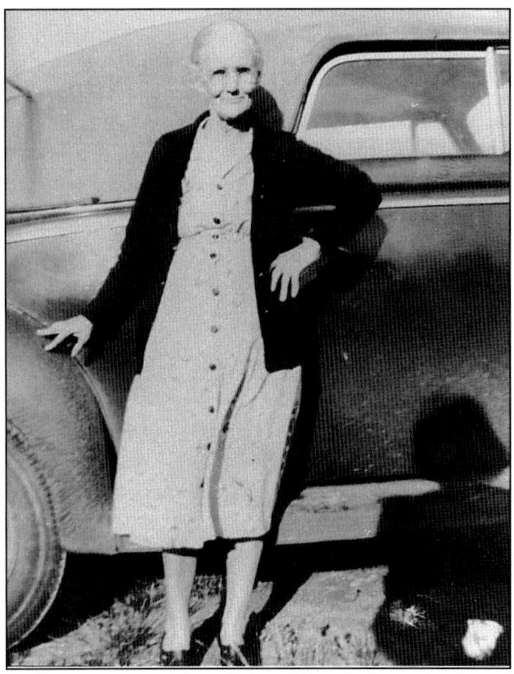

STEELE'S CROSSROADS RESIDENT, 1940. Rosa Mae Stone, the daughter of Tom Eubanks, was a long-time resident of Steele's Crossroads. She is photographed standing beside her 1940 Ford.

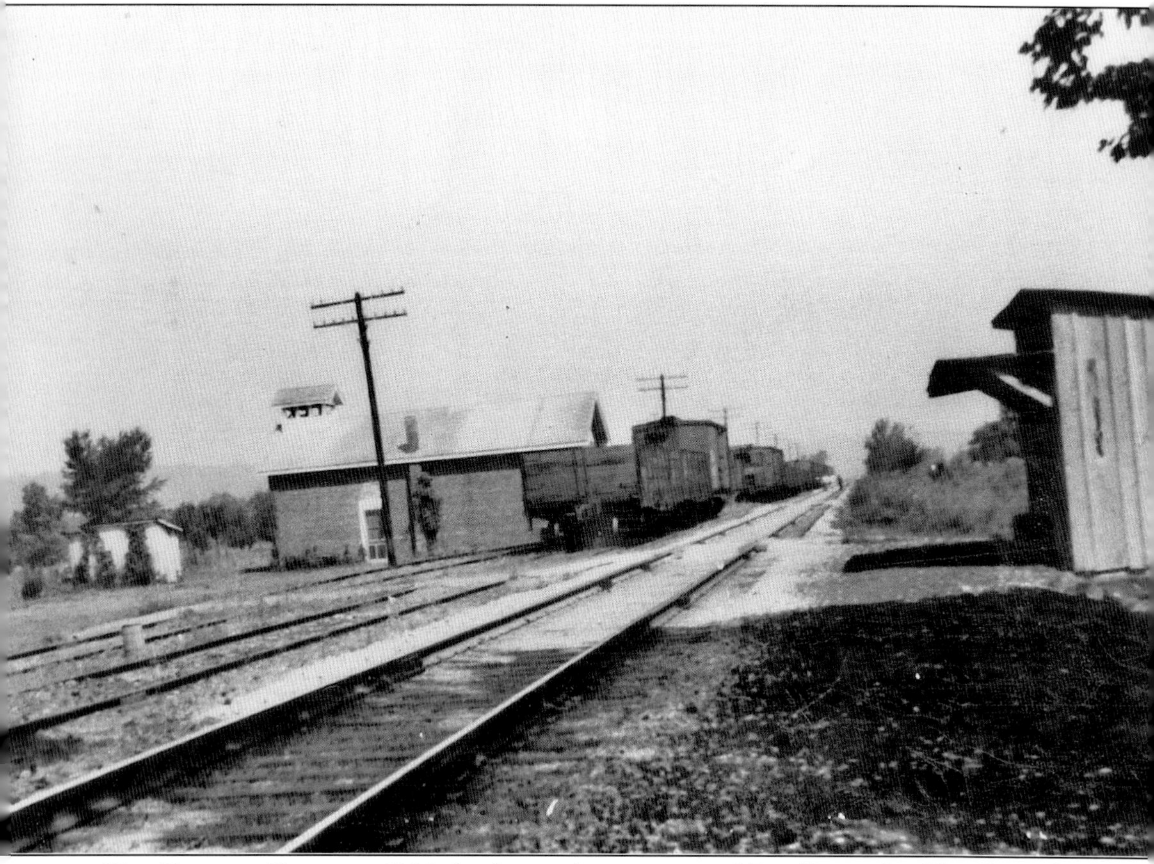

THE TOWN OF BARTLES, 1930. In the northwest corner of Fort Knox, the Ohio River flows west and then takes a sharp turn to the south, then west again. The L&N Railroad went through the area c. 1880 and followed the Ohio River along this loop on the south side of the river. Within this loop, a train depot was built, a post office established, a school and church erected, and a store began operation on the east side of the tracks— enough attributes to earn a place on maps. It became known as the town of Bartles, after Frank Bartles, who ran the depot with his wife "Aunt Tina" (Martha Tina Perry). She stocked and sold groceries from a small store they operated and also ran a post office in the store. A Methodist church was located in Bartles, and Brother Carter was the last pastor. Ten to fifteen families attended church services in the small brick church. The town had telephone service but no electricity. The Streble family (other members of this same family spelled the name Streible) was the last to run the store/post office in Bartles. They were also the last to leave. The last post office cancellation stamp was October 31, 1941—on this date, Bartles became extinct.

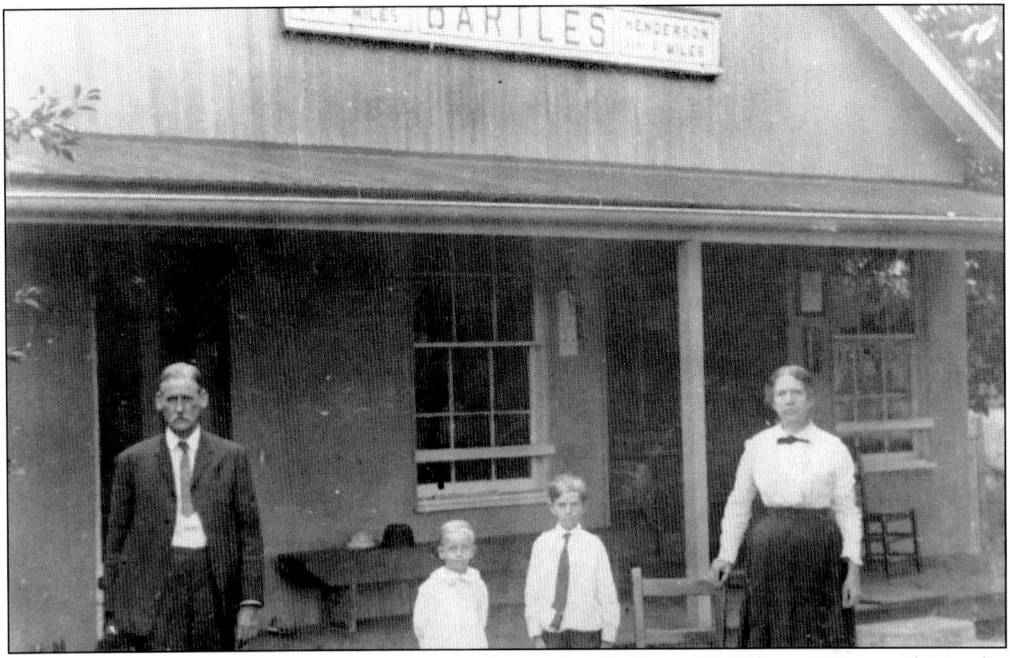

BARTLES, 1925. From left to right are Frank Bartles, Leslie and Gilbert Perry, and Martha Bartles. Frank "established" the town of Bartles sometime after the railroad went through the area *c.* 1880. The area was not heavily wooded as it is now, and fertile farms operated in the area. The building behind Frank was the home, post office, and general merchandise store.

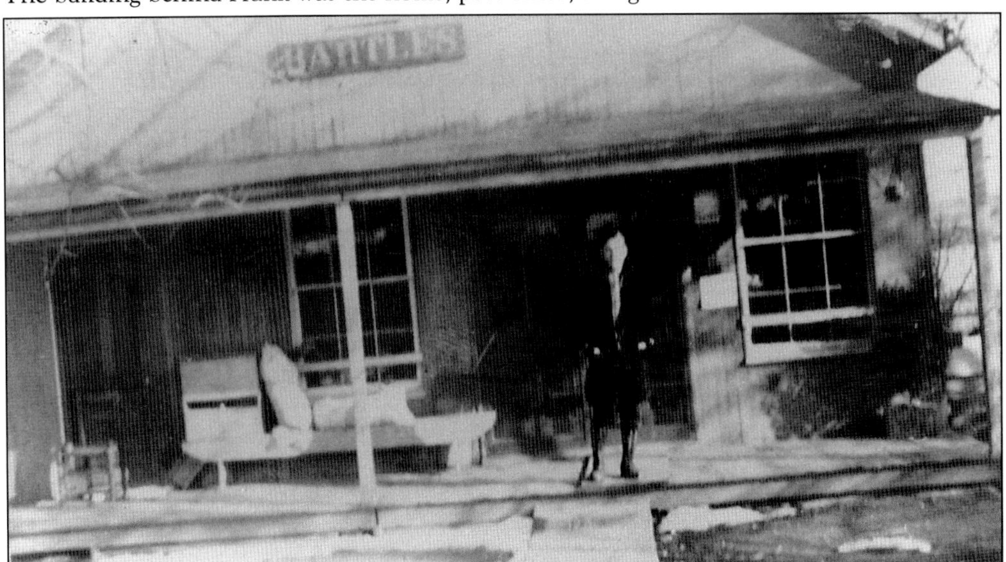

DEWEY STREBLE IN BARTLES, 1935. Dewey Streble purchased the Bartles depot/store/post office operation from Frank Bartles. For a time they had the area's only radio, and neighbors came to listen for news and entertainment. Only one passable road led into Bartles from the east, so the town was quite isolated. A baggage clerk threw the Louisville newspaper from the train. Virginia Able, a one-time resident of Bartles, recalled fetching it from beside the tracks. Trains did not have regular stops here but only stopped when they were flagged down. Incoming mail was dropped from the train, while outgoing mail was snatched from a pole.

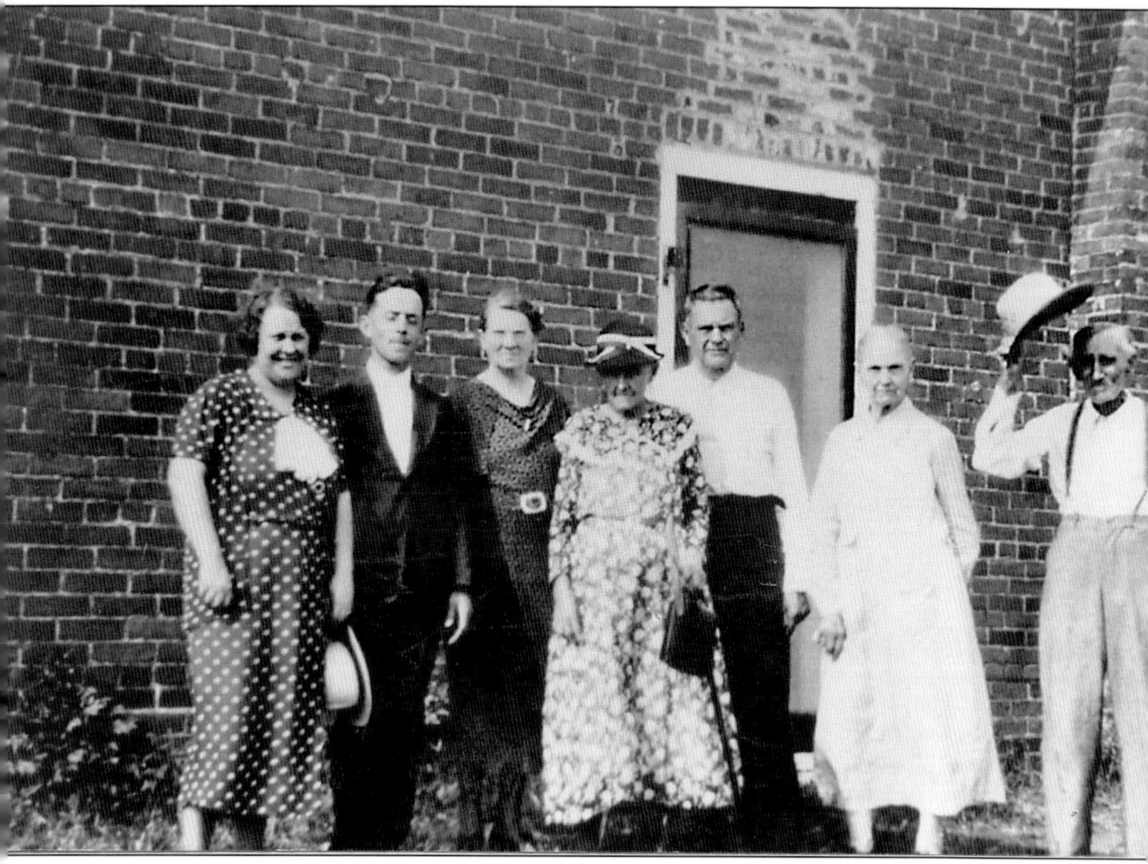

PERRY MEMORIAL CHURCH IN BARTLES, 1933. Pictured in front of the church, from left to right, are Mrs. ? Cooper, Rev. Arthur Cooper, Addie Carter, Amedia Perry, Rev. Charles Carter, Mrs. Isabell Gerkins, and William Gerkins. Rev. Charles Carter, who started the first church in Bartles, was married to Addie McRae. At first, there was no available building, and in the summertime Brother Carter preached from the porch of Frank Bartles' store to residents sitting in chairs in the yard. For several summers a preacher named Bolton brought a tent and held services in Bartles. The brick building that came to house Perry Memorial Church was built by the Louisville Gas and Electric Company on land owned by James Perry. It was originally part of a pumping station used to pump salt water off the many gas wells in the area. When the building was no longer used as a pumping station, ownership reverted to James and Media Perry, who presented it to the people of Bartles as a church on September 21, 1921. A bell that was placed in the church was originally located in the Methodist church in Garnettsville, which was moved to Muldraugh, where it stands today. With the acquisition of Bartles for the expansion of Fort Knox, the church bell was moved to the Bethany Methodist Church on the corner of Dixie Highway (31 West) and Bethany Lane in Valley Station, Kentucky, where it is today.

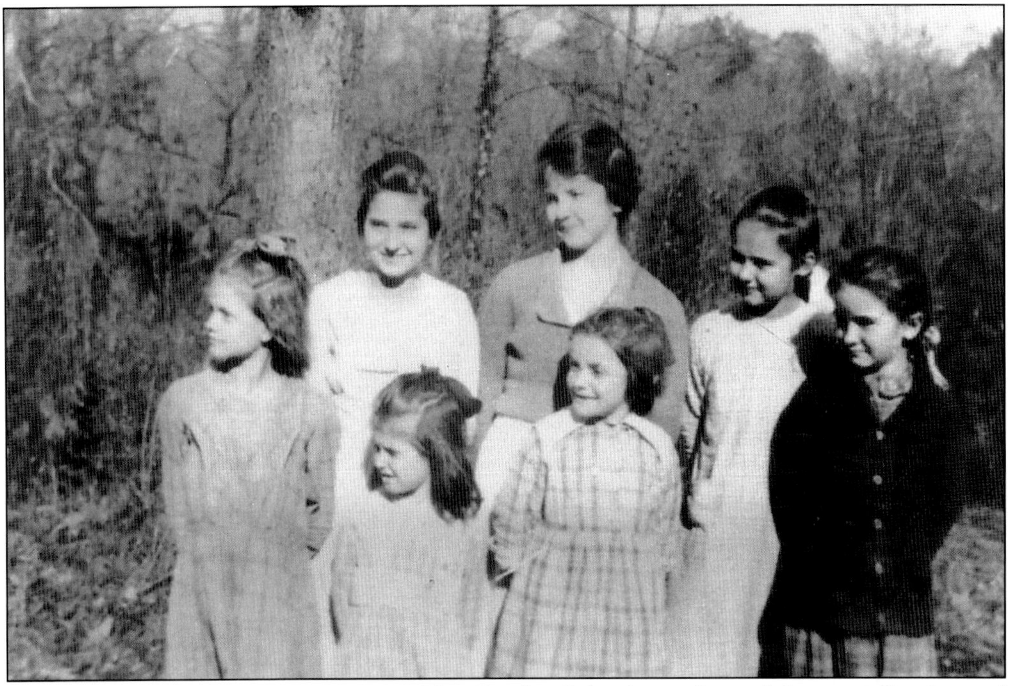

BARTLES SCHOOL STUDENTS, 1919. The Bartles School was located between Bartles and Muldraugh, about two miles from the Bartles train depot. In later years, (Adam) Dewey Streble picked up children along the way as he drove his children to school in a mule-drawn wagon. Pictured from left to right are (front row) Louisa Higby (died shortly after this picture was taken), Lillian Reesor, Emma Walker (married Forrest Basham), and Anna Mae Holloway (married Hays Basham); (back row) Ethel Streble (married George Long), Iva Mae Perry (married Roy Streble), and Mattie Holloway (married Adam Dewey Streble).

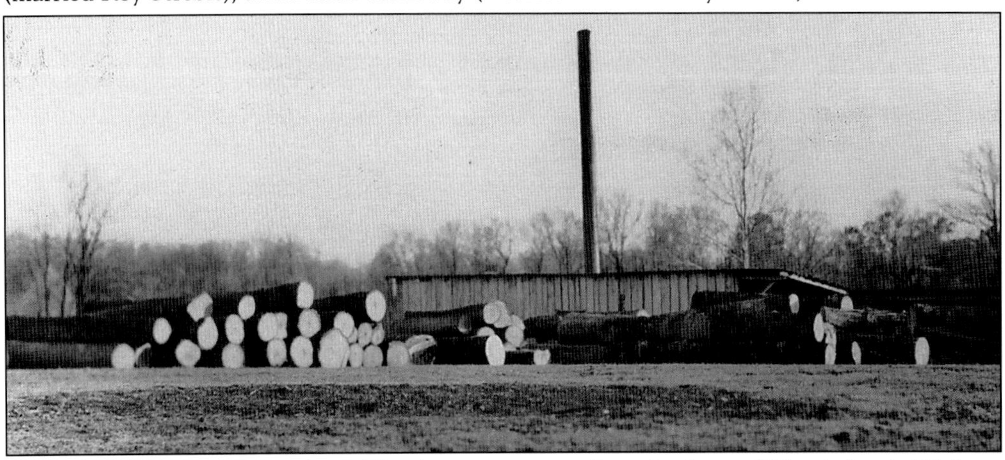

WITHERS SAWMILL, 1940. East of Bartles was a saw mill on the farm of Claude Lewis Withers. Hood Withers operated the mill, which he moved to this location in 1939. The site of the mill is now forested with numerous tank trails carved into the ground, reflecting years of military training in the area. Such saw mills provided part-time work and a source of cash for residents around Bartles. For those not working on Fort Knox, the main occupation was farming. Tobacco, corn, hogs, beef, chickens, and eggs were cash crops shipped from the Bartles depot to markets in Louisville.

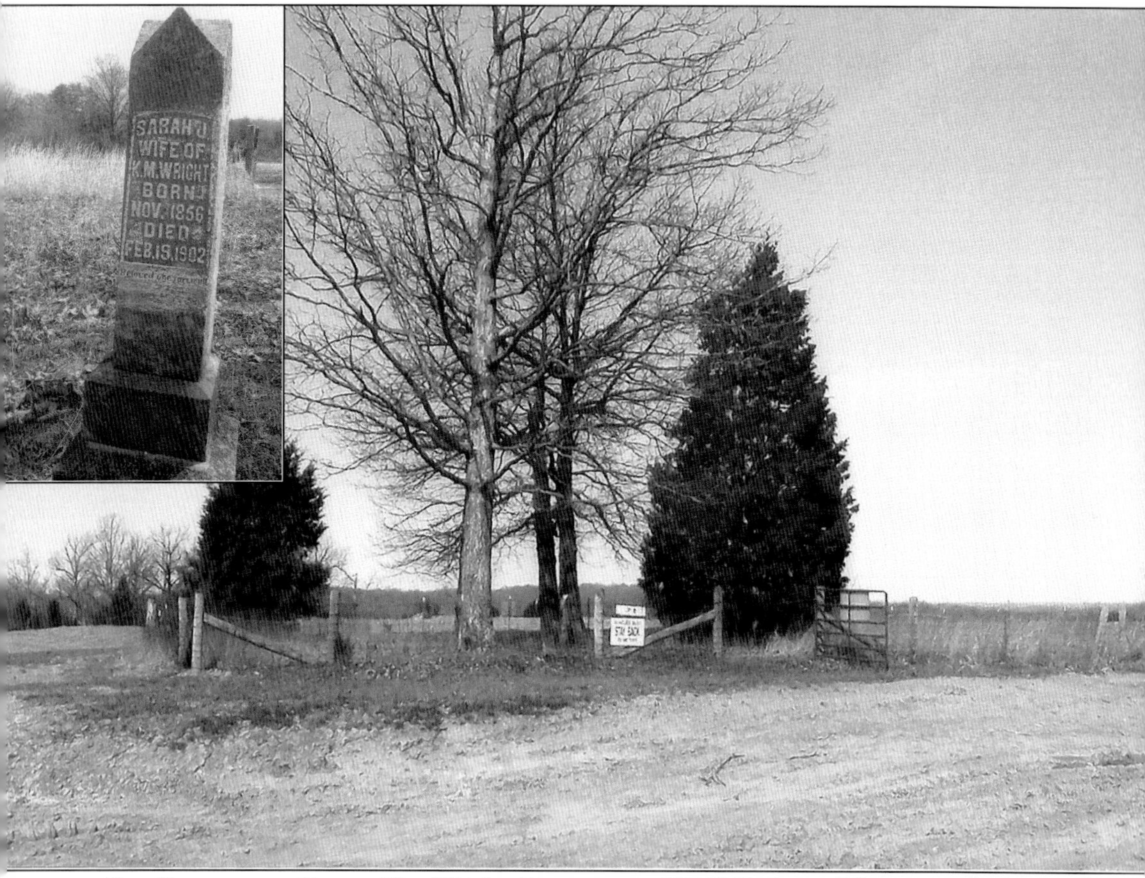

THE FORGOTTEN TOWN. The Wright Cemetery on "Old" Highway 251 just inside the south boundary of Fort Knox is also called the Cedar Creek Black Cemetery, since descendants of slaves who worked the area farms are buried there. In the late 19th century a community of freed African Americans resided around this cemetery. The community established an African Methodist Episcopal Church a few years after the Civil War. A school, merchandise store, and blacksmith shop operated by Henry Miller were established in the early 20th century. During and after the Civil War, John Cowley and his brother, Owen Cowley, along with the Viers family, owned most of the land in the Cedar Creek and Mill Creek Valleys, and both Cowleys owned slaves. Following the emancipation of slaves Owen Cowley gave each of his former slaves a piece of farmland near today's Wright Cemetery. Giving slaves property was not common in slave states, but it occurred in Kentucky with some frequency. Numerous records show former slaves were deeded property in their former "owner's" wills. By the time the community was taken for the expansion of Fort Knox, only six families resided in the area. The African Methodist Episcopal Church that rested near the cemetery had not held regular services for many years. The area was never given a place name and never appeared on maps, though it had all the requisites. The school and church records cannot be found, little was ever written about the town, and few remain who have memory that it once existed. Two additional cemeteries were located behind the Wright Cemetery with graves of African Americans, most marked by uninscribed gravestones.

MONROE AND SALLIE WRIGHT, 1930S. Monroe and Sallie are shown here in front of their home, directly across from the African Methodist Episcopal church. The home was a comfortable two-story frame house with a side porch, kitchen, living room, two upstairs bedrooms, and a large garden. Sallie (Sally/Aunt Sara) was a respected midwife. The Wrights were among the few African-American families remaining in the area just prior to the expansion of Fort Knox.

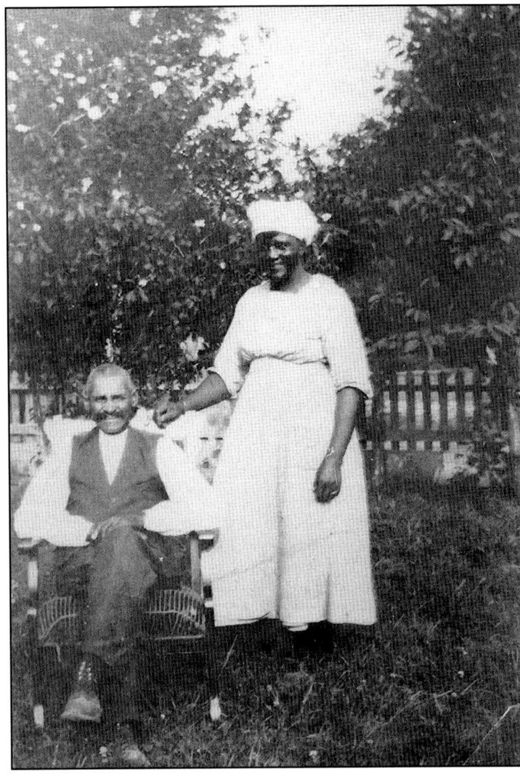

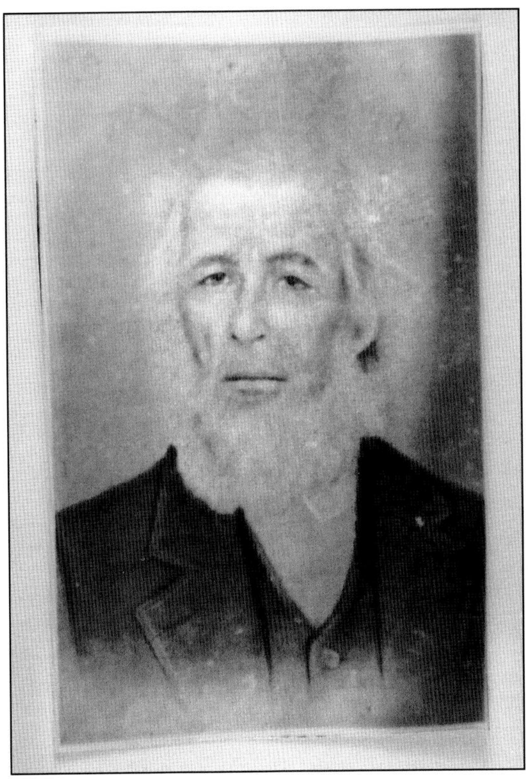

JOHN COWLEY, BORN 1827, DIED 1906. John Cowley and his brother, Owen, were large landholders and slave owners in the Mill Creek and Cedar Creek areas. John is buried in the Owens Cemetery on Fort Knox. Upon the freeing of the slaves following the Civil War, Owen released his slaves and gave each a piece of property in the Cedar Creek area. Other slaveholders in the area are known to have done the same. These former slaves and their descendants established a prosperous community in the Cedar Creek area.

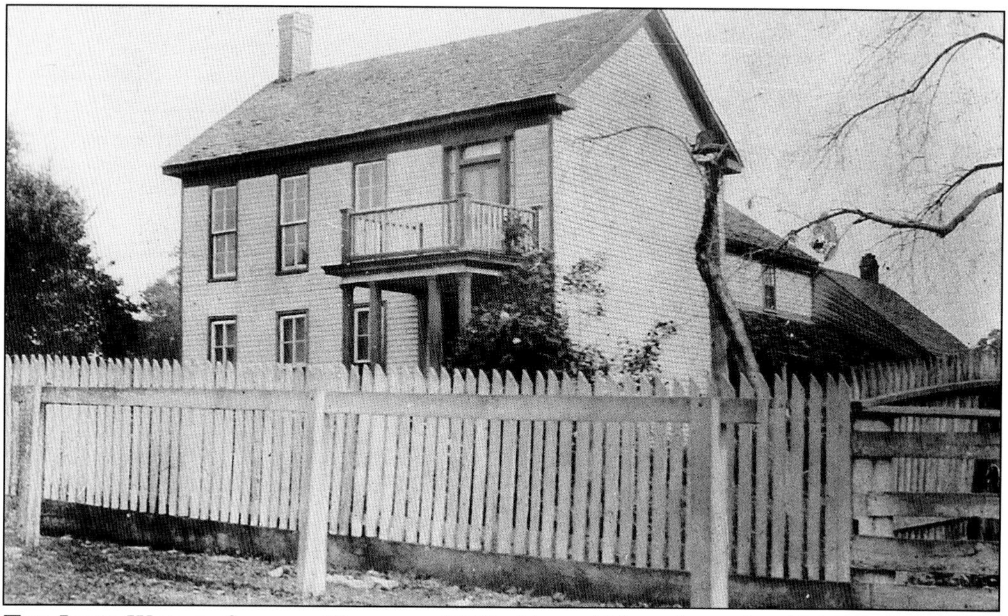

THE JOHN WESLEY COWLEY HOME, C. 1900. About 100 yards south of Main Range Road (once called Bloomington Road) and facing Mill Creek, this farmhouse was a two-story wood-frame house with numerous outbuildings to serve the various farm functions. When this farm was taken for the expansion of Fort Knox, the slave quarters remained, though they had come to be used for other purposes. John Wesley Cowley purchased the house in 1885, and the property passed to his son William Green Cowley, who sold the farm to the government in 1941. The Cowley Cemetery (referred to by some as the Hays Cemetery) lies 100 yards northeast of the house's site. No Cowleys are buried within: it was so named because of its location on the Cowley property at the time of the government's purchase.

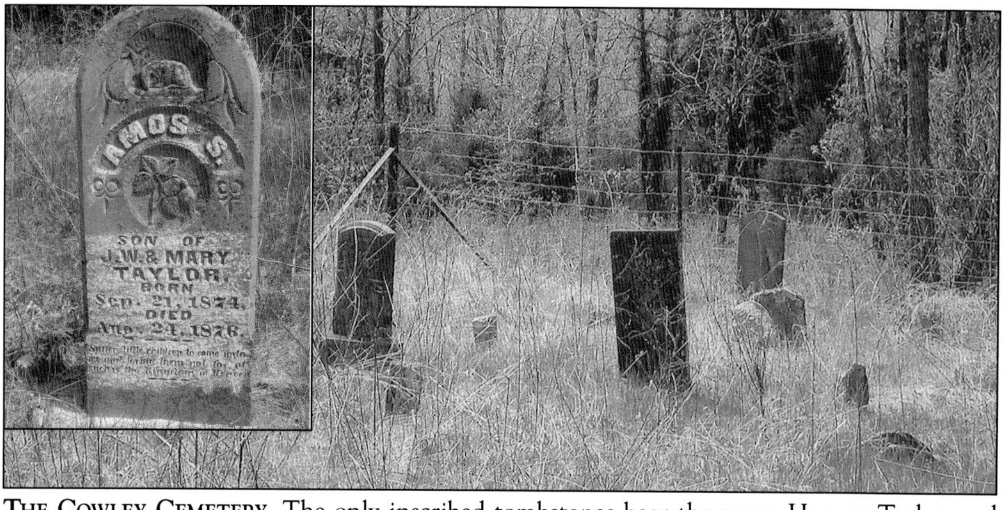

THE COWLEY CEMETERY. The only inscribed tombstones bear the name Hays or Taylor, and the oldest burial noted on the tombstones is that of Hercules Hays in 1855. The cemetery has a small section with numerous uninscribed fieldstone markers, which are probably markers of slaves or freed slaves. It was not uncommon in many of the Fort Knox cemeteries for a section of a family or church cemetery to have graves of slave or freed African Americans within. Remnants of the Cowley home are located about 100 yards southwest of the cemetery.

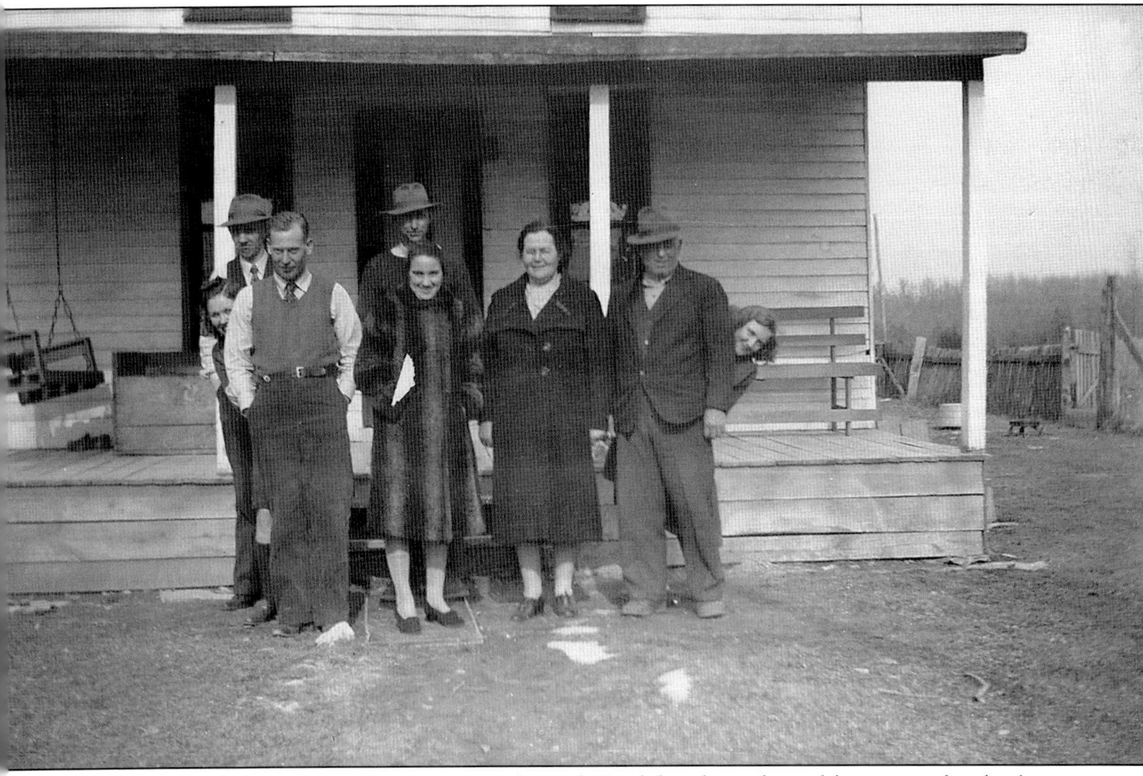

Bird Home in Dorrett's Run, 1941. The Josh Bird family and neighbors pose for the last picture taken at their home in Dorrett's Run, an area between Mill and Cedar Creeks that was named after a stream flowing east to west into Mill Creek, near Atcher Cemetery. The house, originally a log cabin, was later enlarged and covered with clapboards. Three rooms were downstairs—a kitchen, living room, and dining room. Upstairs was one large room that served as the children's bedroom; the parents slept in the downstairs living room. The Bird farm—78 acres—was acquired by the government for the expansion of Fort Knox. A post office was established in Dorrett's Run on February 1, 1869, with Jonathan Owen serving as postmaster. By the early 20th century, the post office had closed and mail came from Vine Grove via mail carriers who dropped off letters in a line of mailboxes. Mr. Sullivan and a substitute mail carrier, Mr. Dunaway, were the last mail carriers. A church arose, and a couple miles away, just east of the Bird home, a school was established. The area had the requisites to be considered a community,- and Dorrett's Run appeared on maps.

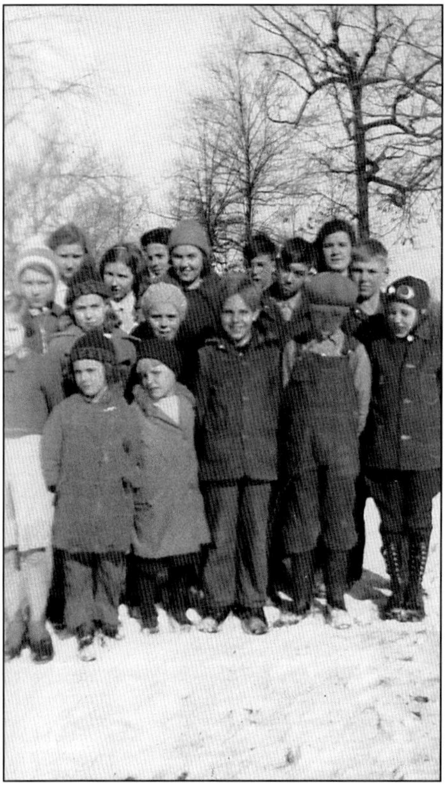

DORRETT'S RUN SCHOOL, 1939–1940. Dorrett's Run school opened by 1891 in a one-room log structure with 38 registered students. Usually only half of the students showed up on any given day. J.C. Hoskinson was the teacher, and school trustees were Chas. French, Jas Sherrard, and Tom Owen. Students from 1939–1940, pictured from left to right are (front row) unidentified (half cut off), Anita Shelton, Margie Bird, Delbert Schumaker, unidentified (bibbed overalls and cap), and Charlie Shelton (cap and goggles); (back row) Alta Bird, Helen Payne, Lila Ann Hargan (directly behind Anita Shelton), Marguerite Payne, Betty Bird (with white cap directly behind Margie Bird), Paul Yates (directly behind Betty Bird), Mildred Bird, Ersal French, Harold Leonard (with head cocked to his left shoulder), Mildred Leonard, and Elwood Leonard

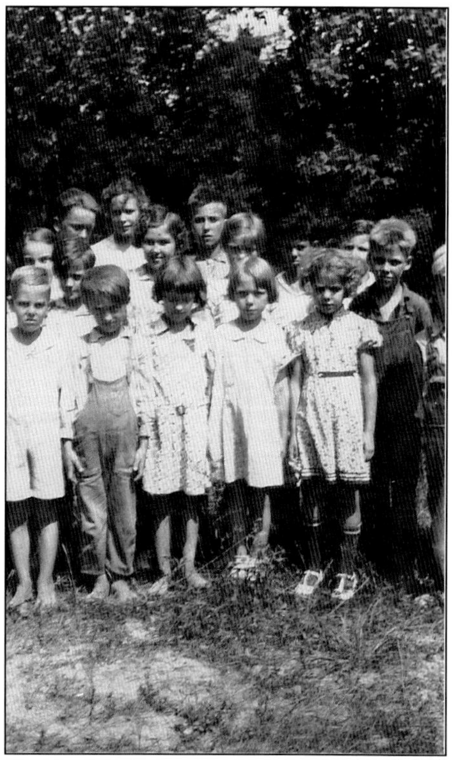

DORRETT'S RUN SCHOOL, 1938–1939. Dorrett's Run school drew children from the area between Mill Creek and Cedar Creek. Part of the class of 1939, are pictured; from left to right are (front row) Delbert Schumaker, Raymond Bird, Thelma Bird, unidentified, and Lila Hargan (with a bushy haired boy behind her left shoulder); (back row) Wanda Crowe (face obscured below her nose), unidentified (boy with dark bushy hair), unidentified (to Wanda's left and directly behind dark bushy haired boy), Marguerite Skeeters (behind Raymond Bird), Mildred Bird, Edward Bird, unidentified (face obscured below his nose), Paul Yates, and two unidentified people (one being the tall, bushy-haired boy with bibbed overalls).